JIDDU KRISHNAMURTI

JIDDU KRISHNAMURTI

A Critical Study of Tradition and Revolution

P. Kesava Kumar

KALPAZ

ISBN: 978-93-5128-099-6

Price : ₹ 790

First Published, 2015

Published by

Kalpaz Publications
C-30, Satyawati Nagar
Delhi-110052
Ph. : 9212142040
E-mail: kalpaz@hotmail.com

Laser Typesetting: Gyan Print (AB-I), Delhi
Printed at: Chawla Offset, Delhi

Cataloging in Publication Data—DK

Courtesy: D.K. Agencies (P) Ltd. <docinfo@dkagencies.com>

Kĕśava Kumār, Pi., author.

Jiddu Krishnamurti : a critical study of tradition and revolution / P. Kesava Kumar.

pages cm

Includes bibliographical references (pages).

ISBN 9789351280996

1. Krishnamurti, J. (Jiddu), 1895-1986. 2. Tradition (Philosophy) 3. Revolutions—Philosophy. I. Title.

DDC 148 23

For

My Beloved Daughters

Akshara and Asmitha

Contents

Foreword

Jiddu Krishnamurti is undoubtedly one of the greatest and the most influential philosophers of our times. He is widely regarded as a radical and insightful thinker who lived through the most tumultuous part of the twentieth century that witnessed not only the phenomenal growth of science and technology but also saw the two World Wars, the collapse of traditions and ideologies, the savage destruction of the earth and rapid deterioration of quality in every aspect of life, in the world. The uniqueness of Krishnamurti as a thinker lies in his uncompromising position that fundamental change in the human consciousness, in each one of us, alone can bring about a lasting and meaningful change in society. He categorically held that pinning our hopes on organised religion, political ideology, science and technology, planned or market economy; including the grand eloquent systems of philosophy not only failed to address the basic human problems but actually created them. The roots of the problems like poverty, hunger, illiteracy, disease, division, conflict, violence, corruption and consumerism, environmental degradation, global warming, fundamentalism, extremism and terrorism, commercialisation and criminalisation and so on, lie in the consciousness, which is in crisis. Crisis in consciousness is its fragmentation in the name of race, nation, religion, region, language and ethnicity. The fragmentation is the source of the content of consciousness which is of the nature of fear, anxiety, ambition, anger, authority, desire, belief, hope, despair and so on. Disintegration 'within' is the disintegration 'without'. Social reality is co-extensive with the human reality, nature and structure of which is consciousness in crisis.

The world as we know, the people world, with all its problems, is not the bolt from the blue but a psychological extension of our being. It is our own creation and we are totally responsible for it. The history of the world is the history of the humanity which has been inheriting the mind as we know it to be. The world is not the creation of any mysterious super-human or sub-human principle but the product of the way we perceive ourselves and others and do the things as we are actually conditioned to do. The world is not only co-extensive but also co-terminus with the consciousness. That is, a change in the society warrants a change in consciousness. Psychological revolution alone can bring about a revolution in the world. No other revolution—cultural, political, economic, or technological—can effect a real change in the society. History is a testimony to the fact that revolutions of all hues—red, green, white, or blue—have not been able to bring about a new world order. There has been a fast degeneration in every facet of life.

Krishnamurti contends that the individual and world problems are due to the fact that we have been living in the background of the traditional mind for millennia. We are the victims of unending suffering, since we are the traditional people all through the history. Tradition means carrying over the content of consciousness, which is the past put together by thought. Our responses to the present are from the past, the memory stored up in the brain cells. Even the so called modern or post-modern people are traditional, for their ideas and actions, too, are traditional in the sense that they are only the reactions of the past to the present. Krishnamurti uses the term "tradition" in its special sense of *'traduce'* besides its ordinary sense of 'tradere'. Traduce means to 'betray, to ridicule and to be untrue' and *tradere* means 'to give, to hand over, to inherit'. According to Krishnamurti, tradition means betraying the 'what is' by meeting it with knowledge which is the past; it is reducing the fact to an idea, truth to thought and translating the new in terms of the old. Tradition also means to hand over the ideas mechanically without understanding and appropriating the spirit of their meaning and living by it. Krishnamurti maintains that, it is only the mind which is absolutely and unconditionally free from tradition in both the senses of the term alone can meet the 'what is', the present, the new as it is. It alone can 'see' truth as truth, false as false and truth in the false. Freedom from tradition is of paramount importance for bringing about a radical change in the social reality. Revolution means the total transformation of the traditional mind, not through time and knowledge but awareness without choice, attention without concentration, or observation without the observer, the product of thought, knowledge and time.

Psychological revolution brings about a new mind which is free from the structure of the known, which is repetitive and mechanical. The new mind is not a novel mind but a creative one in constant revolution of being able to meet the present, the fact, as it is without distorting it. The novel mind which can only react to the past without ever cleansing itself of it may be an idiosyncratic and a bizarre one; but a creative mind in its true sense is supremely intelligent in the sense that its actions are logical, sane and compassionate. The creative mind is of wisdom imbued with a sense of inclusion and integrity and harmony. To Krishnamurti, creativity does not mean creative writing, creative painting, creative cooking and so on, but the birth of something totally new which is possible only when there is freedom from tradition, the known. That which is totally new is precisely the truth which is antithetical to tradition. Truth and tradition do not go together; where the one is, the other is not. Truth begins where the tradition ends; tradition is continuous and repetitious, whereas truth is ever new and from moment to moment; the former is [of] time and the latter is timeless. Tradition is accumulative, evolutionary but regressive, where as truth is negating, denuding, but disclosing. Truth can never be repeated and truth repeated is a lie; truth is totally outside the structure of tradition which is the past modifying itself as the future through the present. A traditional mind which is endlessly chattering with the knowledge/the past can never perceive the truth which is simple and ever in the now. It is only an empty, a still and silent mind that can see the truth of 'what is'. Only a quiet mind can understand the truth or the falsity of a statement.

Truth is not at a distance and there is no path to it, either of knowledge, devotion, or action. There is absolutely no need to confirm to any tradition, philosophical, religious, or scientific to perceive truth. Paths and knowledge and the practice thereof are isolating and exclusive, whereas truth is integrating and inclusive. Fundamentally, truth is a state of being that arises when the traditional mind wedded to the past and naturally seeks to divide and disintegrate the individual and society has come to an end without a vestige. The traditional mind which is basically corrupt in the sense of being fragmented in terms of the maze and the complexity of mutually conflicting, confusing and competing ideas and symbols can never see the truth which is blatantly obvious and right in front of its eyes. Being intrinsically untrue and untruthful to that which is true, the traditional mind is a problematic mind which comes to end only when there in an insight into the whole nature and structure of it. A traditional approach to the transformation of the traditional mind is a contradiction in terms and practice. Truth or the true mind is not a matter of knowledge but a freedom from it. It is not a thing to be remembered and repeated, to be written about or propagated. Truth is that which is the nameless, which a traditional mind cannot approach. Only the mind which is in constant revolution of being ever fresh and new alone can comprehend it. Truth lies in meeting life afresh and seeing things anew which is possible for a mind that does not identify or confirm itself to any pattern of thought or belief and never becomes traditional or old.

Krishnamurti denounces philosophy in the sense of a tradition of theories, ideas and ideals. He does not subscribe to the concept of philosophy as a corpus of justified true beliefs or an activity of advancing arguments to convince others of something. Philosophy is not an intellectual activity of clarifying conceptual confusion, nor a theoretical enterprise, nor an *exegetical* exercise of disputing the prevalent ideas and inventing novel ones. Philosophy is not a speculative activity of system building, a construction of grand eloquent theories which have industrialised the human mind and dehumanised the human being. To Krishnamurti, philosophy is not the love of concepts, not a series of theories, but the love of truth in the sense of its actual realisation and living by it in daily life. It is not a pursuit of abstraction but a practical discipline of bringing about a radical change in the mind by comprehending truth beyond thought, wisdom beyond knowledge. The function of philosophy is discovering intelligence which is holistic, sane and compassionate. Philosophy is the praxis of living in accordance with facts without fiction, truth without reducing it to ideas. Its concern is the creation of a new, a true and an integrated human being who is in harmony in relationship with people and nature. Philosophy is setting out on the voyage of the uncharted sea of truth, a meditative journey into the unknown.

Despite categorical denial of all philosophical traditions as traitors of truth, Krishnamurti's philosophy may be said to be in consonance with the philosophies of *Advaita Vedanta,* Nagarjuna and Wittgenstein. It comes close to the *Advaita Vedanta* if *Vedanta* means the actual realisation of the non-dual absolute truth by ending all knowledge about it. *Vedanta* literally means, the ending of knowledge, and, not merely the *Upanishads,* which are the end part of the *Vedas*. Krishnamurti himself subscribed to the view that his philosophy may be regarded as *Vedanta* if it means, 'freedom from knowledge and practice'. But Krishnamurti does not accept the traditional *Vedantin's* view that acquisition of the knowledge of the *Upanishads* and the practice of the path thereof are the *sine qua non* of freedom or salvation. Krishnamurti maintains that freedom from knowledge which is tradition is absolutely essential at the very beginning of the inquiry into the truth. In this sense, Krishnamurti claims, that he begins exactly where the traditional *Vedantins* stop. To him, freedom is the first and last step in the observation and understanding of truth. Krishnmurti's philosophy is also akin to Nagarjuna's philosophy of emptiness which teaches the absence of inherent being of the phenomena. To Krishnamurti truth is emptiness of everything that thought has put together. He holds that emptiness is the truth of being of everything—things, people and ideas. Nagarjuna's notion of *tathata* is similar to Krishnmurti's truth, the 'what is' which is beyond words, concepts, or systems. To both, truth is all inclusive, harmonious and quiescent which is beyond desire, attachment and hatred. To Nagarjuna, transcendental truth comprehends the absence of intrinsic nature of the phenomenal truth. To Krishnamurti, truth is freedom from the nature and structure of thought which is conditioned and limited. And, Krishnmurti's notion of the silent mind, which is of the nature of truth, may be likened to Wittgenstein's notion of the transcendence which is beyond language. Wittgenstein's statements that 'whereof one cannot speak thereof one must be silent' and 'what is not said is more significant than what is said' come very close to Krishnmurti's view that the unknown is far more profound than the known and being is more important than becoming.

Dr Kesava Kumar, in the present work, has attempted to bring out in clear and simple terms Krishnmurti's views on tradition and revolution. He has discussed many other issues related to the two seminal philosophical problems. He has also made a critical examination of Krishnmurti's insights in the light of the contemporary thinkers and the trends of the East and the West. I must say that this book is a bold venture to present the philosophy of a remarkable thinker whose life is intriguing and the teachings vast and difficult to decipher. This work is one of the few books which seek to bring to light a rare thinker like Krishnamurti who is less known, rather less studied than many other contemporary Indian thinkers in the academic circles. Krishnamurti is more a philosopher of the general public than a philosopher's philosopher, who shunned propaganda and publicity. His philosophy embodies truth which is more concrete and practical than conceptual and theoretical. He is extremely relevant to the resolution of the crisis of the world of ideas as well as of action. He has to be studied more seriously and widely at the college and university level, for his teachings are pregnant with the profound truth which can form a basis for meaningful living with a culture of supreme human values.

I hope Kesava Kumar's work ably serves the purpose of giving a better exposition and currency to Krishnmurti's philosophy both in the academia and outside. However, writers on Krishnamurti should show a diligent restraint in interpreting and commenting on Krishnamurti, lest they may distort his teaching. They should also keep in mind Krishnmurti's last wish—let the teaching be not corrupted. His philosophy is concerned more with the actual and the urgent realisation of truth and the transformation of the individual and society than a mere intellectual or conceptual understanding of it. Let us not reduce the living truth of his philosophy through a dead tradition by repeating it in terms of words and concepts and proliferating books on him. Let us live the teaching more than writing about it. Krishnamurtiy often asked his listeners to live the teaching besides discussing and having dialogues about it. He warned people against claiming authority over his teachings, for truth cannot be a monopoly of anybody.

G. Vedaparayana

Senior Fellow, ICPR
Dept. of Philosophy
Sri Venkateswara University
Tirupati A.P.
PIN: 517502

Preface

J. Krishnamurti (1895-1986) is one of the prominent thinkers of contemporary times. He did not expound any philosophy or religion but engaged in talking about problems of everyday life. His lectures and writings have global appeal. Every word he spoke has been recorded and printed. Krishnamutri's foundations were established and thousands of followers appeared all over the world. He emerged as a phenomenon in contemporary times. As a researcher my fascination for Krishnamurti lies in his being a thinker of Indian origin who was boldly critical about tradition and looked for radical change. His immediate concern throughout his life was human predicament and the way out of the labyrinthine world. He picked up many themes, such as identity, division, conflict, violence, world disorder, education and religious life. I believe that 'tradition' and 'revolution' are the basic themes of Krishnamurti and also invariably are related to each other. Though both these concepts are popular concepts of his time, the way he presented them adds new meaning. Tradition and revolution are historically constructed categories and considerable literature is available in this respect. The discourse of social change and world order are invariably linked with the ideals of tradition and revolution. As a researcher I could not ignore existing theories of both tradition and revolution and at the same time conscious of Krishnamuti's unique usage of these terms. There is a difficulty in doing this as he does not allow any method or approach in understanding world or his teachings. Any scholar of Krihnamurti's teachings is compelled to work with the language and tools used by Krishnamurti. In my study, I have attempted to present Krishnamurti's thought without losing its essence and at the same time engaged him with other prominent philosophical theories of contemporary times on the same issue. I am conscious of my position as a scholar, it is important to depict the philosophical position of Krishnamurti and equally important for me, not to be carried away by him. To bring relevance to his thought, I place him into the socio-political developments of contemporary times of the world. I came to an understanding that Krishnamurti provides new way in approaching the problems of life. His approach seems to be philosophical and logical rather than practical and political in bringing about the transformation of the world order. In this study, I took liberty to locate him in larger philosophical systems and even to explore the limitations of his thought in terms of contemporary relevance.

I see tradition as a problem because of its oppressive and authoritative character in most of the issues of social life. In Indian context, caste system and patriarchy are bound by tradition. Tradition is regulated by religion and its texts, systematically executing by the priestly class in association with ruling class. Tradition and its value systems have manifested through the social institutions and had continuity for generations. The victims of tradition will definitely admire the change, the idea of revolution which is promising a new vision of life. We can see the crisis of contemporary society that has manifested in many forms, especially from the decade of eighties. On one hand, the idea of revolution has been confined to Marxist sense and become limited to economic equality rather than life as a whole. On the other hand, tradition in the form of religious nationalism becomes a rallying point for many struggles in a crisis ridden society. I believe in this historical juncture, Krishnmurti's ideas are relevant in providing broader meaning to the concepts of both tradition and revolution.

Krishnamurti goes beyond known liberal and Marxist positions. For me, the significance of Krisnamurti lies in his ideas to think about the problem of human freedom from repressions and constraints of internal life of mind. Modern ideologies are concerned with well-being in the external world. Identity struggles are also concerned about one's place in the past and future also. Looking at freedom as an issue of mind than the world, he is critical about any other identity other than human. He is critical about all historically, socially, culturally, religiously and politically constructed identities. He argues that any identity based on past, memory, or thought, not only distorts the present (existing reality), *what is*, but also responsible for fragmentation of human consciousness leading to conflict and world disorder. The spirit of universal human consciousness can be appreciable and tends to be logical.

As we are aware, the decade of nineteen eighties are known for identity politics that countered the liberal and Marxist conception of life. For Krishnamurti, individual is central. He treats the individual as rational and universal. He extends this rationality to criticise the tradition, past, religion and belief. In order to understand the reality as a whole in its freshness as *what is*, he even rejects the verbalisation, thought, memory and the social-cultural process. He rejects the *social*, which he considers as a source for the existential problems. He understood the problems are due to partial and prejudiced understanding rather total understanding. He demands *nameless experience* for better understanding of the world. He thinks *choiceless awareness* keeps the individual away from the existential problems and conflicts. He finds the solution to all existential problems in individual. He argues for change in the individual psyche or psychological revolution. He maintains a position that change in the individual psyche will automatically bring in the world since 'you (individual) are the world.' The state of revolution, he identifies, with religious mind is meditative and silent. It is a state of joy filled with love and compassion.

Here Krishnamurti proves himself logical rather than philosophical. On maintaining the scientific understanding of the world, especially on critique of tradition, his thought comes close to a Marxist stream.

Krishnamurti's use of the term 'revolution' has its own historical meaning. He not only extends this word to connote total change in the psychological realm of the individual, which he believes that it encompasses all the fields of life, but also calls it a religious revolution. As we know, in the context of revolutionary change, religion has negative connotation. Though Krishnamurti is critical about organised religions in this sense but upholds the idea of 'religion' by giving it a different meaning. The question arises here, is can't he speak about revolution without referring to religion?

One thing is clear that Krishnamurti has invented new language of his times, which has predominantly liberal tone. He is critical of both tradition and revolution in his own terms, which goes against the historical notions of both of these terms. At the same time, he mediates both tradition and revolution through 'religious revolution'. This kind of position makes it difficult to locate him in known philosophical and political positions. In contrast to western modernity, the western educated Indian intellectuals are engaged with Hindu religion or tradition either by redefining or reforming it. The social reformers tried to reform the religion. The nationalists, such as Gandhi, redefined the Hinduism by making it universal and opposing the problems linked with caste and gender. Another Indian thinker Ambedkar, too, came out with an idea of religion as rational, social, moral and righteous, thereby denying the *Hinduism* as a religion. At an alternative level, he proposes *Buddhism* to fulfill his notion of religion. Krishnamurti goes against all the organised and historical religions but retains the idea of religiousness by redefining it.

Krishnamurti reduces the problems of the world and society to the individual level and provides solutions accordingly. Though he speaks in terms of understanding the individual and change, we can't brand him as a typical liberal. In other words, his philosophical perspective goes beyond known positions on science and religion, modern and postmodern positions and liberal and communitarian theories of contemporary times.

It is a challenge for anybody to capture the essence of thought without understanding the social and political context of the Krishnamurti and its implication to world order. His social and political background may provide some clues to understand him better. Krishnamurti was born in a *Telugu Brahmin* family and groomed by Annie Besant with a mission of making him a messiah through her Theosophical Society. He was trained according to her vision. Theosophical Society was based on the mystical insight into divine nature and claimed to be derived from the sacred writings of *Brahminism* and *Buddhism*. It has its belief in reincarnation and spiritual evolution. It believes in speculative mysticism and occult powers. Its emphasis is on universal brotherhood. It has its organisations both in India and the West. The Theosophical Society in India has become a hub of liberal *Brahmins*. Krishnamurti after disbanding the *order of star* and came out of clutches of Theosophical Society, and with the help of his followers formed the Krishnamurti's foundations all over the world in course of time. These foundations became platforms for his meetings. But there is no significant change in his articulation of various issues and his approach towards problems of the world. We may find a thread of continuity from Theosophical Society to the audiences of his speeches. However, he has become an international figure and got established as a phenomenon. He is a religious *guru* with modern attire and with cosmopolitan appeal.

In the wake of identity politics and my conviction in radical transformation of society, I have started relooking at Krishnamurti's writings. He dismisses any identity other than human which is an abstract and universal ideal that came up with liberalism. This makes me write a 'postscript' to my earlier work after fifteen years. I have observed closely the people engaged with Krishnamurti and found that Krishnamurti provides a solace for a particular set of people. As individuals they proved better than others but collectively Krishnamurti has exercised no impact. As a complementary to struggles against injustice, his thought is helpful in overcoming problems of hatred and egoism within social struggle. He can be seen as going along with theorists in talking of love. He reminds us of the limitation of our struggles by keeping in front of us, the total transformation as an ultimate end. If stretched to the extreme, Krishnamuti's dismissal of identification with any identity may ultimately end us without any struggle against injustice. However, he makes us cautious of limitations of our struggles by broadening our understanding of the reality if we read him properly.

In other words, these struggles came with alternative philosophical frameworks against the dominant liberal position. His ideas expose the limitations of liberal ideas aimed to transform the world on the path of progress and limits of identity struggles. Liberal thought aims to eliminate the traces of the past totally from human memory and identity. Simultaneously, it formulates new bonds of mind in the form of rationality yielding freedom. This freedom is a new kind of bondage tying mind to the world. On the other hand, identity struggles invent new pasts for one self supposedly ensuring a sense of belonging in times of swift changes in the world. Liberalism invents new desires and identity struggles offer securities in times of radical erasures of the past and the construction of delusive ambitions.

Krishnamurthi's ideas can be interpreted to show that it exposes the limits of pastless progress/predatory capitalism and selves inventing new pasts in the form of identity struggles. Krishnamurthi would look at both the streams as offering new forms of bondage. Freedom from bondage does not come from nervously possessing objects in the world. It comes from total cessation of attachments not just to things but to ideas as well. His idea of total freedom from the known is this in brief. It comes close to existentialism of Sartre.

Both the philosophies point to intense self-examination of self to see clearly fragmentations constituting core of it. By looking at divisions within the self, one could go beyond them. Both the streams assume radical individual responsibility for the kind of self one is. Their axis of thinking is internal freedom of the mind, not external freedom. It emphasises internalisation of responses to the external world. Both call attention to be critically aware of thought constructions shaping response to world. But, there are differences as well. Sartre factors in worldly affairs in achieving such freedom while Krishnamurthi totally focusses on the processes of mind for bondage as well as freedom.

Krishnamurthi's ideas have affected a large number of his followers. They have become better persons in relation to others. It also made them introspective humans highly obsessed with ones thought processes. In practical struggles against injustice, they have been found withdrawing from the mud of the routine life. In other words, they view fights against injustice as one more suffocating thought pattern which one needs to be free from. His ideas and followers stand in indifference to the injustices of every day. It cannot encompass liberative catharsis that the oppressed feel in their quest for justice because of extreme subjectivism. It should be enriched and brought in touch with objective world. One should be able to conceptualise the experiences of freedom in criticising injustice and freedom of the self should be seen as freedom of self being in the world.

However, the importance of Krishnamurti lies in his wholistic approach of understanding the reality against reductionistic approaches. For him, any of our understanding must be comprehensive and contemporary without having any distortion. In that process, he is critical about any preconceived notions about reality and demands for the suspension of judgment to understand a thing in its essence. He extends this in rejecting the tradition, belief, self, thought, knowledge and even time (Psychological). He has consciously kept away from the known philosophical categories and approaches in understanding the problems of the human life and the world. But at the same time, he was aware of philosophical wisdom of both eastern and western thought. He has reinvented new language in articulating the issues.

In simple terms, he appealed for freedom from the known for total understanding. He is not claiming as the philosopher or religious *guru*. He may not be a philosopher in technical sense as generally we have understood the term 'philosopher'. But today we are introspecting the very notion of philosophy. Philosophy describes, interprets and comprehends the everyday life experiences and social reality. Philosophy is a reflexive engagement of making meaning of our life. As cognitive enterprises, it differentiates the factual from the conceptual. We often find a gap between concepts and the facts. Our dominant philosophical theories are to an extent disconnected from the concrete contemporary experience. Krishnamurti opposed the binaries, such as materialism and idealism, tradition and modernity, culture and nature, empirical and analytical, conceptual and factual. Major theories are facing challenges from the unfolding of the historical events. Krishnamurti's approach will definitely overcome this kind of philosophical crisis. His notion of philosophy has a role of critical, transformative and emancipator character. He is a philosopher of life. There is a possibility to caricature his approach and its significance in contemporary times. My study is an attempt in this direction.

There is no doubt that his philosophical approach has its novelty and importance in addressing the vital problems of life but the question remains, how far it succeeds in transforming life, society and the world.

P. Kesava Kumar

Acknowledgements

First of all, I am thankful to my research supervisor Prof A. Ramamurthy, University of Hyderabad for helping me in organising the structure and content of the manuscript. I am extremely thankful to Prof G. Vedaparayana, ICPR Senior Fellow, Sri Venkateswara University, Tirupati for giving me the direction in proper understanding of J. Krishnamurti's writings and also for writing a foreword to this manuscript. I am thankful to my teachers in the Department of Philosophy, University of Hyderabad, Prof. Suresh Chandra, Prof Amitabh Dasgupta, Prof A. Raghuramaraju, Prof S.G. Kulkarni, Prof Chinmoy Goswamy (Late), Prof R.C. Pradhan, Dr. K.S. Prasad and Mr. Anand Wazalwar.

I am thankful to Krishnamurti Foundation of India, Chennai and Rishi Valley School, Madanapalle for giving me an opportunity to collect material and to engage in discussion with members of the foundations.

I am thankful to Dr Narayana Reddy (Late) of University of Hyderabad, who helped me with a lot of enthusiasm all the way in finishing this manuscript. I thank Dr Sindhu Menon, Department of English and University of Hyderabad, who unhesitatingly took up the task correcting the proofs. I am thankful to Dr Srividya Natarajan, Dr Nigel Joseph and Dr K.C. Bindu for meticulously going through the manuscript and for their valuable suggestions.

I am thankful to my friends Dr J. Aneel VB Babu, NIPCCD, Bengaluru, Dr S.V. Srinivas, CSCS, Bengaluru,

Dr Suneetha, Fellow, Anveshi, Hyderabad and Raja Indrakaran (Dr J), Dr Illa Ravi, Mr M. Shoban Babu, Mr N. Bhanutej, Dr B. Narendra, Dr Seshagiri Rao, Dr B. Eswar Rao, Dr Y. Srinivas Rao, Kathi Kalyan, Dr G. Lakshmi Prasad, Dr V.V.B.N. Rao, Former Director of Physical Education, University of Hyderabad, Prof R. Vijay, Prof R.V. Ramanamurty, Dr Sudhakar, Dr K.Y. Ratnam and Dr P. Thirumal of University of Hyderabad, Dr T.V. Madhu, Calicut University, Dr Koshy Tharakan, Goa University, Goa and Prof B. Thirupati Rao, Dravidian University, Kuppam.

My heartfelt thanks are to my friend Mr Kanaka Rao, Faculty at Assam University, Silchar for always engaging me in both academic and political discourses. I am especially thankful to my friend and well wisher, Dr J. Ravindranth, Dept. of English, Gayatri Vidya Parishad, Vizag, for giving me valuable suggestions to improve this manuscript and for his note.

I am thankful to the librarians and staff of IGML, University of Hyderabad, JNU Library, New Delhi and Nehru Memorial Library, Teenmurti Bhavan, New Delhi for allowing me to collect the material. I am thankful to UGC for providing me fellowship (JRF/SRF) in completing my doctoral research.

I am thankful to my colleagues at Department of Philosophy, Pondicherry University for their support in the Department and my research students for their help in preparing the index of the manuscript.

I am greatly indebted to my mother late P. Nagendramma and my grandmother late Kattupalli Chandra Mahalakshmi for their immense emotional support in my life. My special thanks to my family members, my brother P. Vijaya Kumar, my sister Dakshayini and my brother-in-law Dr Ramesh Babu for showing their affection towards me.

Finally, I am thankful a lot to my wife Dr P. Rajeswari and my beloved daughters Akshara and Asmitha for keeping me always in good spirits.

P. Kesava Kumar

1

Introduction

Jiddu Krishnamurti is a great thinker of our times. Several attempts have been made to characterise the teachings of J. Krishnamurti or to identify his thought in terms of the known categories of thought like religious, philosophical, psychological etc. It is really a problem to characterise Krishnamurti's thought either as philosophical or religious or psychological. Is it a kind of philosophy dealing with some general problems of philosophy like nature and meaning of human existence? Is Krishnamurti a free thinker generally concerned with the decline of moral values? Are his writings psychological explanation of human behaviour related especially to religion and spirituality? Or is his thought religious with a view to reconcile the traditional religions with the modern thought which is influenced and shaped by reason and positive sciences? Or can we say that his thought is revolutionary in nature which means that his intention is to bring about a radical change in human attitudes and ways of thinking?

Krishnamurti himself does not want to be placed in terms of any traditional categories as he thinks such classification of himself and his thought would be rigid and reductionistic. We find him making a constant effort to keep himself away from traditionally accepted roles and labels which are parochial as he is basically a universal man and his thought is not addressed to any one community, nation or tradition.

According to Krishnamurti the nature of definition is such that it overlooks the richness of the thing defined and to define human life in terms of certain categories is to miss the richness of life and its integral character. For him, there is no distinction between human life, thought and action. Krishnamurti has shown interest in human existence and its problems related to truth, freedom, self-knowledge and revolution. And in dealing with or discussing these problems, he has neither identified himself with any particular viewpoint or school of thought nor does he claim to have propounded a new theory or philosophy about anything. For him reflective understanding must not miss the uniqueness of the situation which may happen when one adheres to certain static notions and theories.

We began our introduction with a set of questions which one would normally like to pose in order to situate or identify a thinker. But *what is* more important, according to Krishnamurti, is not the problems which these questions address but the manner in which one approaches these problems. The traditional way of understanding these problems may not be adequate and inspiring. One must rethink these issues not by caricaturing the traditional understanding of them as it is often done but by revisiting them in their own freshness. It will be paradoxical as well as futile to approach Krishnamurti's thought and analysis in terms of already defined terminologies and accepted modes of analysis. The holism that we find in his reflections is not congenial to any kind of reduction or binary poles of opposition.

He is not a philosopher in academic or 'technical' terms as he does not indulge in arguments and proofs, nor is he interested in maintaining coherence of thought or in system building or in conceptualisation. Questions about epistemology or ontology are of least interest for him. To debate over the cognitive status of values is to indulge in a controversy over the primacy of mind or matter which is to miss the point.

Kishnamurti's main concerns are problems which human beings face and therefore if at all we want to see a purpose and goal to his thought, it is to emancipate human spirit from all types of conditioning. To understand and appreciate the thought of Krishnamurti, one should dispense with accepted philosophical techniques and categories and face the issues directly without too much indulging in conceptualisation etc. Most of the philosophical concepts are not free from presuppositions and prejudices peculiar to the system of philosophy or to the thinker who has formulated them. For instance many of the ideas we have about the world, human existence and social system to which we belong are mostly traditional and accepted uncritically. Because of these reasons Krishnamurti emphasises on looking at the problems and understanding them afresh without accepting the various ideas and values uncritically.

Though Krishnamurti has remained a popular and creative thinker, he has not been taken seriously by the academic community. If we understand the meaning of philosophy in the classical sense as a quest for wisdom, then Krishnamurti is definitely a philosopher and may be regarded as a 'philosopher of life' or of human spirit.

We find that Krishnamurti's thought is well informed by some of the age-old debates in the history of philosophy. We may even characterise him as a free and creative thinker who has tried to reconcile the wisdom of the East and the West. Though he is not a materialist or an idealist in the accepted sense, yet he has something new to offer in understanding the controversy between materialism and idealism. However, the implications of his thought may prove helpful and even insightful in understanding some of the problems of philosophy. He has not generally concerned himself with the problems which worried the academic philosophers or bothered him to revisit or re-interpret the traditional philosophical problems. One may find meaningful solutions from his thought to some of the philosophical problems, but that is not the main concern of his thought. Krishnamurti, on the controversy between idealism and materialism, remarks "Idealism is an escape from *what is* and materialism is another way of denying the measureless depths of the present. Both idealists and materialists have their own ways of avoiding the complex problems of suffering; both are consumed by their own craving, ambitions and conflicts and their ways of life are not conducive to tranquility. They are both responsible for the confusion and misery of the world".[1]

Krishnamurti thinks that in the process of inquiry into any problem concerning human existence, a commitment to any of the existing views would naturally lead to a partial understanding of the problem. Therefore one must suspend one's judgment about any problem and try to be just aware of the problem. One must be wholesome or integral in his approach not to miss the truth. For instance, if one wants to understand the nature of one's own reality one should consider one's conscious and unconscious mind. A suspension of judgment would lead to real self-knowledge which is what Krishnamurti calls the beginning of intelligence. Therefore all our inquiries must be spontaneous and free from preconceived and inherited notions.

Brief Biographical Sketch of J. Krishnamurti

Jiddu Krishnamurti also known as Krishnaji or JK, was born in a modest Telugu Brahmin family, on 11th May, 1895 in Madanapalle, Chittor district in South India. His father was a retired revenue officer who moved to Theosophical Society, Madras along with Krishnamurti and his other three sons, where Annie Besant offered a job for him. At that time accidentally, CF Lead Beater, one of the associates of Annie Besant, the president of Theosophical Society, sensed something unusual in the young Krishnamurti. In 1909 Krishnamurti was adopted by Annie Besant to herald him as a vehicle for the coming messiah and he was groomed for that role. In 1911, he was taken to Europe and was tutored privately under the supervision of learned theosophists like George Arundale, AE Woodhouse and Jinarajadasa. Towards the end of the nineteenth century, the resurgent Europe had bought many diverse people under its colonial umbrella and a niche had opened up for a movement capable of establishing links between separate cultures—Eastern and Western and between science and religion. The theosophical program of drawing these diverse spheres into a unified and peaceful brotherhood attracted a large membership all over the world. Keeping this program in mind, a suitable course of study was drawn up for Krishnamurti to serve the role of world teacher as predicted by the Theosophical Society. England to which Krishnamurti was introduced had been breaking out of smugness of the Victorian life and the growing prosperity helped to foster a liberal, progressive, intellectual and scientifically advanced culture. At the same time people were inspired with socialist ideals all over the world.

The emphasis of Krishnamurti's education was on learning languages like English, French, German and Italian. He was trained to use better expression. He was kept away from the religious scriptures, systems of philosophy and was allowed to think on his own.

The theosophists had been awaiting the advent of a world teacher to prepare for whose coming they had formed a group known as 'The Order of the Star in the East' with Krishnamurti as its head. In 1912, Krishnamurti was formally proclaimed as world teacher, but in 1929 he disbanded the order with his spiritually radical speech, *Truth is Pathless Land.* By doing so he rejected estate, money, power and all claims to authority or guru status. He kept himself away from theosophy and its organisation. In fact, by 1920 Krishnamurti developed doubts about the application of theosophy to human problems. Whereas theosophy had promised an evolution of spirit, Krishnamurti's teachings even in the early period aimed for something more like revolution. His brother Nitya's death brought into focus Krishnamurti's dissatisfaction with theosophy and marked the beginning of Krishnamurti turning away from theosophy. In 1927, on an occasion he wrote "When I began to think for myself, which has been not satisfied by any teaching, by any authority".[2] And he also maintains that "when a most critical moment comes theosophy and all its innumerable books do not help."[3] It is believed that Krishnamurti found enlightenment in 1927. In 1929, he questioned and negated the very idea of his future Messianic role. After keeping away from the shadow of theosophy, from 1927 to 1932 his speeches strongly concentrated on finding an apt form of expression for an effective and faultless delivery of his message while after that from 1933 onwards one discovers within him a certain stability of expression and approach. He adapted himself gradually to psychological probing into the nature of existence, the psychological structure, substance in the function of the mind and the constitution of human consciousness etc.

After disbanding the Order of the star, he declared that truth cannot be found through any sect or religion but only by freeing oneself from all forms of conditioning. He dedicated his whole life to set man absolutely free. For the next sixty years after disbanding the Order of the Star in the East, Krishnamurti travelled to different parts of the world giving discourses on his vision of life. For six decades until his death in 1986, at the age of ninety, he travelled over the world bringing his thoughts to those who were ready to listen. Krishnamurti's entire life was focused on realising and explaining the human quest. In all that time the message of his talks was that truth is pathless land, each one of us represents all humanity and one needs to be a light to one self, free from all authority.

He spent the last sixty years of his life in going all around the world and speaking to the mixed audience of varying temperaments and of different intellectual capacities, of different cultural marks, without distinction of sex, age, class, creed, nation or race. In conveying his teachings, Krishnamurti explored them as of thought, time, suffering, death space, silence and sacredness. In his speeches and dialogues, he addressed the evils of civil society and the irrationality of organised religions, futility of existing social structures, inertia in conforming to beliefs, dogmas and ideas and the failure of temporising reform. By mid-1950, he had developed notions about education, human relations and communications, which were not found in his earlier discourses. The range of his teachings further grew to embrace a number of new concerns such as nationalism, ecological despoliation, unemployment, hunger, poverty, with an almost contemporary sensitivity and the social issues that were once on the periphery of his perceptions came closer to the center stage.

Krishnamurti's language is simple and superb. Though he uses very simple words, yet every word has profound significance and establishes an intimacy with his audience. His teachings are free from all mythical or religious reference. His style is even free from standard terms, which are of having a traditional as well as established meaning and often infuses a word with an unusual and unexpected significance and opens within the most common words depths and heights and expressive charisma. As Aldous Huxley observes, 'it was like listening to a discourse of Buddha, such power, such intrinsic authority.'

Krishnamurti is an uncompromising and unclassified teacher, as his teachings were not linked to any specific religion and were for neither the East nor the West but for the whole world. Krishnamurti embraces within himself life in its totality. He rejects every ideology and every system of thought. He does not hold any viewpoint and so he does not propagate a theory, neither does he preach any dogma, or presents a philosophical doctrine and his teachings do not expand a definite theme. And yet he speaks of life, freedom, revolt and revolution and about suffering and self-knowledge. In the words of a well-known writer, Henri Miller, "His (Krishnamurti) language is naked, revelatory and impressing. It pierces the clouds of philosophy which confound our thought and restores the springs of action. He initiated no new faith or dogma, questioning everything, cultivated doubts and perseverance, freed himself of illusion and enchantment of pride, family and every ...form of domination over others. I know of no other living man whose thought is more inspiring." He spoke to the vast audiences in words that were of vital, catalytic relevance to every individual and every society. He was able to reach the core of the problems with which humanity has grappled for centuries. His teaching explores the reasons why mankind has lived in chaos and misery for thousands of years. The discussion brings to light, as the chief cause, the fragmentation of the mind deeply conditioned by race, nationality, religion and ideology which produces division, fear and conflict.

Krishnamurti humbly says, *I have nothing to offer you* since he views that *people need to be awakened not instructed*. But in reality, his teaching demands not only a self-correctness, a life free of self-centred activity but the awakening of enormous energy, radiating and integral to perception, which alone frees man from the bondage of time. The core of Krishnamurti's teachings is that man has to be a light into him; truth is a process of self-discovery. He advocates self-knowledge in the pursuit of truth. The miseries of the world can be ended only if man changed his own psyche to develop a broader outtook towards all creation, an outlook of love and compassion and sharing—as society and its ills were the creation of the psyche. He challenged the existing patterns of human living, thought, feeling and action. He urges us to look at life directly without the glasses of erudition and traditional wisdom. He perceives the unity of human existence, through insight and intelligence. The perception of truth, of the reality of *what is*—is essentially an individual problem he says. He refuses to accept the role of world teacher. The message of Krishnamurti is the message of love, compassion, self-criticism and freedom from past inhibitions. The aim of Krishnamurti's analysis is *freedom from the known*. He covers the entire gamut of human thought, aspiration and endeavour. He often discusses the relations between idea and action, contradictions of effort, the perils inherent in the acceptance of traditions and dogmas uncritically. His teachings do not propose any ideals since he considers the ideal is always *what is* not.

A careful examination of his works and teaching would reveal both consistency and changes while certain central concepts remain fundamental. Krishnamurti did not hesitate to adopt them to new historical circumstances and spiritual quests. In that way, his teachings are creative as well as without change in the essence despite the use of different terminology to suit the situation.

Human Crisis and World Disorder

We are at the threshold of the twenty first century. No one can deny the fact that there has been an unprecedented advance in science and technology. Even as we make certain claims about the progress that has been achieved, we experience a sense of loss or decline in certain aspects of human life and civilisaisation. On the one hand, there is a definite change in our living conditions while on the other humankind is engulfed in a series of ideological battles—religious, political, or economic. Then in what sense can we assert that our civilisaisation has achieved progress? What does it then mean to say that we have more knowledge about nature, the world and of man than ever before? Can we accept without any reservation or unconditionally the claim about progress?

We cannot deny the fact that the fragmentation of humanity into caste, class, nation, religion, ethnic groups is also unprecedented. Human beings are leading their lives not in a state of joy but under a constant fear of being destroyed. Mankind seems to be obsessed with the idea of domination in various forms like amassing wealth, monopolising trade and colonising nations. This domination is carried out with the help of certain institutions which are supposed to serve as custodians of moral life. Life is no more an expression of joy but a vulgar display of human weaknesses resulting in the increase of human suffering. We find ourselves trapped in activities that are really meaningless.

That humanity is facing a deep rooted crisis, is not a recent revelation and that there is a crisis is one thing on which all the creative thinkers largely agree. The symptoms were recognised long before and there have been many attempts to emancipate man from such a situation. But there is no unanimity among thinkers about the nature of the crisis and the way to overcome it. People from all walks of life—scientists, economists, spiritual leaders and political thinkers are concerned with the problem and their analysis of the situation and also their attempts to solve it are helpful in understanding the complex situation. However, the failure in overcoming the crisis is partly because the various thinkers are not clear in their diagnosis of the fundamental problem, and therefore, their solutions are not comprehensive and lasting. For instance, the economic solution to the problem is limited as human beings cannot be explained in terms of economics alone. The core of the problem lies in understanding the human nature in its totality. According to Krishnamurti, a solution to the crisis would emerge not from politics or religion, but from the insights about the human mind or psyche and also from understanding of the nature of human consciousness.

To understand the nature of man, we have to comprehend the nature of human consciousness. Therefore, Krishnamurti pays more attention to understand the nature of human consciousness. However, his attempt to characterise the nature of human consciousness is not the first of its kind; but what distinguishes Krishnamurti from others is his way of perceiving the problem. Krishnamurti feels that our inquiry must begin with an understanding of our traditional notions and attitudes that we cherish. He, however, feels that the various solutions that have come to us are conditioned by tradition and our past. The tradition, whatever may be its structure, can offer us only a partial view of the problem, and therefore, any attempt to offer a solution based on it would inevitably be conditioned by the limitations of the tradition. Krishnamurti would, therefore, like to encourage us to explore the psychological reasons behind the crisis which, according to him, would alone bring about emancipation of human intelligence and creativity from the limitations, authority and fear of tradition.

So far we have made an attempt to present some of the basic features of his thought and what follows is an attempt to highlight the problem that forms the focus of my study. Along with stating the problem of my study, I also try to point out the limitations of previous attempts by others. Two broad areas in which Krishnamurti's thought has its significant impact are education and human freedom. What forms the core of my thesis are his ideas on tradition and revolution which so far have not received their due attention. The problem of tradition and revolution is one of the most crucial problems that Krishnamurti has tried to analyse and understand in his writings as well as in his talks.

Living in the present, one finds it extremely difficult to ignore one's past. At the same time we also realise that the past which comes to us in the form of tradition has conditioned us and our ways of looking at and understanding things. What is required is clarity in terms used in negotiation with the past in understanding our place in and relation to the tradition. Moreover, the emerging world order also makes us rethink about our relation to the past. Thinkers of various ideological persuasions have tried to address themselves to this problem in their own ways. The objective of my critique is twofold. Firstly, to discuss the various ideologies like Marxism, different versions of liberalism and religion in general with a view to understand their approaches to the problem of tradition and revolution as well as their understanding of the problem itself. Secondly, I have tried to critically examine Krishnamurti's understanding of 'the problem of tradition and revolution' and to present and discuss his views on the problem, in a systematic manner. The second one is the major thrust of my thesis to which the first serves as a backdrop or introduction.

Problem of Tradition and Revolution

Tradition represents the past that is carried over into the present in the form of ideas, beliefs and images. It prescribes certain norms and conventions and stands for certain values which are transmitted from one generation to another. It is not static but something which flows in one form or other and is ingrained into contemporary thinking and practice. Revolution, on the other hand, aims at breaking away with the past or tradition and encourages constant questioning before accepting anything. Its object is to emancipate humanity from the past and its conditioning and to create a new world order. It tries to free mankind from the burden of tradition, so that the creative human energy finds an intelligent expression. By helping in creating a new social order based on human equality, it aims to end the exploitative structure of the traditional society. Thus, we see that tradition and revolution are not completely unrelated, though tradition and revolution are related as 'self' and the 'other'. Tradition tries to negotiate with revolution by appropriating it; revolution demands a total break from tradition. For Krishnamurti, tradition is something one has to do away within order to bring about a new world order. According to him, thought serves as a medium for the continuity of tradition. By the same token one may say that it tries to perpetuate the traditional values and ideas. Krishnamurti views thought as a response of our memory that is conditioned by our modern challenges and situation. Such a response would, therefore, be both incomplete and inadequate and would only help in strengthening the process of conditioning of our minds. The values, ideas and beliefs inherited from the tradition inhibit spontaneous response and free action as they condition our thinking and attitudes. As Krishnamurti says, "Knowledge, belief, conviction, conclusion and experience are hindrances to truth; they are the very structure of the self".[4]

Knowledge, involving thought, does not encourage independence. It hinders the possibility of seeing and experiencing things afresh. The different kinds of knowledge that we have are rooted in tradition and are, therefore, incomplete and limited. Its possibilities are also limited. For these reasons, Krishnamurti equates knowledge with tradition. We generally feel a sense of optimism about human situation with the advancement in science and technology. But to reduce human activity to science and technology is to limit human nature and its possibilities. Science and technology are due to a kind of human endeavour and imagination. Therefore, their claim to solve all the problems under the sun must be examined. Krishnamurti does not fail to acknowledge the progress that sciences have made and their value and importance to the progress of humankind. But the knowledge that sciences provide must be utilised with a lot of caution.

According to Krishnamurti, the emancipation of mankind from the crisis requires overcoming the past, its ways of thinking and understanding. To substantiate his position, Krishnamurti considers religion at length to throw light on the human crisis. Generally, religion is seen as the custodian of moral values and as final authority and solution with regard to human life and its problems. However, as science makes great advances, we find that religions of different kinds are losing their hold and authority over human life. Science has done us a great favour by questioning the beliefs upheld by different religions. In the modern world, science has replaced religion as the final authority but failed to alleviate human misery and suffering. One may even say that it has succeeded in turning human life more miserable. Communism is another major attempt to break away from all existing traditions. It envisages a social order which will be conducive to human welfare, free from all domination and exploitation. However, with the collapse of the Soviet Union and other east European countries, thinkers have started characterising communism as a false prophecy.

Another tendency that we witness in today's world is a journey back to tradition and to an extent traditions are being 'invented' to serve certain political goals. Identities are asserted with the help of traditions. This tendency is exemplified in the various movements that address the problem of cultural identity. The attempts to revive tradition have given rise to a much more complex problem of confrontation between traditional values and secular form of life. In this context, it may not be far from truth to say that secularism is also rooted in the past. One can definitely argue that secularism is motivated by humanism, accepts rationality and tolerance. Various notions like rationality and tolerance may themselves be motivated by not so apparent ideologies. Thus, we find that both the models (tradition and secularism) are equally problem ridden.

What differentiates Krishnamurti from others is his approach. He makes it very clear that ideologies, religions and the so called social reforms cannot bring about any substantive change in the existing situation. While attempting to provide a solution, he raises a few pertinent questions. Is the brain conditioned by scriptures, economic structures and other forms of ideologies? And if the brain presents us with continuity, can we put an end to it? Can the brain be free of psychological time? Is it possible for the brain to be totally free from memory or tradition? Is the brain capable of bringing about its own transformation? If the brain cells are keepers of memory of the tradition, then is it possible to transform the brain in order to get away from the conditioning memory? Does the brain have mechanism to carry this out?

Krishnamurti feels that the answer basically lies in transforming the very structure of human consciousness, which according to him is real 'revolution'. This change should take place in each and every cell of our brain. The revolution must take place spontaneously and in the present moment. It can happen only when the brain is totally free of all patterns and dominating structures. And that puts an end to the continuity of time which is the carrier of the past. Thus, a mind which is capable of transforming itself faces the challenge from moment to moment. And such a transformation enables us to be aware of and experience love, compassion and human relationships in an altogether different light. Thus, the revolution in the individual brains or minds would automatically bring about a change in the world order.

Krishnamurti has left behind a huge collection of writings and audio-visual records of his teachings. My study is concerned mainly with the teachings of post-realisaisation period, i.e., from 1927 to 1986. However, one may find a change only in his expression during this period but not in the essence of his teaching that is to set man unconditionally free.

The first chapter, *'On Tradition'* is a discussion of some of the views of important thinkers about tradition that has come down to us. This discussion provides a significant background for the exposition of Krishnamurti's views on the same problem. It also enables us to have a clear understanding of the issue involved. The role of tradition in our day to day life is highlighted. Krishnamurti holds that man is a product of tradition as well as its guardian. He defends it and strengthens it by his own contributions. Taking up different examples like family, religion, nation and moral values, I tried to discuss, how they act as barriers in attaining a clear understanding of the human nature. The discussion of Krishnamurti's views in this chapter is in no way exhaustive. My effort is only to introduce his thoughts along with the thought of other prominent thinkers who made significant contribution to the problem.

The second chapter entitled *'Traditional Mind'* probes further into the problem of tradition as viewed by Krishnamurti and focuses on the 'operations of the mind' under the influence of tradition. Traditional mind is viewed as a product of psychological evolution and as a shadow of certain images, formulae and conclusions that find their expression in thought. It is argued that the creation of 'I' is instrumental in the affirmation of certain notions. The role of thought in this process is analysed along with a discussion on the construction of certain structures of consciousness which are its correlate. Time, knowledge, memory and thought form a unit and condition the mind. They shape the very structure of mind, which Krishnamurti calls conditioning. Such a conditioning, according to Krishnamurti, results in an inability to respond creatively to different problems humans face in their day to day life. A conditioned mind fails to perceive the truth as a whole. This is because tradition supplies the mind with a sense of security which it does not want to forego in favour of adventure and freedom. Traditional mind by its very nature is fragmented, divisive and full of conflicts. It is rooted in fear, envy, insecurity and jealousy. The discussion of the operation of traditional mind paves the way for a detailed analysis of its implications in giving rise to a world order.

The third chapter is titled *'World Disorder and Traditional Revivalism'*. It begins with a discussion on the predicament of modern age that is reflected in personal relationships, politics and a disbelief in the claims of science, technology and religion. The fragmented responses of a conditioned mind only succeed in the revival of certain traditions. The emphasis on cultural identity is one among many identities. The argument for revivalism results in the 'closing of the mind'. Religions with a long history and political ideologies have failed to make sense of the situation. War and fragmentation of nations, only affirm the point further. According to Krishnamurti, the root of the problem lies in the structure of the human consciousness. The political turmoils that we witness all over the world are only individual's mental conflicts writ large. One can not draw a clear line of demarcation between the individual and society and both contribute for mutual sustenance. As the world, according to Krishnamurti, is an extension of human consciousness, the fundamental problem has to do with the very structure of the human psyche. The outer is the manifestation of the inner. This chapter also discusses the tendency, more explicit today than ever before, to invent 'traditions' in order to find answers to various problems. This becomes clear in the context of various movements that argue for particular traditions and identities. Religious fundamentalism and nationalism are discussed to understand

and illustrate the problem. The chapter ends with a discussion on Krishnamurti's attempt to understand human life as a whole in order to facilitate the emergence of a solution.

While the first three chapters deal with the formulation of the problem, the fourth chapter entitled *'On Revolution'* discusses the possibility of a 'way' out. The chapter begins with a discussion of the different views on revolution held by different thinkers and move on to an elaborate discussion of Krishnamurti's views. According to Krishnamurti, the solution does not lie in the application of a certain model, but in bringing about a fundamental change. A clear understanding of the structure of contemporary society and mind are prerequisites. Revolutions of the past, political or scientific, have only brought about piecemeal reforms. *What is* necessary is a radical and complete change. For Krishnamurti, revolution involves a complete and radical transformation of human psyche. Political systems or moral institutions are incapable of bringing this change. It demands a complete rejection of dominant structures. Such revolution, according to Krishnamurti, means an end to the continuity of time that carries tradition within itself. Revolution, in this sense, is not something that is to be realised in future. It must take place 'here' and 'now'. It is not time bound. It is marked by the absence of thought, memory and time. It is characterised as 'choiceless awareness' that realises 'freedom'. A mind that is capable of bringing about such a revolution is what he calls an 'intelligent mind'. An intelligent mind, according to him, is free and, therefore, capable of perceiving, the reality as a whole. It is both silent and meditative. He calls it, a 'religious mind' in the true sense of the term. It lives in freedom and is free from fear and anxiety. It experiences love and compassion with freshness and that marks the beginning of wisdom.

The final chapter begins with a discussion of the implications of psychological revolution to self-knowledge. An attempt is also made to argue a case for change in the global relationships sans war and violence. The revolution must be at the level of individual psyche. Only then a radical change at the collective level can be brought about. Such a revolution, Krishnamurti says, will establish a new world order. To make the discussion fruitful, I follow Krishnamurti's distinction between reality which is a product of the psychological time and Truth which is ending of past and the beginning of intelligence. He equates truth with 'nothingness'. But his notion of nothingness has not much similarity with that of Sartre and other existentialists. After a brief discussion of views on Brain, Mind and Cognition, I take up a comparison of Krishnamurti's project with some of the major philosophers both Eastern and Western. Thinkers like Plato, Marx, Freud, Sartre and Buddhist philosophy are discussed in order to show how Krishnamurti goes beyond them, though his thought has something in common with them.

Krishnamurti has contributed to the debate on tradition and modernity in his characteristic way. He finds that both of them are equally problematic and must, therefore, be rejected. While rejecting tradition, Krishnamurti does not counterpoise it to modernity, though we may see some of the modernist assumptions in his views. He maintains that there are no dualities and opposites. His only concern is that man should live the present or with *what is*. I discuss his views on tradition and modernity, along with those of Gandhi and Ambedkar, two of the most prominent contemporary Indian thinkers. Krishnamurti is more close to Ambedkar than Gandhi in some respects though he goes much farther than Ambedkar substantially. In the second and last section, I argue that Krishnamurti's notion of religion is a humanistic one. To give an example, one may point towards Zen Buddhism or the ideas that we find in the early writings of Marx. I conclude the chapter with a recapitulation of the controversy about characterising Krishnamurti as a mystic. In all these discussions, I have tried to take an independent stance in contrast to the dominant and the most prevailing views on Krishnamurti. Such a critical study I hope would at least bring into light the extent of relevance of Krishnamurti to the contemporary world.

End Notes

1. J. Krishnamurti, *Education and Significance of Life* (Madras: Krishnamurti Foundation of India, 1992), p. 63.
2. Cited in K. Krishnamurti (Comp), *Krishnamurti for Beginners*, p. 33.
3. *Ibid.*, p. 25.
4. J. Krishnamurti (D. Rajagopal (ed.)), *Commentaries on Living* First Series (Madras: KFI, 1991), p. 89.

2

On Tradition

"...Scientists say man is rational but the fact is that everyday life is irrational. Now we are asking, show us scientifically why it is irrational. That is, show man in what way he has slipped into this irrationality; why human beings accepted this. We can say it is habit, tradition, religion. And the scientists also, they are very rational in their own field, but irrational in their lives."

— J. Krishnamurti

This chapter discusses the concept of tradition in general to provide a significant background for understanding Krishnamurti's views on tradition. In order to place Krishnamurti's ideas in the context of a general debate and to give some idea of their uniqueness, several important definitions of tradition are examined. Some of these definitions are narrow and others broad and lucid and are given to show in what way Krishnamurti accepts or rejects them.

The word 'tradition' has several meanings. In academic circles, it is very often used in contrast with concepts like 'modernity', 'industrialisation', 'westernisation', 'development' and 'progress'. It is often discussed in relation to authority, convention, custom, habit and prejudice, norms etc. It is very difficult to conceptualise 'tradition' because the word conveys different meanings in different contexts.

The word 'tradition' is derived from '*tradere*' which means to transmit. According to the *Oxford English Dictionary,* 'tradition' means the action of handing over something to another. It also means delivery or transfer. It is especially oral delivery of information or instruction. It is the act of transmitting or handing down or being handed down from one person to another or from one generation to another. Transmission may be of statements, beliefs, rules, customs, or the like especially through word of mouth or by practice without writing. It further says that tradition is a long established and generally accepted custom, or method, or procedure, having almost the force of law.

Edmund Burke, an English political thinker of the early nineteenth century, argued strongly in favour of tradition. Reacting to the American and French Revolutions, Burke who represented conservatism, maintained that tradition is the wisdom of ages and that the life of the individual has to be rooted in the past. Institutions and customs are the products of the past. But tradition, in Burke's view is more than just institutions and customs; it is the 'spirit' of the people, defined in the course of a long history. So he feels that tradition has to be preserved and sustained. Institutions must be reformed, in accordance with their original principles and purposes. Burke's reforming impulses were directed towards restoring the legacy of the past and freeing it of corruption.

> "Tradition connotes nature and wisdom. To follow nature is 'wisdom without reflection', because we naturally respect tradition, which contains wisdom of the ages. This wisdom is embodied in custom, which should, therefore, be regarded with deference and even in the 'popular notions' which are not always laughed at".[1]

Burke gave more importance to feelings than to reason or knowledge. Being inclined to preserve tradition, he argues that the French Revolution was against the nature of things, a rebellion against God, a rupture with the universal order. Burke's empiricism leads through traditionalism to a kind of epistemological populism and an obvious leaning towards irrationalism. For example, he thinks that "When our feelings contradict our theories, the feelings are true and the theory is false".[2] Thus Burke prefers tradition to reason because he believes that it embodies more reliable knowledge. Though his traditionalism is surely anti-enlightenment, in its epistemological rationale, it shares a belief in the progress of the era of enlightenment. In that sense he thinks that tradition is to be respected since it represents the 'progressive experience' of mankind. He also thinks that tradition represents the wisdom of God, working through human experience in the course of human history.[3]

Michael Oakeshott, a well-known conservative political scientist, says, "Tradition is not a fixed and inflexible manner of doing things, it is a flow of sympathy". It may be temporarily disrupted by the incursion of foreign influences', or it may "reveal so deep-seated an incoherence that (even without foreign assistance) a crisis appears". But howsoever caused, "political crises always appear within a tradition of political activity". Oakeshott suggests that even a revolutionary crisis invariably appears within a tradition and in order to meet and resolve the crisis a society has nowhere to turn except to the tradition itself. He insists therefore that even in a crisis, however serious it may be, men in a society "have no resources outside the fragments, the vestiges, the relics of its own tradition of behaviour which the crisis has left untouched" and 'salvation' comes "from the unimpaired resources of the tradition itself". He also adds that "this is what no one is without and all, in fact, rely upon".[4]

T.S. Eliot, a famous poet and literary critic of the early twentieth century, attacked romanticism and humanism and so paved the way for neo-classicism in the twentieth century. By 'tradition' he means all those habitual actions, habits and customs, from the most significant religious rites to our conventional way of greeting a stranger. In his famous essay, *Tradition and the Individual Talent*, Eliot suggests that following a tradition is not merely "blind or timid adherence" to the past, but involves "the historical sense...a sense of the timeless and of the temporal together".[5] That is, the poet sees himself as part of a large historical structure of texts and ideas and judges his own work by the standards of the past. "What happens", Eliot writes, "is a continual surrender of him as he is at the moment of something more valuable".[6] This process of being absorbed by a tradition Eliot calls 'de-personalisation'. Neo-classicism, as Eliot sees it, is more than mere slavish imitation, a mere repetition of what has already been achieved, since "novelty is better than repetition". Tradition in the sense of passive is in fact repetition which needs to be discouraged. It represents the accumulated wisdom and experience of ages and its knowledge is essential for really great and noble achievements. For Eliot, tradition is not something immovable, but rather something constantly growing and becoming different from what it previously was. It carries within it both the essential and the non-essential, both the good and the bad. It must therefore be used intelligently and changes in the conditions of life must be taken into consideration so that only the best is preserved and fostered. Eliot believes that the past directs the present and is itself modified and altered by the present. The task of the poet is to make sure that the past is examined critically and only *what is* significant in it is acquired. Tradition in the real sense for him meant, a consciousness 'of the main current', which does not always flow invariably through the most distinguished reputations.

If Eliot confidently claims the poetic right to 'modify' tradition, the German philosopher Hans George Gadamer addressed the problem of how we can *read* and *use* traditions. Gadamer, who studies the problem from the hermeneutic point of view, claims that the historicity of humanity is manifested through tradition. For him, tradition accounts for both humanity's finitude and its openness to possible future. Tradition is not simply a cultural repository for the present; nor is it an autonomous historical realm that has a life apart from concrete human activity. It requires active appropriation, perpetuation and transformation by human subjects. For Gadamer tradition is ontological, which means that an individual comes to grips with tradition through living within it and experiencing it.

Gadamer identifies authority with tradition. Here authority has nothing to do with obedience, but rather with knowledge. Authority is superior knowledge. The recognition of authority is always connected with the idea that what authority state is not irrational and arbitrary, but can be seen, in principle, to be true. That which has been sanctioned by tradition and custom has an authority that is nameless. Our finite historical being is marked by the fact that the authority of what has been transmitted has power over our attitudes and behaviour. Gadamer maintains that tradition is constantly preserved by an element of freedom. Even the most genuine and solid tradition does not persist by itself. It needs to be affirmed, embraced and cultivated and the preservation of tradition is active historically. Our continually negotiated attitudes to the past reveal that we are not distancing and freeing ourselves from what has been transmitted. We stand always within a tradition. Conforming to a tradition is not an objectifying process, that is, we do not conceive of tradition as something alien. It is seen as a part of us. It is a model or an example for us. Tradition is therefore not opposed to freedom and knowledge according to Gadamer. It is actually a legitimate medium through which one can realise freedom. It is a prejudice of the Enlightenment and Romantic eras which assert that there is no rational ground to support the authority of tradition.[7]

Truth for Gadamer means what occurs as a 'fusion of horizons' much like what occurs in genuine conversation. To recognise the horizontal nature of understanding is to recognise differences because there is always something beyond one's own horizon. Perspective, or what Gadamer calls 'prejudice' *(voruteil)*, is not a bad thing to be overcome metaphysically. It is the preconditioned nature of understanding.

Edward Shills, an American sociologist who worked extensively on the concept of tradition in the later decades of the twentieth century suggests in his work *Tradition* that a tradition in its elementary sense is 'anything which is transmitted or handed down from the past to the present. It makes no statement about *what is* handed down or in what particular combination, or whether it is a physical object or a cultural constitution; it says nothing about how long it has been handed down and in what manner, orally or in written form. The degree of rational deliberation which has entered into its creation, presentation and reception likewise has nothing to do with it in a tradition'.[8] The concept of tradition, as we understand it, is silent about whether there is an acceptable evidence for the truth of the tradition or not. The anonymity or otherwise of its authors or creators likewise makes no difference as to whether or not it is a tradition. Edward Shills maintains that tradition is *what is* handed down and includes material objects, beliefs about all sorts of things, images of persons and events, practices and institutions. It includes buildings, monuments, landscapes, sculptures, paintings, books, tools, machines, practices and institutions made up by human actions. Thus traditions are beliefs, standards and rules of varying but never exhaustive explicitness, which have been received from the preceding generation, through a process of continuous transmission from generation to generation. They recommend themselves by their appropriateness for the present situation and a certain measure of authoritativeness which they possess by virtue of their being proven from the past.

Shills further says that the traditional rule possesses authority because its acceptance establishes an attachment to the past of a family, town, country or corporate body to which an inherent value is attributed. Membership in a primordial and a civil body carries with it not merely attachment to the symbol of the body at a particular moment in time but to symbols which expose a sense of creation, of a state of communion with past authority. It is of the same order as any act of communion with one's contemporary society. The affirmation of tradition, tacit or explicit, is an act which binds the recipients to the past. Shills also notes that traditions are slightly modified by both endogenous and exogenous factors.

An Indian scholar V.P. Varma is of the opinion that: Tradition is an inclusive concept. It connotes the initiative character of a certain dominant religious, theoretical, metaphysical and ethical values and beliefs. It also stands for the crystallisation of deference and reverence for certain symbols. Tradition also includes folk ways, mores and semi-institutionalised patterns of action in a society. At a more extended level, tradition may be identified with the totality of the historical heritage of a nation or a community.[9]

Tradition is a generic term and to a large extent identical with historical continuity in the field of social, cultural and interpersonal existence. J. Duncan M. Derret in his paper *Tradition and Law in India* maintains that "Tradition is that element in the present which represents (and re-presents) the past, whether or not people are conscious of it, whether or not they accept it...."[10] For him, an institution is traditional if the present society conforms to it. An outlook is traditional if the present generation approaches the same matter in the same way. He further adds that there are two kinds of traditions as there are two ways of self-consciously employing it. One form of tradition is 'fossilisation' as when a ceremony is retained even when its function has ceased. Another is the opposite of fossilisation. In it the old is continued functionally in the current and thus grows and moves in keeping with the needs and general growth of society. This form of tradition has a furtive and a slightly fraudulent air: it masquerades as the same and yet it is constantly subject to change.

Acton defines tradition systematically in his paper *Tradition and Some Other Form of Order*. He holds that a belief or practice becomes a tradition when, (a) It persists over several generations, (b) If it changes at all, it changes only slightly and gradually and (c) It is not questioned by its adherents nor thought by them to need justification.[11] Thus it may be said that traditions are chronic, continuous and authoritative.

An Indian sociologist Sachidananda holds that tradition is transmitted value and behaviour pattern of a community. Traditions are tested, recalled and esteemed. Their age long succession is an assurance of value which has already occurred in the process of their instrumental functioning as a constituent of social cohesion or social solidarity.[12] Many writers have noted that traditions are not static. Old traditions die and new ones are continually being built up. Leaving aside external influence, there are also, endogenous factors of change in tradition. The famous historian Eric Hobsbawm speaks of 'invented' traditions, which are taken to mean "a set of practices normally governed by overtly or tacitly accepted rules and norms of behaviour by repetition which automatically implies continuity with the past."[13]

After considering different ideas of tradition, now we may use a typology to arrive at an overview of the many meanings of tradition. We will use the typology suggested by S.L. Sharma.[14] S.L. Sharma says that it is possible to distinguish at least three meanings of tradition in sociological literature, i.e., existential, ideal-typical and analytical. As an existential category, "tradition refers to the heritage of a particular community."[15] Here the emphasis is on the historical particularities or the concrete elements of the tradition of a community. Anthropologists frequently use the term in this sense in their field studies of tribes and pre-literate societies.

Another meaning of tradition is ideal-typical which signifies a set of values common to a community or society. In this sense tradition is shorthand for such values as sacredness, ascription and slow change. Such a conception of tradition offers a criterion for determining what a traditional society is like. The last one, which is analytical-referential, is a more acceptable meaning of tradition. Analytically tradition connotes routine acceptance of a body of beliefs and action patterns from the past out of sheer reverence for the wisdom of the past. An excellent exposition of analytical notion of tradition can be seen in Edward

Shils.[16] Thus defined, the constituents of tradition are: givenness, a past, recurrence, filial and more importantly uncritical acceptance. According to the functional approach, all traditional cultures are sustained by a consistent corpus of norms and values.

Traditionalism

When we encounter tradition in our lived experience, especially in our own Indian context, we seldom evaluate it neutrally or classify it according to types; we in fact *live* it, either as an unexamined habit or as an oppressive structure. Very often we see it manifested concretely in strongly held ideas and rigid institutions. In other words we encounter it as traditionalism, an attitude examined below.

Traditionalism is the self-conscious, deliberate affirmation of traditional norms, with full awareness of their traditional nature. It is based on the feeling that the merit of the norms derives from their traditional transmission or from sacred origin. This could be manifested as a revivalistic and enthusiastic attitude. It is usually dogmatic and insists on uniformity. It insists on a thorough-going adherence and, does not discriminate between *what is* workable and *what is* unworkable. It regards all elements of tradition as equally essential.

Traditionalism is not content with the observance of a tradition in a particular sphere only, as in family or in religious life. It is satisfied only if the traditional outlook permeates all spheres—political, economic, cultural and religious and unifies and subordinates them to the sacred as it is received from the past. Traditionalism is almost always ideological and fanatical. It insists passionately on the full and conscious adherence to tradition with a form and elaboration unknown in the ordinary observance of tradition. It treats exceptions, qualifications and deviations as unhealthy or aberrant and wicked. It regards the pristine tradition in all its fullness as an adequate guide to conduct. Traditionalism is not only hostile to liberty, it is also radically hostile to tradition, the vague, flexible tradition which even when it does not include the tradition of liberty at least allows liberty to live on its margin of ambiguity, to grow gradually and to take deeper roots.

In oligarchic societies traditionalism prevents further growth of elements which can give rise to freedom. In the process of an ideological upsurge of traditionalism, tradition may be changed, stretched and modified by unified and national search for a consensual base for political authority and economic development. Traditionalism, as well as healthy development of 'traditions' depend upon the definition or active invention of a past, an idea which we are going to examine briefly.

The Invention of Tradition

The creation of tradition is not a short-term process. What we regard as tradition is the result of a long period of development. The existence of tradition and the persistence of primitive sentiments are shaped substantially by an individual's perception and loyalties from his childhood and adolescence through the process of socialisation. In the course of time, the personal experience of many becomes the collective experience of the community which is then enshrined as a tradition. Time-honoured customs pervade and regulate most aspects of daily routine. Wisdom is often equated with age and knowledge of the past rather than with youth or education or a vision of better future.

To carry forward tradition, certain human agencies and institutions are needed. Generally, tradition is transmitted from one generation to another through the family, schools and religious institutions. At present, the media also play a significant role in this regard. Tradition should be understood in the context of social change. Today, tradition is being revived worldwide in various forms. It is invented by interested groups to suit modern day politics. It is argued that tradition is renewed, created and discovered towards a goal which man aspires for and appeals to in some specific historical guise. As Gusfeild puts it:

"Tradition is not something waiting out there always over one's shoulder. It is rather plucked, created and shaped, to present the people's needs and aspirations in a given historical situation. Men refer to aspects of the past as tradition in grounding their present actions in some legitimating principle. In this fashion, tradition becomes ideology, a programme1 of action in which it functions as a goal or a justificatory base".[17]

Thus tradition is re-invented, re-created, re-enacted, re-represented, re-embodied, re-placed as a new form of tradition rather than the tradition of ancient form. Traditional continuity and authenticity appear as mere shadows of reality, in spite of territorial restoration, genealogical restoration and cultural renewal.

Salient Points

From the above discussion we may say that tradition has the following general features:

1. Tradition is related to the past. It is the knowledge about the past and, by and large, it is a mode of uncritical acceptance of the past.
2. It works as authority, in which an individual believes and regulates his attitudes and daily life accordingly.
3. Tradition generally lacks the total adaptability that would allow its followers to adjust their behaviour to new circumstances.
4. Tradition elevates the cultural and religious aspects of life and its values. It forms a coherent pattern giving men reason, an orderly rationale for a relatively stable life, at whatever level of society they find themselves in.
5. Tradition or a traditional structure pervades intimate human relations; it affects the relationship of an individual's relation to another and to the external world which gives people a degree of security in facing their appointed destiny within a traditional structure.
6. Tradition is a more or less homogeneous body of rules and ideas. As such, it is used as a normative or coercive force upon the people who are subjected to it.

7. Traditional structures can supply skills and traditional values can supply sources of legitimisation, which are capable of being utilised in the pursuit of new goals and with new processes.
8. Tradition has the capacity to evoke conformity even though it has undergone some modifications or changes.
9. It is selective as only some of the elements of the past are useful for fulfilling needs of society.

Krishnamurti's Conception of Tradition

Having discussed some views of prominent thinkers on tradition, we shall now examine Krishnamurti's views on tradition. According to Krishnamurti, tradition, broadly means carrying the past over to the present. It is to hand down, to pass on, to give from generation to generation a certain set of ideas, systems and beliefs. Tradition is a passing on of not only one's particular inheritance but also the weight of all the collective thought of a particular group of people who lived in a particular culture. That is, tradition is following a belief or an idea without much reflection. In Krishnamurti's view, man finds some kind of hope or security in tradition and therefore carries the burden of this accumulated knowledge. Krishnamurti, while reiterating some of the current notions about tradition, also gives a subtle and fundamentally new meaning to the concept. He suggests that tradition means betrayal. It is the betrayal of the present by the past.[18]

Tradition, according to Krishnamurti, is a barrier to living life in harmony and peace. Life in its actuality is in the 'present'. But tradition, which is of the past, cannot understand the beauty of actual life. Krishnamurti says, "To carry the past over to the present, to translate the movement of the present in terms of the past destroys the living beauty of the present."[19]

Tradition may be very ancient or a day old. It may imply a remote or a recent past. Yet all tradition is profane. Krishnamurti says:

"there is nothing sacred about tradition, however ancient or modern. The brain carries the memory of yesterday, which is tradition and is frightened to let go because it cannot face something new. Tradition becomes security".[20]

Krishnamurti holds that the brain or mind as we know it is itself traditional. It is through the brain that an individual carries the past over to the present.

"The brain is the centre of all senses. It is the centre of the past; it is the storehouse of experience and knowledge, tradition".[21]

The human mind has been caught up in tradition since time immemorial. Somewhere along the line of evolution, the mind began recording and repeating the past in the psychological sense. It started creating for itself a tradition by way of security. Thus the mind immersed in tradition has become an instrument which functions in a groove of imitation. The brain or mind becomes traditional by conditioning or programming itself through social, cultural and environmental conditions. It becomes mechanical and interacts with people, nature and ideas mechanically. The traditional mind functions strictly within tradition because it is afraid of public opinion. Krishnamurti says that a person who is born a Brahmin continues to be the same till he dies, moving in the same circle, in the same pattern, in the same framework. The traditional mind is not free from thought that is born of experience, of tradition, of memory; it is anchored in the past and therefore cannot be free.[22]

Tradition as Psychological Inheritance

Human being is conditioned by the past from the cradle to the grave. Apart from the conditioning of the mind by the factual past which is history, the mind is also conditioned by the psychological past, which is tradition. Culture and human environment all over the globe are structured so as to make the mind conform to tradition. Krishnamurti says:

"The imprint of the past on the young mind, the conscious and unconscious conditioning of the student to obey, to conform (the communists are now doing this very efficiently as the Catholics have for generations. other religious sects are also doing it, but not so purposefully or effectively), parents and society are shaping the minds of children through tradition, belief, dogma, prevents the coming into being a new social order".[23]

This psychological inheritance dictates all aspects of life. The brain derives power from this psychological inheritance, defends and limits itself to its own groove. The psychological past is no better than the physical past.

"Psychological inheritance is as conditioned as the inheritance of property; both limit and hold the mind in a particular pattern of society, which prevents a fundamental transformation of society".[24]

Positive Thinking

Many people have argued that in order to free oneself from tradition, one should cultivate 'positive thinking' and a 'positive attitude'. The cultivation of positive thinking involves a somewhat better understanding of the world around us and makes us free of tradition to a certain extent. But this freedom is illusory. The traditional mind always thinks and functions in a positive way. All its actions, however radical or negative they may be, are still traditional. They are the products of the past. They are the continuity of the tradition in a modified form. Positive thinking is no more a thinking; it is merely a modified continuity of what has been thought; the outward shape of it may change from time to time, depending on compulsions and pressures, but the core of positive thinking is always traditional. Positive thinking is the process of conformity and the mind that conforms can never be in a state of discovery.

The traditional mind is the product of time. Its evolution is a process by which the past modifies the present and passes into the future. Krishnamurti says that the past constitutes the background of mind and includes the racial, communal, religious memories and experiences. The patterns of traditions in which the mind is set have not radically changed. The old traditions perpetuate themselves. This has been going on for millions of years and basically, there is no basic change in human beings. Because of this, Krishnamurti says:

> "So the past going through the present, modifying itself, is the future. And that has been our evolution. Though biologically we have changed from millions of years till now, psychologically, inwardly, subjectively we are more or less what we were a million years ago barbarious, cruel, violent, competitive, ego-centric".[25]

It is clear that tradition entails the principle of seeking pleasure and the avoidance of pain. Pleasure lies in the repetition of past pleasant experiences and in the avoidance of the painful ones. The traditional mind lives by hoarding such memories from the past. Krishnamurti says, by way of example; "Suppose I had an affair which gave me pleasure. Then thought comes along and says: 'I would like to repeat it'. So it brings affair, memory, reaction to memory as thought, thought building images, demanding images. All this is part of tradition, the carrying over of yesterday into tomorrow".[26]

The older the civilisation, the greater the pre0ssure of tradition. The habit of repeating the past is stronger in the mind which is ancient. As Krishnamurti observes:

> "The older the civilisation, the greater the weight of tradition, of authority, of discipline which burdens the mind. People who belong to an old race, as in India, are more conditioned than those who live in America (for example, where there is more social and economic freedom and where people have fairly recently been pioneers)".[27]

The ancient past or tradition constitutes the unconscious part of the traditional mind. The mind consciously acts on the basis of the unconscious past. The conscious part of the mind is confined to the immediate present. It constitutes the superficial part of the whole of the traditional mind. The present of the traditional mind is nothing but unconscious determination by the past. "The deep unconsciousness is the past and we are operating from that. Therefore there is the division into the past, the present and the future".[28] Krishnamurti further says:

> "The conscious mind is occupied with the immediate, the limited present, whereas the unconscious is under the weight of centuries and cannot be stemmed or turned aside by an immediate necessity. The unconscious has the quality of deep time and the conscious mind, with its recent culture, cannot deal with its passing urgencies".[29]

The unconscious is hidden. It is more potent than the superficial mind. It is made up of the racial, religious and environmental influences and appears as though it is mysterious. But in fact the unconscious can be understood and revealed. According to Krishnamurti:

> "The hidden or unconscious mind is the repository of racial memories, religion, superstition, symbol, peculiar traditions of a particular race and the influence of literature both sacred and profane, of aspirations, frustrations, mannerisms and varieties of food-all these are rooted in unconsciousness".[30]

Psychologically the unconscious is made up of one's secret desires, motives, hopes, beliefs, pleasures, fears and sorrows. It is the storehouse of all the unreflective factors. It is the past or the tradition which influences the present and the future. Imitations of all this are given to the superficial mind through dreams and in various other ways when it is not wholly occupied with everyday events.

To Krishnamurti, there is in fact no such thing as the unconscious. The unconscious is part of the whole consciousness. The unconscious is *what is* suppressed or pushed behind as it were, by the mind. The mind has the tendency to be conscious of what it likes and it suppresses what it does not like. Everything that is there in consciousness is that which has come from outside. The whole of consciousness is the result of conditioning by external factors. So, the unconscious is not independent of the influences of society:

> "Society influences all of us, it constantly shapes our thinking and this pressure of society from the outside is gradually translated as the inner; but however deeply it penetrates, it is still from the outside and there is no such thing as inner as long as you do not break this conditioning".[31]

Much of the discussion and analysis of the concept of the tradition that we surveyed so far concerns itself with tradition at a superficial level, i.e., as a manifestation of social forces. But Krishnamurti tries to delve deep into the matter and wants to trace the psychic and mythical origins of tradition. He explains the origin and source of tradition, working backwards from a discussion of our immediate perceptions in everyday life. He holds that the 'observer is culture'. Our mind which is conditioned by the past, by culture and tradition, organises the stream of perceptions from the world. Whereas in actuality, truth is changing from moment to moment, as far as the perceptual act is concerned, we experience the world around us without having the total experience.

Krishnamurti maintains that all our experiences and perceptions, however modern they seem to be, are traditional. Our perceptions are traditional since they are based on conclusions and prejudices. They are the products of the mind which is traditional and dominated by the past. Krishnamurti holds that knowledge also is traditional since it is the repository of conclusions and ideas.

Krishnamurti is unique in saying that *'knowledge is tradition'*. Tradition is not only belief but also knowledge. Tradition is knowledge, since it is knowledge of the past. To know is to be in the past. To know is to be in tradition. So science is also tradition-bound in the sense that it works on the basis of the past. Scientific knowledge, however experimental or rational it may be, is still traditional. It is the continuation of the tradition with some modification. Thus scientific knowledge is limited like any other knowledge. Scientific knowledge is essential for biological survival. But it is also destined to be limited and traditional and that which is limited and tradition-bound is always a source of misery. Krishnamurti argues:

> "After all, knowledge is a form of tradition, is it not? And tradition is the cultivation of memory. Tradition in mechanical affairs is essential, but when tradition is used as a means of guiding man inwardly, it becomes a hindrance to the discovery of great things".[32]

Human beings have given undue importance to knowledge. They think that life is impossible without knowledge. Knowledge is treated as the guiding factor in all areas of life. But Krishnamurti contends that knowledge which is limited cannot help us to live a holistic life or in the present. But human beings accumulate knowledge in the hope of becoming secure and certain. In the words of Krishnamurti:

> "We are afraid that without knowledge we would be lost, we would not know how to conduct ourselves. So, through reading what the sages have said, through other people's beliefs and experiences, we gradually build up a background of knowledge which becomes tradition and behind this tradition we take refuge. We think this knowledge or tradition is essential and that without it we would be lost, we would not know what to do".[33]

Tradition regards knowledge as the means of freedom or liberation. But knowledge is itself tradition and freedom is beyond tradition. Tradition or knowledge is the continuity of the past which includes disposition, control, sublimation, suppression. So knowledge, being on the side of tradition, cannot achieve freedom; it is a barrier to freedom. According to Krishnamurti, it is not possible to attain enlightenment through knowledge. He asks:

> "Why did not the gurus, the Gita, question knowledge? Why did they not see that knowledge means the past and that the past cannot possibly bring enlightenment? Why did traditionalists not see that discipline, Sadhana, comes from knowledge?"[34]

Tradition is resorted to for the sake of security and comfort. The mind finds itself secure and comfortable in following a certain kind of belief or idea. By identifying with tradition, the mind feels anchored and ultimately gets conditioned by it. Not content with this security, the mind seeks to make tradition an authority to govern its actions. It has a desire to be secure and therefore strongly defends the authority which is exercised in various forms: the authority of scriptures, parents, gurus, state, law and police etc. Krishnamurti explains how authority comes into being and how it is imposed on young minds by parents, teachers and society. People desire to find a safe and acceptable form of behaviour, or they would like to be guided as to how they should behave in different situations and to be told what to do. Being confused and worried, the people go to a priest, or to a teacher, or to their parents or to somebody else, seeking a way out of that confusion. So it is the desire in us to find a particular way of life, a way of conduct that creates authority.

> "I have the desire to be comforted, to be told what to do. So I create an authority. That authority does not really exist outside me".[35]

Authority may be outward or inward. Outward authority is what others impose on us which comes in the form of rules, regulations and laws enforced by society. Inward authority is living according to one's own ideals. It is disciplining one's mind internally. Discipline and living according to an external ideal is itself tradition. In this, tradition brings about a conflict between '*what is*' and 'what should be' which is the ideal. Krishnamurti wonders:

> "And what happens to you? You get crushed, you are just broken. You never think, act and live vitally, for you are afraid of all these things. You say that you must obey, otherwise you will be helpless. Which means what? That you create authority because you are seeking a safe way of conduct, a secure manner of living. The very pursuit of security creates authority and that is why you become a mere slave, a cog in the machine, living without any capacity to think, to create."[36]

Krishnamurti maintains that the traditional mind can never find freedom or truth; because tradition is the past and freedom is in the 'now'. As it has been already mentioned, tradition and freedom do not go together. Any acceptance of authority is the very denial of truth. Krishnamurti further says, "Truth is never in the past. The truth of the past is the use of memory, memory is of time and in the dead ashes of yesterday there is no truth. It is not with in the field of time."[37]

There is also the authority of the ideal which is not outward but inward. When we say, 'I must be good, I must not be envious, I must feel brotherly to everybody', we create in our mind the authority of the ideal. Do we not? [38]

Krishnamurti says that tradition does not contain truth. Tradition is full of symbols which are of knowledge. And the symbol is an outward sign of *what is* in the past, but truth is in the present. Krishnamurti says:

> "The word, the symbol has become an extraordinary destructive thing for most of us and of this we are unaware. Do you know what I mean by symbol? The symbol is the shadow of truth. The word, the symbol, the image, the idea is not the truth, but we worship the image, we revere the symbol, we give great significance to the word and all this is very destructive; because then the word, the symbol, the image becomes all important."[39]

As mentioned earlier, thought is the source of tradition. Tradition has its continuity through thought. Thought gives permanence to symbols, words, images of the tradition. Krishnamurti maintains that thought ensures the continuity and persistence of tradition in the present. There is nothing permanent either on earth or in our mind. But thought can give continuity to something it thinks about. It can give permanency to the word, or to an idea which is tradition. It can build an image and give to that image continuity and permanency. It is the tendency of the human mind that it "wants permanency in everything, in relationship, in property and in virtue. It wants something which cannot be destroyed. That is why we say good is permanent, or truth is absolute."[40]

Thus, all our conditioned knowledge and traditions are barriers to the discovery of truth. In its nature, tradition is divisive and is a source of conflict. Tradition not only conditions our thinking but also separates us from others. If one identifies oneself with a particular tradition, which he claims as real, it means he isolates himself from the whole or that which includes all other traditions. As Krishnamurti says:

> "Knowledge is a hindrance when it has become a tradition which shapes or conditions the mind to a particular pattern, because then it not only divides people and creates enmity between them, but it also prevents the deep discovery of *what is* truth, *what is* life."[41]

For Krishnamurti, life is in the present. Life is discontinuous whereas tradition is associated with the past and maintains continuity. Traditional life which is irrational and incomplete is no life at all. Krishnamurti declares that man is basically irrational, for he is tradition-bound. Man gives undue importance to thought and knowledge which are the source as well as the expressions of tradition. Being based on thought man's life goes on mechanically and thoughtlessly.[42]

According to Krishnamurti even the 'self' or 'I' or the 'me' is the product of tradition, for the 'I' is the product of thought which tradition is and the 'I' is the source of division and conflict. Where there is the 'self' there is incompleteness which necessarily leads to sorrow. 'I' is related to thought and its continuity. The 'me', survives by the maintenance of thought. It has the tendency to separate the 'I' from others; it is divisive. 'Me' exists due to desire, or it represents the desire for security. The desire is the product of thought, or when the desire takes the form of 'me' the duality is created. Duality is the root cause of all our problems. So far tradition has been discussed in its psychological and subtle sense.

Krishnamurti also explains tradition as manifested in human relations, comprising the institutions like society, religion and family etc. To Krishnamurti society is the psychological extension of the traditional mind. Society does not have an independent existence. Krishnamurti says, "Society by itself is non-existent. Society is what you and I, in our relationship, have created; it is the outward projection of all our own inward psychological states."[43]

In course of time, man developed certain social structures and institutions. But many of the structures and values that have been built in the course of human development are inhuman and anti-developmental. That is why there have been movements struggling against political, social and cultural structures which are inherently violent and oppressive. These institutions flourish because of the individual's assumption of power through them. It is a fact that where the power-relations exist, there the conflict starts. Krishnamurti says, our social structure is based on the principle of pleasure. The individuals who are powerful dominate and exploit others for the sake of pleasure and they build institutions or structures starting from the individual to the collective level. The dominance, the authority, is institutionalised, which can be seen in the form of state, law and justice. As Krishnamurti puts it:

> "The powerful families build themselves into high positions, they acquire big properties, they have more money, more clothes, more cars; they get together and frame the laws, they tell the rest of us what to do. So gradually there comes into big society with laws, regulations, policemen, with an army and navy."[44]

In the course of evolution man has evolved not only biologically but also psychologically. Biological evolution is a fact whereas the psychological evolution is a product of thought. It becomes internalised in our psyche and this becomes potentially violent also. There is also violence pervading institutions like family, caste, religion, education and so on. These institutions perpetuate violence through very well-developed methods of internalisation. Internalised violence does not look like violence even to those who are subjected to it. In the words of Krishnamurti:

> "We are violent people, aggressive, not only physically but also psychologically, inwardly, Violence is not merely physical action, violence is also psychological—aggressive, imitative, comparing oneself with another and so on, all that is a form of violence".[45]

With the passage of time there has definitely been a change in these institutions. But it is only a modification and the basic structure of the mind has never changed. One of the reasons is that these institutions, not only have limited transformation, but also sustain themselves due to human failure to change. Ultimately they are tradition-bound and perpetuate exploitation. For all these institutions combine in themselves necessity, stability, emotion and sentiment. Several of these institutions are human at one level and violent at another level. That is precisely the reason why none of these institutions remained the same either in form or content.[46] Many of these institutions are powerful, authoritative and hierarchical. All these are characteristics of tradition. Krishnamurti, in all his talks, refers particularly to religion, family, state and nationality, where one can locate tradition in an effective way. They have a divisive character and they are being continued, because they lack creative potentiality.

Human Relations

To be is to be related. Relationship is the basis of our existence and of our society. The relationship may be with people, property and ideas. The relationships between man and woman, among different castes, among different religions, among different classes, constitute our life. Krishnamurti says, "Our life is movement in relationship, however much one may think, we live alone, one is always related to something or other, either to the past or to some projected images in the future".[47]

Relationships are tradition bound. They are rigid, hierarchical, authoritative and divisive. These relations are exploitative, prejudiced and preconceived. They are based on images which are the product of thought. In the words of Krishnamurti:

> "In relationships which are moving, not static we form a relationship and later get into the habit of looking at it from a fixed point of view-whether the relationship is with one's wife, or one's children, or one's neighbours. Such relationship ceases to be creative, they become dead. Habit of any kind dulls the mind".[48]

Our relationships are based on images and we continue to see things with the help of images which prevent us from directly seeing the reality. The image is nothing but the memory which conditions our everyday life. So the relationships are superficial. Krishnamurti says, "The relationship is between these two verbal pictures in memory, it is not actual and therefore, there is always division and conflict. When you have been hurt in that relationship; it is the image you have built about yourself that has been hurt".[49]

Relationships are put together by thought. Thought, which regulates relationships, is always rooted in the past, so that relationship is not real and fresh but dead and old. The relationships are also often traditional, in the sense that they are based on mutual need and use. They involve exploitation and violence. So the very basis of society is violence. As Krishnamurti says, "As long as social structure is based on mutual need and use, it is bound to be violent and disruptive".[50]

Human relations, in general, are based on cultural background and economic foundation. As Marxists have argued, all human relations are economic in character. They hold that the uneven distribution of wealth and resources is responsible for social conflicts. Though Krishnamurti does not discuss much human relations from the economic point of view, he recognises the fact that economic factors also play a role in human relations. He reiterates that human relations are bound by political, social and economic factors.

Religion as Tradition

Religion, according to Krishnamurti, is the product of tradition. It is put together by thought and is rooted in the past. All our religions are organised sets of beliefs and superstitions and are conditioned by the tradition which carries beliefs and superstitions to the future. Religions are institutions which affect all aspects of human life and demand conformity with tradition. As Krishnamurti puts it, "Religion as we generally know it is a series of beliefs, dogmas, rituals, superstitions; it is the worship of idols, of charms and gurus and we think all these will lead us to some ultimate goal. Belief will never free your mind, belief only corrupts, binds, darkens."[51]

Belief in the existence of God is fundamental to most religions. God is believed to be omniscient and omnipotent. God is also believed to be the creator, the sustainer and the destroyer of the people and the world. But God, according to Krishnamurti, is an idea invented by man as an escape from his misery, anxiety, despair and loneliness. Krishnamurti says, "God is your invention because you find life so dull and boring. It is such pain. So you invent God who is all perfect, all living; you worship that which you have put together by thought".[52]

For Krishnamurti, the question whether God exists or not is meaningless. God is the outcome of the individual's running away from reality. God is the product of thought, an abstraction of the hopes and feelings of the people. God is the product of human thought and knowledge and as thought and knowledge are limited, God is also limited. Krishnamurti says:

> "Shut your eyes and close your ears. You can still think. Thinking about God is within the field of thought. The man who has not thought at all, to him there is no God. The ancient ones, thinking about something superior, wanting

something greater, said that was God. That was the product of thought. So that was within the field of knowledge".[53]

Religion is mostly an imitation and repetition of what others did in the past. There is no scope for free inquiry and understanding in religion. In religion, rituals are repeated and symbols are copied.Why do older people perform rituals? Because their fathers did it before them and also because it gives them certain feelings, sensations, it makes them inwardly quiet. They chant some prayers, thinking that if they do not do so, they might be lost. And young people copy them, so your imitation begins.[54]

Tradition in the form of religion is being transmitted from one generation to another. There is no place for skepticism or doubt in religion. Krishnamurti holds that organised religion with its set of beliefs is irrational. According to Krishnamurti, religion is not doing pooja or performing ritual, nor is it wearing a particular kind of dress. Organised religions with all their paraphernalia have nothing to do with *what is* truly religious. Doing pooja, performing rituals in front of an idol or altar may give one a sense of satisfaction but it is not religion. Krishnamurti says:

> "Putting on the sacred thread, calling yourself a Hindu, a Buddhist, or a Christian, accepting certain traditions, dogmas, beliefs—has all this thing, anything to do with religion? Obviously not".[55]

The traditional or the mechanical character of the human mind is clearly revealed in the case of organised religions. The fact that an ordinary stone or stick becomes God is testimony to the traditional attitude of the mind. The mind hypnotises itself in the name of religion. It tends to believe anything to be sacred and divine. It deceives itself into believing as God *what is* not really so. Krishnamurti explains:

> "Take a stick or a piece of stone, put it on a mantel piece and every day place a fresh flower in front of it at the same time saying something like 'Om' or 'Amen'. Do this for a month and you will see how holy those stick or stone has become, although of course only your devotion has made it so and it is

> not really different from any other you might pick up by roadside".[56]

Prayer is one of the characteristic religious activities. The religious man prays for the grace of God and totally surrenders to him. Prayer is supplication. It is a kind of begging to fill one's empty bowl of the confused and insecure mind. In prayer, the person underestimates himself. He suppresses his own potentialities. Prayer is self-hypnosis. It works like a drug which calms the superficial layers of the mind for the time being. It helps one to escape from the actuality of life. Being repetitive and mechanical, prayer in fact renders the mind dull and inactive. According to Krishnamurti:

> "Prayer is a sedative which enables us to continue in our psychological prison without feeling the need of bursting it open and destroying it. The mechanism of prayer ...gives a mechanical result....It has all kinds of ideas, concepts and beliefs about the unlimited and is enclosed in a system of explanations, locked up in a mental prison. Prayer binds, it does not liberate."[57]

Religious people abide by their scriptures and treat them as sacred. They approach it for the answers to their problems. The sacred book is one of the basic requirements of religion in the sense of tradition. Every religion considers its scriptures as the ultimate authority. Scriptural authority is considered the source for religion. Scripture means the written word, which is past. Religious people exploit other people in the name of sacredness. Krishnamurti says:

> "Through fear you create a spiritual authority and to administer that authority there are priests who exploit you through belief, dogma and creed, through show, pomp and pageantry, which throughout the world is called religion. It is essentially based on fear, though you may call it the love of god or truth; it is if you examine it intelligently, nothing but the result of fear, therefore, it must become one of the means of exploiting man."[58]

Krishnamurti however admits that religious scriptures do contain *what is* sacred. But the sacred is adulterated by the profane. Since the scriptures are ancient, they are interpreted and re-interpreted several times and in the process they are deprived of their original core or essence. Ultimately what remains are the rituals and dogmas in all religions and the seekers get caught in their net:

> "It would have been a most interesting task to find in the various religious scriptures the old authentic teachings. Some traces remain and it is because of them religions (are) still attracting men of integrity and goodwill. This is regrettable indeed, for the earnest spirits get trapped in the net of rituals and dogmas".[59]

Tradition in the sense of religious dogmatism has been reduced with the advent of science and some of the religious beliefs have been proved to be irrational. But yet the religions have not disappeared and hold on to their symbols, rituals and beliefs in the name of eternity. The religious world-views are proved to be irrational and baseless and yet they maintain their dogmas through propaganda and force. On one hand, the religions try to come to terms with science and on the other they claim to be the custodians of eternal truth. In the words of Krishnamurti:

> "They continue their propaganda in order to maintain their power over minds. They seek to get hold of children to condition them better. The religions whether of church or of state demand from man every virtue, but their history shows a succession of violence, terrors, tortures, massacres, horrors beyond imagination."[60]

Belief is the fundamental feature of religion and belief is where truth is not. Belief and truth do not go together. Therefore, beliefs divide people. "So belief brings enmity, division, destruction and that is obviously not religion",[61] according to Krishnamurti. [61]

Family as the Extension of Tradition

Family is the centre of tradition. It is the most effective and powerful institution in carrying out tradition. It is the embodiment of traditional values, morals and customs. All kinds of conditioning start within the family and family is the source of continuity of tradition from generation to generation. It is through the elders in the family that the beliefs, culture and values are handed down to successive generations. In the family, the relationships among members are fixed and defined and individual members have to play their parts accordingly. The relationships among them may be close and intimate but still are authoritative and hierarchical.

The family dictates the code of conduct to the individual according to his background. The customs, ceremonies and norms are part of tradition and in the family they are carried out without questioning their validity. The individual adheres to them because his family gives a kind of security to him. In the family, the ownership of property and its protection are involved. Obviously, the family is an institution which seeks power and domination, thus leading to oppression. Though some families claim that they are totally free, in practice, the freedom in them is very limited, for essentially, the family as an institution is tradition bound. And the tradition is bound to the past which is limited.

At present the family and its values are contested due to their traditional character. The family is an especially oppressive institution for women and in most traditions, the family is patriarchal in character. Women are treated as second-rate human beings. They are used as objects for the pleasure of man. Krishnamurti says that it is a tradition to treat women contemptuously, almost like a door-mat. He asks, "Are you conscious, for example, why you treat women differently from men? Why do you treat women contemptuously? At least men often do".[62]

The life of women is controlled more by tradition than that of men. There are more restrictions upon women in the name of tradition. Tradition dictates their lives in several aspects. Krishnamurti says:

> "You are controlled by tradition—you must do this and not that, you must wear your sari in a certain way, you must

not look at the boys or at the girls. Tradition tells what to do."[63]

Family dictates everything in the name of tradition, not only to women, but also to children, who are moulded according to the patterns of tradition through family.

State as the Continuation of Tradition

State is also a product of time, which is tradition. People form the state to protect themselves from others. It is the collective interest of individuals that is exercised in the form of the state. It is the extension of the individual's belief system. As Krishnamurti puts it, gradually, through centuries, we establish a system of law, of authority, the state, the government, the police, the army to protect 'me' and 'mine'.[64]

The state, like the family, is authoritative. The authority of the state is derived from the tradition of the dominant sections of the society whose interests are sought to be imposed on others. The state functions according to traditional norms and becomes an exploitative institution in the hands of the powerful people. In the words of Krishnamurti:

> "There is the outward authority of the state, of the law, of the police. We create this authority outwardly because we have property which we want to protect. The property is ours and we don't want anyone else to have it, so we create a government which becomes our authority; it is our invention, to protect us, to protect our way of life, our system of thought."[65]

The state expects the individual to conform to its norms and rules. It reduces an individual to a citizen. The citizen is one who obeys the rules of the state. The citizen is not free to think and act as he wishes to. He has to abide by the ideology of the state even though the ideology is irrational and authoritative. Krishnamurti argues:

> "Whether it is communist, capitalist or socialist, the state has ideas as to how I should behave. There are those who say the state is all important. If I live in such a state and do

anything contrary to the official ideology, I am coerced by the state—that is by the few who control the state."[66]

Nationalism is another powerful and destructive manifestation of tradition. Nationalism, like family, religion and state sets up its own ideas, symbols and sentiments. Krishnamurti thinks that nationalism is a form of glorified tribalism. It is a very narrow and primitive conception. Though it gives a certain identity to the individual, it has the tendency to cause separation and division. It puts a group of people in opposition to other groups and this gives rise to conflict, violence and war. Nationalism is basically a product of thought and therefore has all the possibilities of making human beings conditioned and destructive.

Social Morality

Even the morality that people observe is traditional, in the sense that it is mechanical and inauthentic. Morality that is dictated by society means conformity to the existing social structure. Social morality is based on self-centeredness and mutual exploitation. It is based on norms of respectability which are merely expedient. Krishnamurti contends that social morality is no morality at all. In his words:

> "Today all morality is to be moral, for the accepted morality is the morality of respectability and I am afraid we all crave to be respected—which is to be recognised as good citizens in a rotten society. Respectability is very profitable and ensures you a good job and a steady income. The accepted morality of greed, envy and hate is the way of the establishment".[67]

Thus tradition is authoritative in all its dimensions. The institutions of family, religion, state and society or the world as a whole are authoritative. The individual is conditioned and controlled by authority under the garb of tradition. Men are bound by tradition 'within' as well as 'without'. Krishnamurti declares, "Everything about you, if you have observed it, reflects a way of life in which authority is very established. There is the authority of Gurus, the authority of political group, the authority of the parents and of public opinion."[68]

Tradition as authority kills the initiative of the individual. Tradition means copying and following the past in a variety of ways, which are barriers to clear understanding and creativity. It acts as a hurdle to the discovery of truth which is sacred. Krishnamurti says that tradition, or carrying the past over to the present and future deprives man of the rare privilege of comprehending the highest form of intelligence:

> "Initiative is destroyed, when you are merely copying, when you are bound by tradition, following a political leader or a religious Swami. To follow anybody is surely detrimental to intelligence. The authority destroys intelligence. It conditions freedom."[69]

Individuals identify themselves with tradition for the sake of psychological security. But as there is no such thing as psychological security, the tradition becomes a threat to the physical security of men. Seeking security through traditional institutions like family, state and nationalism often results in threats to physical security.

End Notes

1. Edmund Burke, "Works and Correspondence" Vol. V. p. 360. Cited in, Michael Freeman, *Edmond Burke and the Critique of Political Radicalism* (Chicago: University of Chicago Press, 1980), p. 29.
2. Edmund Burke, "Works and Correspondence" Vol. IV, p . 406. Cited in Michael Freeman, p. 30.
3. Edmund Burke, "Works and Correspondents" Vol. IV. p. 388. Cited in Michael Freeman, p. 29.
4. Quoted in Randhir Singh, *Reason, Revolution and Political Theory,* New Delhi: People's Publishing, 1976, pp. 119-120.
5. T.S. Eliot, "Tradition and Individual Talent", M.H. Abrams (ed.) *Norton Anthology of English Literature*, Vol. 2, New York: W.W. Norton, 1993, p. 2294.
6. *Ibid.,* p. 2296.

7. Prejudices are significant in as they are the cultural anticipations that make possible our understanding texts, cultural products, human actions and ourselves. Prejudices are neither suspended, nor dogmatically maintained but are corrected or modified through the dialectical movement of understanding in the relationship of part to whole.
8. Edward Shils, *Tradition,* London and Boston: Faber and Faber, 1981, p. 12.
9. V.P. Varma, "Conceptual Framework for the Study of Tradition and Modernisation" In S.K. Srivastava (ed.), *Tradition and Modernisation*, Allahabad: Indian International Publications, 1976, p. 35.
10. J. Duncon M. Derret, "Tradition and Law in India" In R.J. Moore (ed.), *Tradition and Politics in South Asia*, New Delhi: Vikas Publishing House Pvt. Ltd., 1979, p. 32.
11. Acton, "Tradition and Some Other Forms of Order" cited in Andrey Cantle, "*The Concept of Tradition*" In Moore (ed.). p. 1.
12. Sachidanada, "Tradition, Modernity and Modernisation in India" In Srivastava (ed.), p. 41.
13. Eric Hobsbawm "Introduction: Inventing Traditions" In Eric Hobsbawm and Terence Ranger (eds.), *Invention of Tradition,* Cambridge: The University Press, 1984, p. l.
14. See S.L. Sharma, "Concepts of Modernisation", In Rajendra Pandey (ed.), *Modernisation and Social Change,* New Delhi: Criterion Publications, 1988, p. 17.
15. See E.E. Evans Pritchard, *Social Anthropology,* London: Routledge and Kegan Paul, 1972.
16. See Shils, *Tradition.*
17. Joseph. R. Gusfeild, "Tradition and Modernity: Misplaced Polarities in the Study of Social Change" In Claude E. Welch Jr. (ed.), *Political Modernisation: A Reader in Comparative Political Change,* California: Wordsworth Publishing Company Inc, 1971, p. 56.
18. J. Krishnamurti, "4th Public Talk, Bombay 29th January, 1978". *The Krishnamurti Text Collection* (CD-Rom) (Madras: KFI).

19. Mary Lutyens, *Second Penguin Krishnamurti Reader*, Harmonds Worth: Penguin Books, 1982, p. 71.
20. *Ibid.*, p. 71.
21. J. Krishnamurti, *Krishnamurti's Notebook,* Madras: KFI, 1991, p. 9.
22. J. Krishnamurti, "9th Talk to Students at Rajghat, January 14, 1954". *The Krishnamurti Taxi Collection* (CD-Rom) (Madras: KFI).
23. J. Krishnamurti, *Commentaries on Living,* 3rd series, Madras: KFI, 1992, p. 57.
24. *Ibid.*, p. 57.
25. J. Krishnamurti, *Last Talk at Saanen,* 1985, Sanfranscisco: Harper and Row Publishers, 1986, p. 85.
26. J. Krishnamurti, *Tradition and Revolution,* Madras: KFI, 1972, p. 78.
27. J. Krishnamurti, *Life Ahead,* London: Victor Gollencz, 1987, p. 49.
28. J. Krishnamurti, *The Flight of the Eagle,* Madras: KFI, 1988, p. 77.
29. J. Krishnamurti, *Life Ahead*, p. 23.
30. *Ibid.,* p. 23.
31. J. Krishnamurti, *This Matter of Culture,* Madras: KFI, 1964, p. 66.
32. *Ibid.*, p. 122.
33. J. Krishnamurti, *Life Ahead*, p. 92.
34. J. Krishnamurti, *Tradition and Revolution*, p.77.
35. J. Krishnamurti, *Life Ahead,* p. 36.
36. *Ibid.,* p. 12.
37. Mary Lutyens, *Second Penguin Krishnamurti Reader*, p. 11.
38. J. Krishnamurti, *Life Ahead*, p. 37.
39. *Ibid.*, p. 121.
40. *Ibid.*, p. 110.
41. J. Krishnamurti, *This Matter of Culture*, p. 123.

42. J. Krishnamurti and David Bohm, *The Ending of Time,* Madras: KFI, 1992, pp. 62-66.
43. J. Krishnamurti, "First and Last Freedom" and *Total Freedom, The Essential Krishnamurti.* Mary Cadogan, Alan Krishnamurti, Mark Lee and Ray Mc Coy (eds.), New York: Harper San Franscisco, 1996, p. 65.
44. J. Kirushnamurti, *Life Ahead*, p. 58.
45. J. Krishnamurti, *Last Talks at Saanen*, 1985, p. 47.
46. G. Haragopal, *Political Economy of Human Rights: Emerging Dimensions,* New Delhi: Himalaya Publishing House, 1997, p. 195.
47. J. Krishnamurti, *Network of Thought*, Madras: KFI, 1992, p. 39.
48. Luis S.R.Vas (ed.) *Mind of J. Krishnamurti,* Bombay: Jaico Publishing House, 1989, p. 53.
49. J. Krishnamurti, *Total Freedom*, p. 292.
50. J. Krishnamurti, *Commentaries on Living*, 2nd series, Madras: KFI, 1991, p. 69.
51. J. Krishnamurti, *Life Ahead,* p. 135.
52. J. Krishnamurti, *Mind without Measure,* Madras: KFI, 1990, p. 130.
53. J. Krishnamurti, *Tradition and Revolution*, p. 133.
54. J. Krishnamurti, *Life Ahead,* p. 50.
55. *Ibid.*, p. 98.
56. Quoted by Stuart Holroyd, *The Quest of The Quiet Mind: The Philosophy of J. Krishnamurti,* Wellingborogh and Northamptenshire: Aquarian press, 1983, p. 65.
57. Luis S.R. Vas (ed.), *Mind of J. Krishnamurti*, p. 97.
58. J. Krishnamurti, *Total Freedom,* p. 13.
59. Maurice Frydman, "The Basic Truth" In Luis S.R. Vas (ed.), *The Mind of J. Krishnamurti,* p. 273.
60. Luis S.R. Vas (ed.), *The Mind of J. Krishnamurti,* p. 95.
61. J. Krishnamurti, *This Matter of Culture*, p. 25.
62. J. Krishnamurti, *Life Ahead,* p. 33.
63. *Ibid.*, p. 38.

64. *Ibid.*, p. 36.
65. *Ibid.*, p. 36.
66. *Ibid.*, p. 37.
67. J. Krishnamurti, [Mary Lutyenes (ed.)], *Only Revolution*, p. 144.
68. J. Krishnamurti, *Life Ahead*, p. 33.
69. *Ibid.*, p. 30.

3

The Traditional Mind

All theory is grey, life alone is green.

— Goethe

The problem of mind is one of the seminal philosophical issues and philosophers have given it prominence in understanding man, life and the world. The thinkers of the East as well as of the West have dealt with the problem of mind in great depth. Jiddu Krishnamurti is one of the prominent thinkers who has delved deep into the nature and structure of mind. His discoveries in the field of mind/brain are comparable to the discoveries of the physicists in the field of matter. Krishnamurti's analysis and understanding of mind are insightful and instructive.

Krishnamurti's conception of mind is psychological as well as philosophical. He understands human mind as a product of biological evolution. He also considers it as a product of history. The thought that operates in the mind is conditioned by the past. This memory is retained in the mind through time. It is a storehouse of knowledge and experience. Mind, an organ of intellect and reasoning performs activities such as comparison, imitation, effort, discipline, beliefs and ideas etc. Krishnamurti calls this aspect of mind as the traditional aspect and characterises it with several aspects like division, conflict, contradiction, self-centeredness, fear, pleasure, envy, jealousy, competition, comparison, desire, choice and sorrow. He also terms this as an ignorant mind which is working against itself. It, by its nature, fosters self-contradiction and conflict.

The traditional mind is confined to the realm of the known which constitutes images, formulae and conclusions. All its responses are based on the past, on accumulated knowledge. It is the result of culture and beliefs and is brought about by thought and therefore is confined to the activity of thought-process. Thought ensures its continuity through symbols, images and ideas etc. The traditional mind is an 'old' mind and so it tries to find security in the past, instead of coping with the new and the present. It accumulates knowledge and experience and acts on their basis. All its activities are limited since it is limited by the past. Krishnamurti regards memory, experience, knowledge and thought as more or less synonymous with tradition.

Krishnamurti says:

> "The brain is the centre of all the senses... It's the centre of remembrance, the past; it's the storehouse of experience and knowledge, tradition. So it's limited, conditioned. Its activities are planned, thought out, reasoned, but it functions in limitation, in space- time."[1]

Human Mind as the Product of Evolution

Mind is the product of evolution psychologically as well as physically. Physically it has grown larger in size in the course of time. Psychologically human brain has evolved in the sense of accumulating more knowledge and more experiences. But both psychological and physical aspects of mind have evolved through time. The brain that has evolved through millennia has gathered tremendous knowledge and experience. As Krishnamurti explains:

> "My brain which has evolved through a long period of time, that brain with its consciousness is not mine because my consciousness is shared with every other human being."[2]

The evolved mind which is the brain of mankind is part of mankind genetically and in the course of evolution it has had all kinds of destructive and pleasant experiences.

Mind as the Product of Thought

The traditional mind is the product of thought; it is put together by thought. Thought is the outcome of knowledge or memory and knowledge or memory is the word, the symbol, the process of image-making, Krishnamurti says, "Thinking starts from experience which becomes knowledge stored up in the cells of the brain as memory, then from memory there is thought."[3]

Thinking is not personal, according to Krishnamurti. It is common to all human beings. It is the capacity of the brain which expresses itself in words and forms. As Krishnamurti puts it: Thinking is not yours or mine. There is no individual thinking; there is only thinking. You may think in one way, another may think in another way. It is still thinking. So the thinking consciousness is shared by all human beings.[4]

According to Krishnamurti, the thinker is not different from the thought. There is no independent existence for the thinker apart from the thought. *Thought creates the thinker*. The activities of thinker like observing, thinking, reasoning, analysing, rationalising are possible only through thought. All the activities of the thinker are within the field of thought and the thinker adjusts and modifies himself along with his thought. Thought binds and conditions the mind. Therefore, it is important to discuss the origin and structure of thought and its limitations. Krishnamurti also holds that thought arises from memory and memory is the result of knowledge which in turn is the product of experience. He says, "The experience may have been from the beginning of man, which we have inherited, that experience gives knowledge which is stored up in the brain; from knowledge there is memory and from that memory, thought. From that you act."[5]

Human mind as it exists now has programmed itself to function in the cycle of experience-knowledge-memory and thought which again is responsible for experience. Mind is the constant repetition of a process of thought and by constantly repeating itself, or its content, it acquires a pattern and it learns or perceives mostly in terms of the past. Thought is in a way the response of the past to the present. As Krishnamurti puts it, "When thought is functioning it is the past, therefore there is no new living at all, it is past living in the present, modifying itself and the present."[6]

Thought is mostly conditioned by experiences, knowledge, memory and culture. Therefore tradition determines the structure and nature of even the brain cells. The traditional brain functions only in the field of the known. Thought is the whole structure of the known in which it conditions itself, or it creates its own prison by operating within the boundaries of the known. Krishnamurti says, "Thought is always working in a prison. It can call it freedom, it can call it beauty, it can call it what it likes! But it is always within the limitations of the barbed-wire fence."[7]

> "Thought is consciousness.[8] All thinking is conscious activity. Thought is not something separate from consciousness. Thought constitutes the content of consciousness. The movement of thought is the movement of consciousness. It comprises of all experiences, beliefs, dogmas and divisions".

> "The essence of the content of our consciousness is thought. Thought has brought about a structure in consciousness, of fear, of belief. The idea of a saviour, faith, anxiety, pain – all that is put together by thought and is the content of consciousness."[9]

The thought process is a material process; it is essentially a physical and chemical process. Mind, the seat of thinking, is materialistic in character and that which is material is also mechanical. It acts with limited energy. Krishnamurti says:

> "Thought is a material process because it is held in the very brain cells themselves that whatever thought thinks about or invents, is the result of material process."[10]

Thought is verbalisation. It operates in terms of formulae and conclusions, words, symbols and images without which it cannot function. It verbalises all the reactions, memories, abiding incidents, ideas, pleasure, pain and sorrow. They are all verbalised when mind thinks about them. Krishnamurti says, "Verbalisation is thought. The word, the symbol retards action and idea is the word, as memory is the word. There is no memory without the symbol, without the word."[11]

Thought is a continuous process. Being conditioned by the past, it perpetuates itself in all its activities. So it gives continuity and permanence to everything it thinks about and thus makes itself permanent.

> "Thought can give continuity to something it thinks about; it can give permanency to a word, to an idea, to a tradition. Thought thinks itself permanent, but is it permanent?"[12]

Mind is always occupied with something or the other since thought is thinking about something. It is never empty of content. It is always of something. Preoccupation with its object gives continuity to thought and because of this fact the traditional mind by itself is problematic, as thought creates problems which it cannot solve. The traditional mind is a problematic mind, since thought itself is problematic. Thought is responsible for many problems like division, conflict, separation, violence and war, as by its nature, thought is divisive, conflictive and separatist, "thought cannot solve any human problem, for thought itself is a problem."[13]

Thought creates the sense of 'Me' and 'Mine' in the thinker. It gives rise to the sense of 'I' in all activities; as the sense of *'I'* is articulated in terms of self-acquisitiveness. It is thought that is responsible for the construction of the whole structure of the psyche. In the words of Krishnamurti, "Thought has built the psyche, the psychological structure, which me my ego."[14]

The sense of 'I' or 'Me' is not natural but acquired. It is *what is* brought about by thought. Krishnamurti suggests:

> "My name, my form, how I look, my qualities, my reactions, all the things that are acquired, are all put together by thought. Thought is 'me'. Time is 'me', the self, the ego, the personality, all that is the movement of time as me."[15]

Thought and Time

Thought can function only in the field of time. Thought is movement in time. Thought is memory and remembrance of past things through time. The sense of time is built into the nature of human mind, since mind sustains itself in terms of time or past. It is the psychological becoming of the mind that creates the sense of time. Time, knowledge, memory and thought form a single unit. They are not separate but form a single movement. Thought as time always tries to achieve something and in trying to become something, thought gives permanence to time. Tomorrow is the invention of thought in order to achieve its aspiration and ambitions and to achieve fulfillment. Thought is bound by time.

> "Thought is time, the thought that has been and the thought that will be that which is an ideal. Thought is the product of time and without the thinking process time is not. The mind is a matter of time."[16]

The traditional mind is corrupt and contaminated because thought is itself corrupt and contaminated. It is corrupt in the sense that it is divided within itself. It is contaminated in the sense that it is not whole and integral. It is fragmented within itself. As Krishnamurti explains:

> "Ideals corrupt the mind; they are born of ideas, judgments and hopes...we are using the word mind to imply senses, the capacity to think and the brain that stores all memories as experiences, as knowledge.....we said ideas corrupt. Knowledge also corrupts the mind. Knowledge is the movement of the past and when the past overshadows the actual, corruption takes place. We are using the word corruption to mean that which is broken up, that which is not taken as a whole."[17]

> "Thought contaminates that which is ever new and fresh and with its ideas and words colors the unknown. It is thought as memory, the conditioned thought that contaminates the past, straining the purity of the new and

the unknown thought. Of course memory is essential for all practical purposes."[18]

The traditional mind is incomplete because thought is incomplete. Thought is incomplete as it is based on the past or on knowledge which is not holistic. Knowledge is partial, cumulative and is relative in terms of ignorance. Thought which is incomplete interferes with or influences all the perceptions and experiences and prevents the experience from being complete. The more thought influences/interferes the more experience remains incomplete. The completion of thought-process is a meaningless idea, as any effort to complete the thought-process is only an extension of its continuance.

Thought in Daily Life

Life moves in the realm of thought. All the human activities and relationships are based on thought, or are based on the images which thought creates. According to Krishnamurti, thought has two dimensions: the physical and the psychological. Physically, thought has been helping man in biological survival. The advancement of science and technology has contributed to better living conditions in the realm of health, communication, transport etc. But psychologically thought brings about chaos in human life. It divides the human mind and humanity by creating various kinds of images, symbols, organisations and structures. It is responsible for poverty, violence and war. So Krishnamurti thinks that thought other than the factual leads to sorrow.

Thought is capable of creating great structures like cathedrals and temples. It can invent the idols, the rituals and gurus but it is still limited, for it cannot comprehend the Truth. Thought, being conditioned, is limited. It builds its own limits and seeks security in the known only. "Thought is anchored to memory and it can never be free to discover the truth of any problem," says Krishnamurti.[19]

Thought, born out of knowledge, must inevitably be fragmentary. Whatever is limited will definitely generate conflict. "Thought is limited, because all knowledge is always limited, that very image brings about conflict that feeling of reverence to a person, to a symbol, or to a certain long established tradition."[20]

The traditional mind is the product of psychological time. Psychological time is the mind's sense of constant becoming. It is the movement of thought from *what is* to what should be, or from the present to the future. Krishnamurti admits the existence of factual time which is measured by the watch or the calendar. It is useful for biological and practical purposes. Psychological time is the internalisation of chronological time, is a barrier to the immediate understanding and solving of human problems. The traditional mind is caught up the network of psychological time. Chronological time is time necessary for doing certain work: anything from learning a skill or going to the moon. It is required for biological existence, whereas psychological time is an inward reflection of the outward movement of evolution. It is the time needed by the mind for the fulfillment of its unfulfilled desires. Psychological time arises when one thinks of learning or changing oneself. For instance, one thinks: "I must have time to learn about myself. I must have time in order to change myself from what I am to what I should be. In it memory plays an important role."[21] Psychological time is the product of the mind's urge to improve itself in the future. It is the result of the mind's effort and struggle to become or achieve the ideal as against the fact. It is born due to the conflict between *what is* and *what should be*. It is the source of contradiction in the mind. Psychological time is responsible for the endless continuity of *what is* and therefore it does not allow '*what is*' to alter itself radically. It may allow some modification in '*what is*'. But it is a barrier to a complete change or transformation of *what is*. Krishnamurti says:

> "Existence may entail efforts, but all considering process of becoming, the psychological urge to be better, to become something, the struggle to change *what is* into its opposite. This psychological becoming may be the factor that makes everyday living painful, competitive, a vast conflict... And

> this becoming that is without end and so conflict is without end."[22]

In reality, psychological time is something fictitious and superimposes itself on chronological time with the demand that the latter move according to its requirement. When this does not happen, the mind experiences tensions and frustrations. Psychological time destroys the beauty of *what is*. And the one who is caught in psychological time and operates with its limited energy is an example of the traditional mind. The traditional mind is narrow and limited and cannot handle the vast energy. It is always guilty of the avoidance of fact.

Traditional Mind is the Mind of Knowledge

Knowledge is derived from human experience. The human brain acquires knowledge through acknowledgement or recognition of facts. It also acquires knowledge through accumulation of experiences, analysis, incidents and through information. The constant accumulation of information and acquisition of various forms of knowledge involve the assertion of knowing. Knowledge knows a thing by recognition. The traditional mind is the storehouse of knowledge and operates in the field of the known. The known is in the form of beliefs and ideas. The brain, when it struggles with nature, or when it meets any challenge, derives knowledge through that struggle on the basis of experience. Krishnamurti says:

> "Knowledge is having ideas, having opinions about things, having a sense of continuity as in relation to the known and no more. Ideas are memories, the result of experience, which is response to a challenge."[23]

The traditional mind is sensation, experience and memory. The experiences either inherited or accumulated in the present become knowledge. In the words of Krishnamurti:

> "Knowledge is always of the past. What you know is already in the past, is it not? You do not know the present or the future. The strengthening of the past is the way of knowledge. What may be uncovered may be totally new and your

knowledge, which is the accumulation of the past, cannot fathom the new, the unknown."[24]

The traditional mind finds security in knowledge or the past. It assumes that knowledge frees the mind/brain from the bondage and leads to wisdom. But knowledge is only the accumulation of ideas/words-and through this it strengthens only the beliefs and prejudices. Knowledge with its beliefs, hopes, frustrations and illusions always conditions the brain. Knowledge implies process in time as the past. Because of this Krishnamurti says there is no future-knowledge. Krishnamurti explains:

"Knowledge is always limited. There is no complete Knowledge about anything. The scientific knowledge is limited. Every kind of knowledge in any field is limited-biological, sociological, technological and in the world of religions with all their Gods and all Gods are invented by thought."[25]

Krishnamurti also writes:

"Knowledge both in the scientific world and in human existence is based on experience. This experience is gathered for millions of years or for the last 3000 years. And that knowledge is used to accumulate further knowledge, further exploration but knowledge is always past. There is no question about that. And knowledge is never complete about anything. That is fact."[26]

Knowledge is the projection of thought. As thought is divisive, knowledge brings about duality. Krishnamurti says:

"Knowledge, the division between the known and the unknown is itself divisive. The division of yesterday, today and tomorrow: the today, modified from yesterday's knowledge which is the past, modifying the future, is divisive. Knowledge is also my image of you and my consciousness about you–my senses that I knew you, when you in the meantime may have changed. My image of us divides us."[27]

Krishnamurti differentiates between two kinds of knowledge—psychological and factual. Factual knowledge consists of experiences and judgments about facts. It contributes to our efficiency and helps in our struggle for survival. Psychological knowledge consists of past valuations or judgments of value, each heavily charged with emotions. It strengthens the sense of me, or the ego. It is the essence of the traditional mind. Psychological knowledge is illusory whereas factual knowledge is real. Factual knowledge includes knowledge which is well reasoned and proved by experiment. The scientific, technological, mathematical and linguistic disciplines come under the category of factual knowledge. Psychological knowledge is a product of speculation or thought. It is what thought abstractly creates. It is fictitious and irrational. Psychological knowledge is of me, the ego or Psyche. It is based on images. It brings about image patterns through time and these images are continued further. Knowledge generated through images of the traditional mind even impedes relationships. It is a hindrance to understanding. Krishnamurti thinks that factual knowledge, like the skill to drive a car, to learn a language, etc., is essential for our biological survival, but the psychological knowledge is problematic. It makes the mind traditional.

> "Knowledge at a certain level is essential, but psychological knowledge about oneself, one's experiences etc, becomes routine. The image I have about myself also obviously becomes routine and all that helps to bring about shrinkage of the brain."[28]

Memory

The traditional mind is full of memory. Remembrance of past experiences is memory. Memory is the reservoir of knowledge. It operates on the basis of previously acquired knowledge, or remembered knowledge. Memory is structured information and includes visual images, sound sequences, motor programmes, abstract concepts, relationships, values and attitudes etc. It also includes the incidents from the remote past (tales, ancient signs and symbols) as well as the recent past (activity of immediate past). Memory is both subconscious and unconscious, or both these layers of the psyche are composed of memories. While the conscious mind reflects the immediate acts of the brain with its conditioning, the unconscious mind which is also a part of traditional mind, is a storehouse of relics and memories of the past, which work unconsciously.

Being burdened with past experiences, the mind is selective in its operation. It ignores most of the information which comes through the senses. It allows only a small portion of information to reach the stage of active processing. Depending on the individual psyche and its plans, values and goals, the mind selects certain information and rejects certain other information. In this sense, the traditional mind is selective in its cognitive activity.

The traditional mind fails to experience anything completely. All its experiences are unfinished or incomplete. An unfinished or incomplete experience which is stored as memory makes the mind dull and it responds to the new situation incompletely. It searches restlessly for completeness within memory. But it always remains incomplete, for memory continues to influence it in all its activities. The traditional mind keeps memory alive and gives continuity to it. Krishnamurti says:

> "Marks left on the brain cells. See what happens–unfinished experience leaves a mark on the brain cells is matter–the brain cells are matter. So every incomplete experience leaves a mark which becomes knowledge. The brain as accumulated knowledge has received information and information is knowledge. Its weight makes the mind dull."[29]

The Traditional Mind is a Conditioned Mind

Krishnamurti explains that the traditional mind has been a conditioned mind for centuries. Krishnamurti says, "It is the tradition that has been imposed upon you from the childhood or the beliefs, the Experiences, the knowledge that one has accumulated for oneself. They are all conditioning the mind."[30] In its desire to be secure the traditional mind conditions itself and always wants to become something or the other. Behind this striving to become something there lies a deep sense of insecurity.

A conditioned mind cannot think freely. All its Arguments, conclusions, justifications and reasoning are within the boundaries of conditioning. The very structure of the conditioned mind is limited. It isolates itself from actuality and operates within the limitations of conditioning. Krishnamurti says: The mind through propaganda, through tradition, through the desire to be secure, begins to condition itself."[31]

It programmes itself like a computer. The programming is not only factual or biological but also psychological. Krishnamurti says, "We have been programmed biologically, physically and also programmed mentally, intellectually. This brain has become as a computer but not so capable because its thought is limited.[32] Because of psychological conditioning, the traditional mind isolated itself from *what is* and is not therefore free to understand '*what is*' there actually. It cannot perceive the reality as it is. The conditioned perception creates division and conflict which are responsible for all kinds of problems at the individual and social levels. The conditioned mind is partial, prejudiced and swayed by desires and fears, hopes, likes and dislikes. It is constantly disturbed and distorted. The conditioning leads to the partial use of the brain, as more attention is given to what was and what will be rather than to that is, it also connects all sorts of divisions and distractions like thinker and thought, experience and experienced and deeply affects human relations.

Conditioned Perception

The traditional mind cannot perceive the truth as a whole. Instead of perceiving *what is* the traditional mind approaches it with preconceived notions and prejudices, for it operates with the help of symbols, images, ideas and beliefs. It considers these as more important than *what is* actually there. Krishnamurti says:

> "Everything that is recorded–conscious as well as unconscious sensory impressions, various images, conclusions, prejudices–

is involved in perception. I see you and the various images that I have, been built through perception, through association and through prejudice emerge. Thousands and thousands of images are recorded and are held in the brain cells. When I meet you, I turn on attention and an image emerges. That is what we call perception, is not it?"[33]

The traditional mind finds security in conditioned and partial perceptions. The conditioning gets strengthened in the course of experience. The mind conditioned in a particular way gets further conditioned as it responds to more and more stimuli. Krishnamurti illustrates this thus:

> "You are conditioned as a Brahmin in accordance with tradition which has been going on for centuries and you respond to stimuli, to social change and conflict as Brahmin. You respond according to your conditioning, according to your past experiences, knowledge, so new experience only conditions further. Experience according to a belief, according to an ideology, is merely a continuation of that belief, the perpetuation and the idea. Such experience only strengthens the belief."[34]

The traditional mind is a mind of attachment and identification with *what is* other than the actual, what actually is. Attachment to something or the other is a means of escape from its own emptiness; such experience, according to Krishnamurti, strengthens the conditioning of the mind. The traditional mind desires to be successful, or to achieve what it wants.

The Traditional Mind is a Believing Mind

Belief, according to Krishnamurti, is the denial of truth. Belief is where truth is not. It is the product of thought. Belief is the extension of desire and leads to faith. Belief gives the mind a peculiar strength which arises from necessity. Krishnamurti says that belief in anything is the expression of the mind's desire to become something, feeling uncertain, the traditional mind clings to beliefs in which it finds certainty. Belief is prejudice and being burdened with beliefs, the traditional mind fails to see the truth as a whole. Belief symbolises and verbalises the object of perception and binds and isolates the brain from reality. Krishnamurti says the activity of belief leads to confusion. The conventional mind believes in order to overcome its fear. But belief is itself the source of fear. It is the insufficient response of the traditional mind to a challenge.

The actions of the conventional mind are incomplete as they are based on thought which is inherently incomplete. Thought is action which is conscious. The conscious action has always an end in view. It is self-centered and the sense of the actor is implied in it. It is influenced by ideas; or the ideas condition action. It moulds the action according to its goals. The action based on thought is divided between *what is* and what should be.

This division breeds conflict. Explaining this, Krishnamurti says that action based on an idea is no action at all. It is only an imitation and a repetition of the past. The conventional mind is incapable of real or total action, for it is based on the past which controls action. Real action, according to Krishnamurti, is action without an idea, an end in view. Real action is that which is devoid of the sense of an actor.

The Traditional Mind is Fragmentary, Divisive and Conflictive

The traditional mind is not holistic, but fragmentary, for thought is fragmentary. Thought is divided within itself and holistic thought is a contradiction in terms. Where there is fragmentation and division, there is conflict. Fragmentation implies conflict, logically as well as factually. Krishnamurti says, "Thought being divisive whatever action it creates must be fragmented, which therefore gives rise to conflict."[35]

The traditional mind is divided 'within itself', for thought cannot remain content with *what is*. Unable to remain content with *what is*, thought invents its opposite, that is, *what should be*? Traditional mind sustains itself in terms of the conflict between *what is* and what should be. In the words of Krishnamurti:

> "What should be is a division which thought has put together in the avoiding or overcoming the reality of *what is*. Hence the struggle between the actual and abstraction... *what is* actual is *what is* and everything else is non-real. It is the non-real that brings about the fragmentation, not the actual."[36]

The traditional mind is slow for there is wastage of energy in conflict and self-contradiction. In its struggle to avoid *what is* and to attain the ideal, the traditional mind loses its energy. Krishnamurti says, "As long as there is duality between *what is* and what should be-man trying to become something else, makes an effort to achieve what should be- And as long as there is conflict between opposites, man has not enough energy to change."[37]

The traditional mind divides itself into various fragments. It approaches the actuality not only with verbal and psychological imagination but also partially through beliefs and distorts the actuality. This further narrows down the mind. Any action from the conditioned part of the mind will breed further fragmentation of mind. The traditional mind is conditioned to choose. It cannot act without choice. Choice is possible only when there is the background of the past. It is through thought that the mind chooses a certain direction to act. Choice implies motives and ends in view. Choice therefore involves conflict. It is only the confused mind that chooses. A clear and intelligent mind never chooses. It is the mind which is conditioned by the past that chooses. The choice is the projection of thought which is the result of the past. Choice is the reaction of the past to the present. Obviously it does not have the understanding of life as a whole. Krishnamurti says, "There is never a direct comprehension but always the tedious process of accumulation, of the capacity to distinguish, which is really based on memory, on the accumulation of knowledge and, therefore, there is this constant effort made through choice."[38]

Krishnamurti argues that choice is ambition. It implies conflict. It prevents the understanding of *what is*. According to Krishnamurti, "All existence is choice... choice, in every form, is conflict. Contradiction is inevitable in choice, this contradiction, inner and outer breeds confusion and misery."[39]

The traditional or the conditioned mind is full of desires. Desire is the response of the past to the stimuli. It is the interference of thought with is. Desire is the want of something, the lack of something, the missing something. Desire begins with sensory responses. Biologically desire is the sensory response to stimuli. However, it is necessary for life. Psychological desire arises when thought creates an image of the sensory experience. Krishnamurti explains "Suppose one sees something at the window. It may be a shirt... while seeing sensation takes place, then one touches it and then thought says if you put on that shirt how nice you will look, that creates the image and then begins desire."[40]

Krishnamurti maintains that if there were to be no thought there would be no desire but only sensation without desire. Thought dominates the sensation and creates the urge, the desire and the will to possess. Desire is the movement of thought as time and measure. Desire leads to comparison and imitation. It is the expression of identification of mind with something other than itself and does not exist in isolation. It is always related to something. Desire is an urge to become or attain something and breeds dependence. Becoming and dependence both bring about fear.

Desire is time and is an important aspect of becoming through which the mind projects an ideal. Having identified itself with the ideal the mind creates psychological time to attain it. Desire involves effort. Desire as the means of becoming conditions the mind in different ways. It limits the mind to the attainment of the object and is responsible for insufficient response and incomplete action. Desire shows itself in various ways such as disagreement and fighting as ambition, jealousy, envy, hope and so forth and because of all these various emotions, the traditional mind is distorted through desire. Krishnamurti says:

"The mind has created, through its desire for self-protection and comfort, many hindrances and barriers, thus bringing about its own incompleteness, its own sorrow. To free itself from this sorrow the mind begins to battle against these self-centered resistances and limitations. In this conflict there is born and developed will, with which the mind identifies itself thus giving birth to the I-consciousness. If these barriers do not exist there would be continual fulfillment in action."[41]

The traditional mind is an embodiment of factors like fear, envy and jealousy etc. Mind is self-centered. The human mind has put up with fear for generations and lives with it. The mind tries to escape from fear and resorts to rationalisation; it tries to forget it by trying to attain something that is not fear. All these involve movement of thought in time and time is fear. Psychological time meant to achieve or become something, is the cause of fear. The traditional mind, being in doubt, confusion and uncertain of achieving what it desires, gives birth to fear. The brain both at the individual and collective level is nurtured in fear for many years. Though based on fear, it always makes efforts to escape from the state of fear. Efforts to overcome fear may be in the form of developing beliefs, ideas, symbols, Gods, nationalism, etc., thus the traditional mind is the network of thought and thought is self-centered. It works from the *centre* called the *me* the *self*, the *I*-consciousness or ego. The self is the seat of fear, envy and jealousy. According to Krishnamurti, Fear is in the movement away from *what is*, in flight, the escape, the avoidance of actuality. It is this flight away that brings fear. Also when there is comparison of what you are with what you think you should be.[42]

Fear arises in the process of the mind's struggle to become something, or when the mind interprets *what is* in terms of what should be. It is the result of the conflict of opposites caused by comparison and measurement. Fear exists always in relation to the known only. Krishnamurti writes:

"Fear can exist only in relation to something, not in isolation. My fear is always in relation to the known, not to the unknown."[43]

Fear distorts action and hinders clear perspective. It makes the mind to follow, imitate and conform to some pattern or other. It creates inhibitions and breeds division.

> "If there is the slightest fear, there is a contraction of all our senses. And most of us live, in whatever relationship we have, in that peculiar form of fear."[44]

Fear causes fragmentation and division in relationships. It expresses itself in the form of violence. According to Krishnamurti, where there is fear there will be violence, aggression and a tremendous urge to succeed, both in the physical and psychological world.[45]

Fear is the other aspect of pleasure. The traditional mind is conditioned to pleasure and works on the principle of pleasure. Pleasure is the product of remembrance and repetition of the past, which is thought. As already mentioned, the traditional mind works on desire which is the product of thought. Desire is pleasure-oriented. Pleasure is invariably associated with fear since it arises out of thought which wants to avoid *what is*. It is the escape from *what is*, which causes pleasure and fear. Pleasure is different from the joy that comes out of being with *what is*. Krishnamurti says, "Pleasure is related to the past, there is no pleasure at the moment when it happens. It comes later, when it is remembered and remembrance is past."[46]

Pleasure is registered in the brain as memory and the pursuit of that memory is pleasure. The brain is occupied with many forms of pleasure. Thought projects pleasure into the future and pursues it. The repetition of pleasure is the movement of thought. Krishnamurti says, "Thought is the movement of pleasure, the brain registers incidents, pleasurable and existing, with remembering and thought projects them into the future and pursues them."[47] He maintains that pleasure is associated not only with fear but also with pain. He says that the very demand of thought to repeat pleasure involves pain. The repetition is mechanical, monotonous and painful. Therefore, the mind conditioned by convention suffers psychologically.

Sorrow is of many kinds. Grief, pain, anxiety and loneliness are sorrowful. The suffering may be due to the failure of not being successful, not being able to fulfill and having no identity and so on. Sorrow may be due to the idea of death. It may be due to poverty, ignorance, attachment and to not being loved. Suffering is both physical and psychological. Physical suffering is physical pain which is natural and the fear of its repetition in the future is psychological suffering.

Suffering has become a fact of human existence. The human being has been living with the mind which has been caught in suffering. Man has accepted suffering as something inevitable and permanent fact of life. But Krishnamurti asserts that suffering is not natural and inevitable. It is not an irredeemable part of mind and life. He views that suffering is due to the conditioning of the mind to the past, to tradition. It is thought which is responsible for suffering and therefore, the change of mind by putting an end to thought helps in overcoming suffering. Is radical transformation in mind, in the brain-cells, going to bring about a new mind which does not suffer? The ending of tradition is the ending of sorrow.

End Notes

1. J. Krishnamurti, *Krishnamurti's Notebook*, Madras: KFI, 1991, p. 9.
2. J. Krishnamurti, *Last Talks at Saanet* 1985, San Fransisco: Harper and Row Publishers, 1986, p. 37.
3. J. Krishnamutri, *The Flame of Attention* (Madras: KFI, 1987), p. 15.
4. J. Krishnamurti, *Mind without Measure* (Madras: KFI, 1990), p. 75.
5. J. Krishnamurti, *Network of Thought* (Madras: KFI, 1992), p. 15.
6. Mary Lutynes, *Years of Fulfilment* (New York: Avon Books, 1983), p. 172.
7. J. Krishnamurti, *Awakening of Intelligence* (New York: Avon Books, 1976), p. 21.

8. J. Krishnamurti, (Pupul Jayakar and Sunanda Patwardhan (ed.)), *Tradition and Revolution* (Madras: KFI, 1972), p. 209.
9. J. Krishnamurti, *The Flame of Attention,* p. 70.
10. J. Krishnamurti, *Mind Without Measure*, p. 44.
11. J. Krishnamurti, (D. Rajagopal (ed.)) *Commentaries on Living, First Series* (Madras: KFI, 1991), p. 138.
12. Mary Lutyens (ed.), *Second Penguin Krishnamurti Reader* (Hormondsworth: Penguine Books, 1982), p. 28.
13. J. Krishnamurti, (D. Rajagopal (ed.)) *Commentaries on Living* (New Delhi: B.I. Publications, 1972), p. 233.
14. J. Krishnamurti, (Mary Cadogan, Alan Kishbaugh, Mark Lee and Ray Mc Coy (eds.)), *Total Freedom, The Essential Krishnamurti* (New York: Harper San Francisco, 1996), p. 300.
15. J. Krishnamurti, *The Wholeness of Life* (Madras: KFI, 1990), p. 188.
16. J. Krishnamurti, (D. Rajagopal (ed.)) *Commentaries on Living* Second Series (Madras: KFI, 1991), p. 107.
17. Mary Lutynes, Krishnamurti: *The Open Door* (London: John Murray, 1988), p. 43.
18. Mary Lutynes, *Years of Fulfilment,* p. 172.
19. J. Krishnamurti, *Commentaries on Living* First Series, p. 159.
20. J. Krishnamurti, *Krishnamurti to Himself* and also in *Total Freedom*, p. 145.
21. J. Krishnamurti, *Total Freedom*, p. 80.
22. J. Krishnamurti, *Commentaries on Living*, p. 195.
23. J. Krishnamurti, *First and Last Freedom*, London: Victor Gollencz.
24. J. Krishnamurti, *Commentaries on Living* Second Series, p. 208.
25 J. Krishnamurti, *Mind without Measure,* p. 73.
26. *Ibid.,* pp. 43-44.
27. J. Krishnamurti, *Tradition and Revolution,* p. 50.
28. J. Krishnamurti and David Bohm *The Ending of Time* (Madras: KFI, 1992), p. 187.

29. J. Krishnamurti, *Tradition and Revolution*, p. 74.
30. J. Krishnamurti, *Total Freedom,* p. 171.
31. J. Krishnamurti, *The Flight of Eagle* (Madras: KFI, 1988), p. 58.
32. J. Krishnamurti, *Network of Thought*, p. 8.
33. J. Krishnamurti, *Tradition and Revolution*, pp. 145-146.
34. J. Krishnamurti, *Commentaries on Living*, p. 208.
35. J. Krishnamurti, *Total Freedom*, p. 267.
36. Mary Lutynes (ed.), *Second Penguin Krishnamurti Reader*, p. 98.
37. J. Krishnamurti, *The Flight of Eagle*, p. 56.
38. J. Krishnamurti, *Total Freedom,* p. 198.
39. J. Krishnamurti, *Krishnamurti's Note Book*, p. 192.
40. J. Krishnamurti, *Network of Thought,* p. 48.
41. J. Krishnamurti, "Talks, Latin America 1935", As cited in R.K. Shringy, *Philosophy of J. Krishnamurti: Systematic Study* (New Delhi: Munshiram Manohar Lal, 1977), p. 258.
42. J. Krishnamurti, *Beyond Violence* (Madras: KFI, 1992), p. 64.
43. J. Krishnamurti, *First and Last Freedom*, p. 83.
44. J. Krishnamurti, *Truth and Actuality* (Madras: KFI, 1992), p. 77.
45. J. Krishnamurti, *Network of Thought,* p. 23.
46. J. Krishnamurti and David Bohm, *The Ending of Time,* p. 213.
47. J. Krishnamurti, *Network of Thought,* p. 55.

4

World Disorder and Traditional Revivalism

In the Nineteenth Century the problem was that God is dead; in the twentieth century the problems, is that man is dead. In the Nineteenth Century inhumanly meant cruelty, in the twentieth century it means schizoid self-alienation. The danger of the past was that men become slaves. The danger of the future is that, men may become Robots.

— Erich Fromm

The first section of this chapter discusses the predicament of modern age that is reflected in our outer world, i.e., in the domains of science and technology, environment, social relationships, politics and religion etc. The next section discusses the fragmentation of humanity and its partial response which has only succeeded in revival of certain traditions. It also elaborates that this tendency, more explicit today than ever before, is to invent traditions in order to find answers to various problems. Reflecting on all these, Krishnamurti considers that the core problem is with our consciousness since the world is an extension of human consciousness. According to him, the outer is only a manifestation of inner psyche.

The Modern World in Crisis

Modern world is passing through a serious crisis. A number of factors have influenced the modern world. Scientific advancement and industrialisation have affected the psyche of the contemporary individual. Capital investments, the market, Western civilisation with its scientific advancement and tyranny, also have had an impact on the human mind.

The twentieth century has experienced devastating wars, the prominence of dialectical materialism and skepticism about religious beliefs, activities and rituals and so on. The rationality of scientific thinking has penetrated into the structures of the society and the individual. The rapid increase of technology and the capital market have introduced many changes all over the world.

> "The old social order is breaking down, the various religious organisations, the beliefs, the moral and ethical structures in which we have been brought up, are all failing."[1]

It seems that the world is in a transitory phase. The present-day human being is caught up in transition and is in a state of terrible confusion and chaos. On one side science has brought about changes in life and on the other, man is still conditioned by or is not free from beliefs and traditions. The crisis is manifesting itself in all the facts of life-the political, religious, moral, social and psychological. Man is not able to overcome his cruelty and confusion despite scientific and technological advancement. There is a deepening crisis in almost all the fields of human life. Krishnamurti says that the crisis which we are facing today cannot be solved by the politicians because they are not aware of the root cause of the crisis, namely, thought. The crisis cannot be solved even by the scientist for the scientist too is confined to the realm of thought which is conditioned and limited.

The Moral crisis is evident from the fact that values have been fast changing in the modern world. The swift change of values is due to the shrinkage of the world affected by scientific and technological advancement. Rajini Kothari, a well known social scientist, in one of his discussions with Krishnamurti, says that a moral crisis arises from time to time essentially due to breaking down of institutions. He also holds that crisis is because of rapid transformation of everything and as a result of which everything is being restructured.[2]

However, Krishnamurti thinks that the crisis is essentially the crisis in consciousness. It is because human consciousness is divided and confused that the life and the world are in deep crisis. The outward crisis is the projection of the inner crisis.

> "The crisis is in our consciousness, the crisis is what we are, what we have become. Unless we meet that crisis, that challenge, we are going to perpetuate wars, destruction and there will be outward chaos".[3]

The crisis continues because we are approaching it with a conditioned or traditional mind. The crisis in consciousness is on the increase. It is continuing because we are trying to approach it and solve it with a traditional mind. Therefore an inward psychological transformation is essential to overcome the outer crisis or to change the outer world. All the regulations, sanctions, decisions which one may have outwardly are shattered by psychological desires, fears, anxieties and by the longing for security. Krishnamurti says:

> "Inward disorder always overcomes that which is outwardly conforming, disciplined, regularised. There may be carefully constructed institutions—political, religions, economic—but whatever the construction these may be, unless our inward consciousness is in total order, inward disorder will always overcome the outer. We have seen this historically, it is happening now in front of our eyes."[4]

Crisis in Science and Technology

Science and technology have brought many changes in society. The innovations in technology have helped in the progress of industrialisation. However, science has its own adverse consequences too. There is increasing evidence to show that the knowledge of science is a threat to civilisation and to human survival itself. Modern science, with all its applications, has the potential for a holocaust that could wipe out mankind.

The advancement in computers and bio-engineering are remarkable. They are going to revolutionise the whole structure of society. Computers are going to outstrip the human being. They have the capacity to minimise human labour or even to render it practically unnecessary. The world is becoming more mechanistic and science is going to make human relations mechanical.

Though technology has a dehumanised face, it also provides more leisure for man. More leisure brings its own perversions. It gives much scope for the alienation of the human being from himself, from nature and from fellow human beings. This is even extended to science and technology since man's psyche has not changed basically. Science and technology aimed at and used for domination and destruction can also complicate the human situation instead of solving the problems of society.

Many people have expressed the idea that modern science and technology are in crisis. For instance, the advancement in genetic engineering has its adverse consequences on the future of society. Socio-biology seeks to promote a notion of humanity that sees intrinsic inferiority in the genes of certain racial and social groups. Sperm banks containing the sperms of intellectually superior people are being established. Those with the means and the desire to produce offspring of a certain racial and intellectual purity will have access to appropriate sperms in the near future.

It has been argued by many people that domination and control are an integral part of the current scientific and technological enterprise. Scientists are not free from their beliefs and cultural ethos which may compel them to reject diversity and complexity in favour of uniformity. The uniformity that is born of their own ethos is being extended to all other areas. Science and technology also help in fulfilling the economic designs of dominant powers. There is also an active alliance of modern sciences with the nuclear weapons industry and the nuclear arms race leading to the consequences well-known. There are major high-tech disasters such as the Three Mile Island nuclear accident in the USA, the Chernobyl nuclear explosion in Soviet Union, the Bhopal gas leak in India, the Challenger tragedy in USA, the SMON and Minamate tragedies of Japan.

It is ironical that more than half of the world population is still living in subhuman conditions, deprived of basic needs such as food, clothing and shelter. But even with all scientific and technological advancement, man's condition is not wholesome. Instead of solving the intractable problems, science is being used for the exploitation of the poor.

Krishnamurti makes a distinction between material progress of man and his psychological well-being. Material progress can be achieved by the scientific and technological advancement but it does not guarantee the psychological well-being of man. Man may be comfortable but it does not mean that he is happy and sane. There has been conflict 'within' man and 'without' despite the material progress. Psychologically, man is what he was a million years ago. The proper use of science and technology depends on the nature of the human psyche. If there is no change in the psyche, science and technology will be used only for destruction. Krishnamurti says that there is an unbridgeable gap between technology and the human psyche. He puts it strongly:

> "Technologically we have progressed, advanced so rapidly and psychologically our behaviour, our attitudes and actions, are more or less unevolved. We are still aggressive, brutal, cruel, thoughtless, for thousands and thousands of years. Apparently man is still behaving more or less as he behaves, 40,000 years ago."[5]

Ecological Crisis

Mankind is facing challenges even on the environmental front. The ecological crisis is global and pressing.

Environmental pollution is all—encompassing. It is spreading to every aspect of life. During the last two decades, rapid and indiscriminate industrialisation all over the globe has destroyed the natural environment and depleted the earth's material resources. It is a paradox that all development is accompanied by environmental degradation. It is man's greed for wealth and comfort that has resulted in the destruction of a number of natural cycles resulting in environmental pollution and health hazards.

The pollution and ecological degradation are a result of the greed. Human demands are increasing with the growth of population and modernity, but the resources at our disposal are limited. Reckless exploitation of natural resources is causing a serious ecological imbalance. The natural environment is fast disappearing. The spread of deserts, soil erosion, flood, drought, urban congestion and extinction or the threat of extinction of countless species of plants and animals are visible phenomena affecting the eco-system. The pollution of air and water is now recognised to be a global problem.

The green-house effect, acid rain, Ozone depletion and drought—all these reflect human interference with the environment. Man is responsible for this ecological catastrophe. Krishnamurti says:

> "Man is destroying nature, cutting down trees to build more houses, polluting the air with cars and industry. Man is destroying the animals; there are very few tigers left. Man is destroying everything because more and more people are born and they must have more space. Gradually man is spreading destruction all over the world."[6]

If we do not realise the problem of ecological imbalance, humanity may face the collapse of the life styles that different societies presently enjoy. This situation is not due to the growing needs and comforts of human beings. It is because of greed and the aspiration for luxury of human beings. All this is leading to the destruction of humanity by itself. In the words of Krishnamurti, "When man destroys nature, he is destroying himself."[7]

Chaotic Society

Society is the relationship of individuals. Its structure and nature are entirely determined by individuals. It is based on a set of beliefs, traditions, which we call religion, nation and certain economic values. In this sense, society is the extension of the individual self in various forms and it is the psychological projection of human beings.

Society is not only bound by traditions, rules and regulations but is also divided into numerous groups. Such division is the outcome of man's acquisitiveness, envy, greed and possessive pursuits. The institutions and patterns of living are dividing factors of humanity and are rooted in the depths of envy and acquisitiveness. Led by possessiveness and self-centered motives, man creates a society that is ruthless, chaotic and destructive.

In the present society human relationships are strained. There is a constant conflict in our relationships. Life is the process of relationship with people, ideas and things. All relationships of human being are self-centered and end-oriented. The 'me' or the 'I' or the ego is the center of human relations. The 'me' creates the image in our relationships. It strives to achieve its ends by means of ideas, things and people—and thus it generates disorder in society. The individual is ambitious to be successful and treats others as means to his ends. Ambition is the struggle to become respectable and to be recognised in society. It is a form of self-assertion which is the cause of conflict in society. To be respectable, men identify themselves in terms of nationalism, religion, class, ethnicity etc.

The whole society is structured on the principle of pleasure and where there is pleasure, there is pain and sorrow. Seeking pleasure in relationships is a barrier to love. As Krishnamurti puts it, "The way we treat our wives, children, neighbors, friends, is an indication that in our relationship there is no love. It is merely a mutual search for gratification."[8]

Society is the product of our relationships and if the latter are confused, ego-centric, narrow and limited, we project that and bring chaos into the world. Since the individual is ambitious and seeks success, there is exploitation in human relations. The structure of society is founded on the structure of exploitation. According to Krishnamurti:

> "Exploitation implies fear and fear inevitably leads to all kinds of illusions and misery. Conflict exists only in exploitation and not in relationship. Conflict, opposition, enmity exists between us when there is the use of another as a means of pleasure, of achievement."[9]

There is a deep crisis in society. The culture and the values on which the society is based are not genuine. There is a tremendous conflict and violence in society which is being crystallised, becoming static and is therefore fast disintegrating. The crises in society are the outward manifestations of the individual's inner consciousness. Since there are division and disintegration in consciousness, they also arise in the world. For, after all, the world is the relationship among individuals. It is the nature and structure of the relationship that constitutes the world. Human being with all his or her wants, ideals and innumerable motivations, becomes the prisoner of his or her own desires. As Krishnamurti puts it, "The society is ourselves, the world is ourselves and the world is not different from us. What we are we have made the world because we are confused, we are ambitious, we are greedy, seeking power, position and prestige."[10]

Political Turmoil

Political conflicts and struggles are going on all over the world. Whatever divisions, confusions, conflicts and interests exist in society, all of them find their reflection in the political realm also. In fact, any social relationship which involves a power differential is political. Political problems are about the nature and distribution of power. It is a fact that the power holders, generally the dominant groups, will tend to use power to further their own interests. They safeguard their power through the available institutions of the society and those who are suppressed through that power form another social group and they struggle against that dominance and for sharing power. An individual or group does not hold power in isolation; they hold it in relation to others. Power is therefore power over others. Power affects every aspect of social life. Owing to unequal and authoritarian human relationships in society, there are many political identities emerging all over the world in terms of caste, religion, race, language and ethnicity. All these condition human beings and therefore political activities are conditioned responses which bring about conflict. The political groups that organise and come close on the basis of common culture, shared historical experiences and a combination of ethnicity, religion and language, struggle with their distinctive and persistent collective identity. Identity of this kind divides humanity and whenever there is division there is conflict. There are many political groups in the world today and they are in conflict with one another over their cultural and material interests. With the increasing number of sects and groups all over the world, there are also more and more 'isms' and conflicting ideologies coming up. Man is totally absorbed into the ideology in which he believes. He is ready to sacrifice himself and also prepared to kill others for the sake of his ideology. He becomes a slave or an instrument in the hands of ideology, the system of ideas, whether it is left, right or center. Systems and ideologies are overpowering the individual. Krishnamurti says, "Systems become important, the philosophy of ideas becomes important and not man and for the sake of idea, of ideology, you are willing to sacrifice all mankind, which is exactly *what is* happening in the world."[11]

Human beings are getting enslaved by the power of ideological regimentation. The individual finds security in ideology, whether political or religious. Ideology is one kind of framework through which groups of people, nations and classes express their self-interest. But actually it is the self-interest of the individual identifying with that of the group or nation. Krishnamurti maintains that all the ideologies are stupid. They represent the conceptual thinking of the conditioned human being. By conditioning human beings, ideologies separate them. The mind which is identified with an ideology cannot see the actuality. According to Krishnamurti:

> "You know, ideologies have no meaning whatsoever, whether they are communist, socialist, capitalist or religious. Ideologies—conceptual thinking with its words—have separated man and man. You all have different ideologies and do not see clearly for ourselves the idiocy of having ideologies. They prevent seeing what actually takes place, what actually is."[12]

Krishnamurti contends that human beings have experimented with many kinds of ideologies to bring about change but failed. There are many ideologies which promise the welfare of the people but when it comes to fulfilling the promise, ideologies bring about more confusion. They complicate the life and fail in the eradication of poverty, starvation, slavery etc. The communist governments with their ideology promised to bring change in the whole of humanity but except for small changes, they have not succeeded. The communist countries have also experienced constant dissent and revolt. Krishnamurti does not appear to be interested in judging ideologies. For him the question is not which is right out of the several opposing ideologies and views—but whether opposites are at all there.

Every nation is paying lip service to the unity of humanity and world peace. Every nation with all its motives, with all its army prepares for war, as each nation dubs other nations as its enemy. The feeling of envy is developed by the politicians, who cultivate the nationalistic feeling in people from childhood. The very division of the world into nations is a hurdle for the possibility of uniting humanity. Every nation is strong in its commitment to nationalism. Nationalism is a glorified tribalism and there is no possibility for the brotherhood of humanity within the framework of nationalism. Krishnamurti argues, where there is nationalism, there must be war. Where there are several governments there must be war.[13] All governments are corrupt. Every nation is concerned with its own advancement and wants to be supreme in the world. Nations are working for the economic exploitation of each other. All countries, particularly the advanced countries are interested in capturing the world market and are monopolising technology and communication media. But the politicians and nationalistic governments can never bring about a new world order. He further says:

> "Politicians will never bring the world together, on the contrary; there may be no actual war but there is an economic war going on. If you are scientist you are a slave to the government. All governments are more or less corrupt, some more, some less, but all are corrupt."[14]

Political life is not disconnected with the psychological life of the individuals who constitute society. Therefore politics have to understand the psyche of the individuals in order to bring about a new social order. Society is the reflection of the inner being of the individual. It is the extension of the individual's mind. As Krishnamurti says:

> "Surely, if the political action is separate from the total action of man, if it does not take into consideration his whole being, his psychological as well as his physical state, then it is mischievous, bringing further confusion and misery and this is exactly *what is* taking place in the world at the present time."[15]

Irrelevance of Religion

Religions are the product of history and geographical conditions and are therefore conditioned. Every religion has its own beliefs, rituals and dogmas. Religion has importance when man is in misery, confusion, sorrow and fear. It is out of fear and desire for some kind of permanence that man accepts religious beliefs.

The world is also fragmented religiously or according to the religious beliefs of people. Religions provide certain patterns of behaviour. The mind is programmed to believe in certain doctrines and beliefs—Christian, Muslim, Hindu and so on. Basically man is conditioned by religion whether it is Christian, Hindu or Muslim and each religion is antagonistic to other religions. However, all the religions claim to strive for universal brotherhood and preach love. Every religion demands virtue and love from its believers. But the history of all religions shows that they have been destructive and have exploited people. In the words of Krishnamurti:

> "Apparently religion has lost its meaning, because there have been religious wars; religion does not answer all our problems, religions have separated people."[16]

Man believes that religion and gods will solve all his problems. In fact, it has never happened. As Krishnamurti observes, religion throughout the world has lost its credibility. It has no longer any significance in daily life. The religions are irrelevant because they are rooted in the past. A religious man responds inadequately to the present through a mind conditioned by the past. Religious dogmatism has been persistent despite the tremendous explosion of knowledge in the realm of science and technology. People are not ready to see the irrationality of religions. Religions preach love and brotherhood. But at the same time, they resort to violence and war. People are being killed for the sake of religious beliefs, dogmas and false gods. Krishnamurti says, "All religions, organised or unorganised, have said, 'Don't kill and love someone'. But you go on killing; you go on worshipping false gods which is your nationalism, your tribalism. So you are killing each other. That is what you all call religion."[17]

Fragmentation of the World

Apart from the psychological fragmentation that human beings experience, the outer world is also divided into various fragments. The outer fragmentation manifests itself in the form of geographical, political, religious, national, linguistic, economical, racial, ethnic and other divisions. Each fragment acquires its own identity and is in conflict with other fragments. There is hierarchy and authority among these fragments. However, these fragments are not natural and real. They are carefully constructed in the course of time. They are the expressions of psychologically built social categories.

Everywhere in the world human life is 'fragmented'. The fragmentation exists in each individual; it is nothing but the internalisation of the divisions already existing in the psychological structure of the society. The mind has divided existence into numerous social categories. The historical application of these categories makes real all kinds of differences—religious, economic, racial, cultural—which are rationalised, not only in a technical sense but emotionally, considered as 'givens' and then perpetuated.[18]

This is also the case with man's self identity. The so called individual comes to gain self-identity only by sharing in the divided mind of the collective or when he comes to own all the divisions. And in the process, he alienates himself from the natural wholeness or unity of humanity; while the divisive forces assert and proclaim their identity and claim meaningfulness and validity to themselves. The world is divided on the basis of beliefs, castes and classes resulting in conflict and cruelty and creating the necessity to fight with each other or among themselves. Such conflict and disharmony are evident in our political religious, ethnic, linguistic and sectarian conflicts.

The fragmentation of the world is due to division at different levels. The divisions are the result of images, concepts, ideas and opinions. Human beings are encouraged to fit themselves into these patterns from childhood. Parents, school and the whole social atmosphere make the child conform to the established patterns. Each fragment operates with its limited energy and from its conditioned background and by comparing and measuring itself with others.

Since time immemorial there has been a conflict among individuals and among groups. The source of conflict is the unequal and authoritative structures and institutions that are carefully constructed in the course of time. These established patterns and institutions are the basis for the domination and exploitation of one group by another for the sake of its own comfort and security. Krishnamurti thinks that conflict is growing more and more and is uncontrollable in the present day world because of the selfish acquisitiveness of human beings. One is used as a means for the pleasure and achievement of others.

The poor are collectively struggling for physical survival; for the fulfillment of basic needs like food, shelter and clothing they organise themselves in the form of caste, class, language, religion, tribe etc. But according to Krishnamurti, through the fragmentary approach, we cannot get even physical security. He maintains that, "There must be physical security for everybody, not only for the few, but that security is denied when psychological security is sought through nations, through religions through the family."[19]

According to Krishnamurti disorder means conflict. It is accepting authority, copying, imitation and all that.[20] Firstly, there is conflict where there is a difference between thought and action, that is, thinking one thing and doing something totally different. Secondly, while pursuing ideals, whether political, religious or moral, there is scope for conflict. The inner division due to neglecting an actual state and pursuing an ideal causes conflict and disorder. And thirdly, conflict is generated by an acceptance of authority, whether of the book, or of the guru, or of the leader, or of spiritual people. In other words, disorder is due to an individual's attempt to become something. The pursuit after an ideal, or 'what should be' and the avoidance of the actual, or '*what is*' can cause conflict and disorder.

The present day world is static, mechanical and lacks creativity in its true sense because the individual is conditioned by tradition and its authority. The individual is not able to respond to a situation without depending on accepted authority as he finds security in the authority of the tradition. To rely on authority is to rely on the past. Education, religion, politics, culture are all the forms of authority which make the individual a machine with conditioned responses. Krishnamurti says:

> "Our responses are conditioned according to the patterns of society whether it is Eastern or Western, religious or materialistic, so one of the fundamental causes of disintegration of society is imitation and one of the disintegrating factors is the leader, whose very essence is limitation."[21]

Violence and War

Violence has been on the increase all over the world. Violence is the result of political, racial, national, ethnic and religious divisions. Wherever there is fragmentation, there is bound to be conflict and violence. Violence is both physical and psychological. In all human relations, violence is growing or is becoming more and more widespread. One man is treating the other in terms of use and human relations are being based on mutual exploitation and destruction.

Broadly speaking, there are two schools of thought which have tried to explain the origins of violence. One school maintains that violence is innate in human nature while the other school holds that violence is the result of the social and cultural heritage in which man lives. The two World Wars bear testimony to man's inward violence. It is the inward confusion, struggle, hate and antagonism of the individual that manifests itself in the form of war.

Krishnamurti says that nationalism is the primary source of war. Nationalism is the product of thought which seeks security in a limited circle. The nationalistic mind cannot treat the vast movement of life as one unit. That is why each one has been killing others for thousands of years in the name of nationalism, the flag and the country. At present, every nation is allocating considerable part of its budget to defense. The scientific and technological discoveries are being used mostly for the purpose of war. Even after thousands of years of civilisation, mankind is still brutal and violent. From the highly educated to primitive beings, everybody is violent. As Aldous Huxley rightly pointed out, "All civilised societies are warlike in the present day world".[22]

There are some thinkers who contend that peace is possible only through war. Krishnamurti totally disagrees with this position and holds that there can be no peace through war. Any kind of effort based on ideology and aggression is of no use for achieving peace and all organisations that are born to promote peace have proved themselves to be ineffective. World peace is a myth as long as the desire for supremacy is in the heart of every nation.

Krishnamurti maintains that war is the outcome of the desire the human beings to be powerful and secure in the psychological sense. In fact there is no such thing as psychological security.

Quest for Constructing Identities

Identity building is an important issue in the contemporary world in the background of the resurgence of nationalist and ethnic conflicts. The problem of modern man is how to establish an identity for himself and maintain it. The past is used as a means through which ethnic, religious and national identities are formed and reinforced in the present. The group which is in identity formation uses the past to play a legitimising role in the present, since the past is accepted as a source of identity without question. Many thinkers have explained the phenomenon of identity formation and we may consider some of their definitions:

> "According to Brackette Williams, the racial, ethnic and class identities are ambivalent, provisional and simultaneously defined through the changing relations of power groups in control of nation building and groups whose is reified by that process.[23] He stresses that discourses of race and ethnicity are deployed in third world states in order to build national cultural identity and to cloak the material conditions defining class and class exploitation simultaneously".

John Camaroff has recently outlined and analysed the political economy of ethnicity, making clear that "Ethnic identities have over time developed as naturalised social forces autonomous from and perpetuated by factors different from the economic structures and divisions of labour from which they originally sprang".[24]

Every disputed identity undermines a basic element of a group's self-esteem and thus poses a threat to the very existence of collectivity. This existential fear in turn breeds an aggressive stance towards other groups. Thus identity-building is a potential source of strife and devaluation of others. Identity-building always differentiates 'self' from 'other'. And also the identification does not take place in vacuum but in previously occupied space. A newly created identity impinges upon others as it makes room for itself. With reference to identity construction, it is argued by Friedman (1992) and Hobsbawm (1994) that, "The situation is a response to political instability and the break up of the existing, very particularly about the resurgence of religious nationalism, hegemonic powers that held at least over conflict in check".[25]

Modern man's search for the past also can be understood from the psychological point of view. J.C. Jung, the famous psychologist discusses the reasons behind modern man's search for the past. He explains that modern man is subjected to cultural forces such as urbanisation, specialisation of labour, industrialisation and loss of contact with native soil which create the social need for energy discharge. Modern man's consciousness is caught up in a conflict between natural, archaic and institutional endowment—found expression in the form of traditional religion—and his contemporary need to adopt rationalistic and collective norms.[26]

Jung defines this conflict as the collective unconsciousness. To provide modern man with a living relation to himself and to his past, Jung devised the concept of a pure self that stayed in touch with tradition—(the archetypes) but also transcended the erosive social and political forces of modernity.

However, Krishnamurti says all identities are unnecessary except 'human being'. Any kind of identity is limited and divisive since it is fragmented from the wholeness of human being. All identities are conditioned and conditioning breeds dogmatism. With identification comes the struggle to hold to it and identities seek the continuity with the past. As Krishnamurti says:

> "If I want to be secure psychologically as a Hindu, with all the traditions, superstitions and ideas, I identify myself with the larger unit which gives me great comfort. So I worship a flag, the nation, the tribe and separate myself from the rest of the world. And this division obviously brings about insecurity physically."[27]

Revivalism of tradition is a worldwide phenomenon. These revivalist movements have considerable popular appeal and are centered on the search for solutions to the present day social, economic and cultural problems. These movements also draw attention to the refusal of modern societies to move beyond the authority of tradition. Though these movements seem to have arisen as a response to real problems, Krishnamurti thinks that they cannot solve any problem. He maintains that they will create a whole set of new problems in their wake. Traditional revivalism is relevant as far as the persistence of the past is concerned. But the problem, according to Krishnamurti, is much more deep-rooted. Revivalism can be understood as part of a much larger problem, as far as Krishnamurti is concerned.

Here we will discuss some of the movements of traditionalism to show Krishnamurti's approach and understanding. It is beyond the scope of this study to carry out a detailed analysis of revivalism in the world as a whole. We discuss below briefly three concrete instances of the revival of tradition, namely, the Sinhala and Tamil identity formation in Sri Lanka, Christian and Islamic revivalism in former Soviet republics and the case of Hindu revivalism in

India. Although these movements are different, they share the significant similarity of invoking tradition and the past as a means of solving the problems of the present.

Hindu Identity in India

Modern Indian society faces a serious crisis due to many problems which came to the forefront in the 1990s. The prominent issues in 1990s are the legislation for the reservation of jobs for other backward castes (OBCs) and the demolition of Babri Masjid which is a product of modern politics. The 'Hindutva' ideology rejects the secular state which for long has had unquestioned legitimacy. Hindutva ideology is an attempt to maintain continuity with the past especially with the Hindu culture.

Hindu means many things. It is the name for India's traditional culture and a specific religious community. There is no clear distinction between religion and general culture of a region. Even the words 'India' and 'Hindu' are etymologically linked. Although 83 per cent of India's population is supposedly Hindu, it is difficult to identify specifically *what is* Hindu. There are far too many internal differences within what has been called "Hindu religion and culture. Despite numerous differences within, there is the possibility of a common identity to a certain extent. Gabriella Fichinger Ferro-Luzzi, an anthropologist, has attempted to establish the continuity of the category 'Hindu' by recourse to the Wittgensteinian idea of 'family resemblances' which allows a greater flexibility in accommodating changes in the definition of this category...[28] Regarding the definition of 'Hindu' there is no clarity and so it is problematic. One can agree with Lawrence Babb's conclusion that, "Despite the diversity of beliefs and practices vaguely labelled as Hindu, "Hindu means something when they call themselves that, what they mean goes deeper than mere matters of sub continental politics or cultural chauvinism".[29]

Though this militant Hindu identity appears to be rooted in the historical past of the country, it is argued that this assertion has taken place in a particular political context in which the traditional forward castes claim of consensus, pluralism and harmony in the system are being challenged by a revised vision of Indian history put forward by Dalits, Buddhists and others.[30]

It is also to be considered that the challenge to secularism in India has come both from within and from external sources. Within the country the identity of Hindu is strengthened by pointing to the Muslims in Kashmir, Sikhs in Punjab, Christians in some North Eastern states and some others. And at the same time, in South-west and South Asian regions, Islamic revival has been taking place. So the task of delegitimising secularism in India has become easier by pointing to Islamic fundamentalism as sufficient justification of the need for a *Hindu Rashtra.* Therefore the language of Hindus is alienating the non-Hindu minorities and is aimed to integrate the majority Hindu community.

Sinhala-Tamil Identities in Sri Lanka

Sri Lanka, like India, was once a part of the British Empire. In both countries, there is a protest against secular nationalism and a demand for a national identity more in touch with the nation's cultural past. The Buddhist majority Sinhala population usually represents itself as heir to an ancient tradition of Sinhala-Buddhist nationalism. Historically, the country is the major center of Buddhism, specifically the form of Buddhism known as Theravada. In the pre-colonial period ethnic and religious identities were not stressed whether in language or in culture. They were dormant during the colonial period. The most prominent view of national past in modern Sri Lanka is held by the majority Sinhala population which has exercised power since independence. The dominant view among them is that, "The Buddha himself entrusted the island's destiny to the Sinhala people as guardians of the teachings. This view is now instantly proclaimed in the press, in the speeches of politicians and in school books and history lessons".[31] As for legitimising the Sinhala rule over Tamils, they put forward a history of pre-colonial period through the source of

Mahavamsa, a Buddhist chronicle. The Sinhalese thrust towards communal identity takes the forms of a revival of Sinhala as the national language and Buddhism as the historical national religion of Sri Lanka. The characteristic pattern of Sinhala nationalism could be seen clearly in 1956, when a new coalition government headed by R.P. Bandaranayike who was elected on the wave of Buddhist nationalism and made Sinhala the official language.

The revival of Tamil culture is outwardly similar to that of Sinhalese Buddhism. In recent times, the separatist minority movement of Tamil has taken an aggressive militant form and they are agitating for the founding of a new state of Eelam in the 'traditional homelands' of the North and East of Sri Lanka. Tamils not only protested against the Sinhala dominated Sri Lankan state, but also the Sinhala Buddhist claims on the national past. Alternative Tamil histories have been put together and propagated in the Tamil speaking North and East of the island. Both official history and opposition history agree on the basic terms of the argument that the present conflict can only be explained by reference to the past.

In the Sri Lankan context the past is a highly contentious, contested and prised commodity that is often used for contradictory purposes by different and often mutually antagonistic groups. This phenomenon clearly manifests the importance of legitimising the present on the basis of what they consider to be the authentic past:

> "The construction of the past (through myths, legends, history or *what is* understood as history), is essentially a political and moral resource that has become an expedient tool in the hands of politicians, nationalists and scholars (sometimes of course these different agents are the same), who use it for their own political projects involving nationalist religions or ethnic hegemonic and legitimisation processes".[32]

Legitimising the Myth of Ravana

The legitimising the Ravana myths were completely new phenomena in Sinhala society currently it appears that both

Sinhalese and Tamils claim Ravana as their own personal ethnic and cultural hero.[33]

On the Sinhala side, a much more sustained effort was made to resurrect Ravana in the context of the Hela movement. The main aim of the Hela movement is to 'purify' Sinhala by purging the foreign influences like Sanskrit and Tamil. Ravana has been presented as the most famous of these early Hela (or yaksha) Kings. It has also been suggested that Ravana's mythical capital Lankapura was located within Sri Lanka. One of the main endeavours of activities involved in historicising Ravana has been the attempted location of this capital.[34]

The Tamil nationalistic side also tries to use the myth for its own ends. The construction, or rather the reconstruction of such political myths has to be understood in the context of Sinhala myth-making when the Sinhalese trace their ancestry to Vijaya; the Tamils trace their origin more easily by using their version of the Ravana myths. The tendency here is clearly to assert that Tamils arrived in Sri Lanka prior to the Sinhalese and therefore they should have equal (or better) rights than Sinhalese.

It is true that the respective political identities have developed from old materials used in new ways as circumstances, ideas and institutions have changed. The use of these may provide some continuity with the past. However it should be understood that:

> "Both sides in the present political context back their respective claims through the selective use of histories and through the selective and competitive use of archeological evidence. Factions on each side have been willing to destroy, or reinterpret, evidence which would support the other party."[35]

Religious Revivalism in the Former Soviet Union Republics

With the disintegration of the Soviet Union the stage was set for a confrontation between religious nationalism and Soviet forms of secularism. Now, in the former Soviet Republics a substantial proportion of the population is asserting its religious identity. The republics are facing a severe crisis. The people there are living with poverty, unemployment and a crisis in the economy. Out of this crisis, in each republic, religious nationalism comes to the forefront.

Indeed, the Soviet state was built on the principles of Marxism. After the Bolshevik Revolution, it aimed at a socialisation process, which in turn aimed at the creation of the new Soviet man. Following Marxist theory, it called for large, international political identities that are based on alliance of working class people rather than any local religious or ethnic allegiances. It implied that the religious identities and all other parochial forms of social organisation should have been subsumed under the political relationship to the state. Karl Marx regarded the practice of religions as "The best expression of the trivial, 'the sign of the oppressed'. At its worst it was an 'opiate'—a narcotic that used to ease the pain of exploitation"[36]

Following the Marxist ideology, the state closed down many churches and mosques and condemned any kind of religious activity. In the 1930's a great number of churches were closed, monastic communities were dissolved and theological schools were abandoned. Perhaps the most rigid symbol of the anti religious moods of the time was the burning of the icons in public squares. Similarly the religion was repressed in Muslim areas and in Central Asia, of the Soviet Union—by closing down the mosques and Islamic schools and confiscating the wakf lands. They even changed the alphabets in which their sacred writings and teachings were published. In the former Soviet Union the old ethnic and religious identities persisted despite Marxist doctrine and various attempts to enforce that ideology. The religious atmosphere even influenced the Soviet State, to the extent that they took a liberal attitude towards religion.

During the late 1980's the political elite began to realise the futility of repressing religion. In such circumstances, it was perhaps inevitable that a new leadership committed to the renewal and humanisation of the Soviet Union should address the religious repression.[37] In the time of Gorbachev, it could be seen that there had been a fundamental liberalisation of state policy towards religion, along with political and economic liberalisation. By the end of 1990s, the Soviet State had in effect dropped its assault on religious values and institutions and provided a legal frame work from within which religious groups could exercise freedom of consciousness.

After the disintegration of the Soviet into different republics, religion played an important role in the resurgence of rational identities in each republic. As it is observed in republics such as Lithuania, Lativia and Tajikistan, the campaigns for religious freedom were often closely linked to the emerging nationalist movement. In Ukraine also the renewed campaign for the legalisation of the Ukrainian Catholic Church provided a major starting point for the emergence of nationalist activity in that most pivotal of republics. In Albania, both Muslim and Christian movements were part of the resurgence of the Albanian national identity, which began in 1990. After claiming Independence, in many of the republics religious holidays were turned into national holidays. Even the democrats and nationalists were keen to be seen participating in major religious festivals. Religious communities themselves also had to adapt to the radical changes brought about by political culture and religious pluralism. In many of the republics, the Church continued to be in the forefront of the nationalist cause rejecting Russian domination and Soviet control. In claiming a nationalistic identity, many people look to the Church as a source of inspiration and support.

Parallel to the revival of Christianity, there was the phenomenon of Islamic major resurgence. By the late 1980s, the possibility of Islamic political activity had been increased by the general reform process. Religious activists began to organise movements and parties aiming to strengthen Islamic influence in the daily life of the region. On occasion this took the form of attempts to 'purify' the existing Islamic establishment.

Although in India, Sri Lanka and the former Soviet Union, the exact causes for and the concrete manifestation of traditionalism differ; one observes recourse to tradition in time of crisis which has social, political and economic causes. By projecting the vision of a glorious or golden past, revivalism tries to generate a hope for a better future. Thus, the study of the revivalist movements shows that the 'past' is selectively appropriated to construct a specific, monolithic tradition which, even as it attempts to remove divisions within one community results in exclusion of other groups, some of which may be projected as an 'enemy' (the Muslim for advocates of Hindutva, 'Tamil' for Sinhala Buddhists). The result is a mass mobilisation often based on distrust and hate.

Traditional Revivalism

When man is caught, in confusion, crisis, uncertainty, or faces a challenge; he turns to tradition. All over the world revivalist movements have been active in the name of religion, nationalism, language, culture and so on. It is true that *what is* sought to be revived is not a living tradition. It is only the dead that need revival. The revivalist movements are spreading all over the world—it is taking place both in advanced western countries and also former socialist countries without any exception.

Revival is the perpetuation of confusion; to turn to the dead past in the movement of a living crisis is to seek a pattern of life which has its roots in decay ... if you cling to the past, you prevent the quickening experience of the new.[38] Krishnamurti is against all kinds of revivalism and religious revivalism in particular. That which is revived is not wholesome and real religion is not that which is revived. That which is revived cannot be new and living. He differentiates between true and false religion and according to him true religion is in the present, it is living. Therefore, religious revivalism is not really religious. People simply carry over the dead past in the name of religious revivalism, for security. But there is no security in religious revivalism or in nationalism or in the knowledge of the sacred books. Krishnamurti says:

> "The mind has invented, the brain has invented, various forms of security—nationalism, religious figures and the so-called sacred books. They have all given a certain quality of security. Actually, there is no security at all. It is an illusion."[39]

The problems of the world cannot be solved through religious revivalism or nationalism. A Hindu state, for instance, cannot solve the problem of poverty. In fact, there is no need for a state or a nation to become theocratic in order to solve the problems of the people. The problems are global and are therefore to be solved on a global level. Krishnamurti says:

> "In India, for example, there are millions starving. The Hindu who is nationalist says 'Let us first become intensely national, then we shall be able to solve this problem of starvation'. Whereas to me, the way we solve the problem of starvation is not to become nationalist, but the contrary, starvation is a world problem and this process of isolation but further increases starvation."[40]

Individual and Society (You are the World)

To Krishnamurti, there is no difference between the individual and the society. He regards the whole world as humanity. The sense of separation one feels as an individual, as an Indian, as an American and so on is illusory. The individual and the world are not separate. Therefore, the individual's problem is the problem of the world and vice versa. The world is the outcome of the individual's inner nature or the extension of the consciousness of humanity. As the consciousness is fragmented and conflicting within itself, the world is full of divisions and conflict. As is the consciousness of the individual, so is the world. The outer is the manifestation of the inner. Whether one is in Asia or in the West, or in the Middle East, or anywhere in the world, basically all are human beings. Basically human beings are not Hindus, Muslims, Americans, Russians; these are all the labels for human beings. The consciousness is similar in all human beings. The content may be different superficially, but essentially all human beings suffer; feel fear, insecurity, anxiety, uncertainty, agony, despair, depression. The individual and the society are not different. Krishnamurti says, "World problem is our problem because we are the world. What we think does affect the world. What we do does affect the society; the individual problem is directly related to the world problem".[41]

Krishnamurti, time and again, says that divisions are illusory. The earth belongs to humanity, but not to the Buddhists, Americans, Christians, Muslims and Hindus, Russians etc. It does not belong to any ideological group.

Krishnamurti views life as a process manifested in each individual. His view of life is integrated as he sees the social, outer, or objective phenomenon as a projection of inner, subjective, psychological structure of the individual. In this way he perceives the conflict as a process of human consciousness. As he puts it:

> "We generally approach this kind either objectively or subjectively, do we not? We try to understand it either on the objective or the subjective level and the difference is that the problem is neither purely subjective nor purely objective, but is a combination of the two. It is both a social and psychological process, One must approach it in its totality."[42]

To overcome the crisis and chaotic human situation, there should be change in the consciousness itself.

End Notes

1. J. Krishnamurti, *Krishnamurti's Journal* and also in Mary Cadogan, Alan Kishbaugh, Mark Lee and Ray Mc Coy (eds.) *Total Freedom, The Essential Krishnamurti* (New York: Harper San Francisco, 1996), p. 168.

2. C.f. Rajini Kothari, In J. Krishnamurti, *The Way of Intelligence* (Madras: KFI, 1984), p. 66.
3. J. Krishnamurti, *Mind Without Measure* (Madras: KFI, 1990), p. 72.
4. J. Krishnamurti, *Network of Thought* (Madras: KFI, 1992), p. 10.
5. See J. Krishnamurti, *Mind without Measure,* pp. 34-36.
6. J. Krishnamurti, *Krishnamurti on Education* (Madras: KFI), p. 11.
7. J. Krishnamurti, *Letters to the Schools,* Second Volume (Madras: KFI, 1981), p. 73.
8. J. Krishnamurti, *First and Last Freedom* (London: Victor Gollancz, 1987), p. 179.
9. J. Krishnamurti, *Commentaries on Living,* Second Series (Madras: KFI, 1991), p. 31.
10. J. Krishnamurti, *You Are the World* (Madras: KFI, 1986), p. 42.
11. Mary Lutyens (ed.), *Second Penguin Krishnamurti Reader*, p. 23.
12. J. Krishnamurti, *Talks with American Students* (Boston: Shambala, 1988), p. 11.
13. Cf. J. Krishnamurti, *Awakening of Intelligence* (New York: Avon Books, 1976), pp. 286-87.
14. J. Krishnamurti, *Beginnings of Learning* (Harmondsworth: Penguin Books, 1978), p.174.
15. J. Krishnamurti, *Commentaries on Living*, Third Series (Madras: HI, 1992), p. 55.
16. J. Krishnamurti, *Awakening of Intelligence*, p. 72.
17. J. Krishnamurti, *Mind Without Measure*, p. 30.
18. M.M. Aggrawal, *Consciousness and Integrated Being, Sartre and Krishnamurti* (New Delhi: National Publishing House, 1991), p. 3.
19. J. Krishnamurti, *The Flight of Eagle*, p. 57.
20. Cf. J. Krishnamurti, *Truth and Actuality* (Madras: KFI, 1992), p. 62.
21. Mary Lutyens (ed.), *Second Penguin Krishnamurti Reader* (Harmondsworth: Penguin Books, 1982), p. 40.

22. Aldous Huxley, *Ends and Means* (London: Chatto and Windus, 1937), p. 90.
23. As cited by Les. W. Feild, "Constructing Local Identities in a Revolutionary Nation: The Cultural Politics of the Artisan Class in Nicaragua 1979-90", *American Ethnologist,* Vol. 22 (4) November 1995, p. 787.
24. *Ibid.*, p. 787.
25. Cited in Reinhard Bernbeck and Susan Pollock, "Ayodhya, Archaeology and Identity", *Current Anthropology* Vol. 37 Supplement, February, 1996, p. 5138.
26. Peter Homans, *Jung in Context; Modernity and the Making of a Psychology* (Chicago: Chicago University Press, 1979), p. 180.
27. J. Krishnamurti, *The Flight of The Eagle* (Madras: KFI, 1988). p. 57.
28. Cited Cynthia, Keepley Mahomood "Rethinking Indian. Communalism Culture and Counter Culture" *Asian Survey,* No. 7, July 1993.
29. *Ibid.*, p. 726.
30. *Ibid.*, p. 726.
31. Jonathan Spencer (ed.), "Introduction: The Power of the Past", *Sri Lanka: History and Roots of Conflict* (London: Routledge, 1990), p. 3.
32. Sasanka Perera, *Living with Torturers and Other Essays of Intervention; Sri Lankan Society, Culture and Politics in Perspective* (Colombo: International Centre for Ethnic Studies, 1995), p. 66.
33. *Ibid.*, p. 63.
34. *Ibid.*, p. 67.
35. Elizabeth Nissan and R.L. Stirret, "The Generation of Communal Identities." In J. Spencer (1990), p. 19.
36. Mark Juergensmeyer, *Religious Nationalism Confronts Secular State* (New Delhi: Oxford University Press, 1994), p. 111. Cited from Neihhold Niebuhr (ed.) *Karl Marx and Fredrich Engels on Religion,* (1964), p. 42.
37. John Anderson, *Religion, State and Politics in Soviet Union and Successor States* (Cambridge: Cambridge University Press, 1994), p. 180.

38. J. Krishnamurti, *Commentaries on Living,* Third Series, p. 43.
39. J. Krishnamurti, *Mind without Measure*, p. 27.
40. J. Krishnamurti, *Total Freedom*, (Ohia Talks, June 30, 1934), p. 47.
41. J. Krishnamurti, *Total Freedom,* p. 191.
42. J. Krishnamurti, *Talks, Seattle,* 1950, p. 40, cited in R.K. Shringy, *Philosophy of J. Krishnamurti: A Systematic Study,* (New Delhi: Munshiram Manohar Lal, 1977,) p. 124.

5

On Revolution

A man who is passionate about the world and the necessity for change, must be free from political activity, religious conformity and tradition which means, time, free from the burden of the past, free from all actions of the will; this is the new human being. This only is the social, psychological and even the political revolution.

— J. Krishnamurti

General Conception of Revolution

The term 'revolution' stands for a family of ideas that share some vague qualitative overtones rather than having a precise meaning. 'Revolution' is widely employed without a clear definition either in speeches or in historical and sociological writings. Despite the variations in the use and usage of the word 'revolution', attempts have been made to find some meaning common to all or most of them.

It is since the French Revolution of 1789, that the word revolution, has more specifically come to mean major change in the political and socio-economic structure of an individual state, brought about by (the spontaneous as well as conscious) efforts of its citizens. A revolution tries to bring about fundamental changes even in the mode of thinking and basic beliefs of people. Revolution differs from reform and rebellion. The process of revolution can be understood in terms of the goals of revolution and the means used to achieve these goals. Keeping this in view many people have tried to define revolution. Some have tried to explain revolution in sociological terms; some in political terms and, some others on grounds other than political and sociological.

According to the Oxford English Dictionary, revolution is a complete overthrow of the established government in any country or state by those who were previously subject to it, or a forcible substitution of a new ruler or form of government. This definition implies that revolutions take place on the political level, involving governments and rulers and that they must be 'complete' and successful in order to bring new governments or new rulers to power. It is interesting to note that Aristotle too had defined revolution in a similar fashion. In *Politics,* Aristotle says that there are "two sorts of change in government, the one affecting constitution and the other involving the capture of administration."[1]

In the book *States and Revolution*, Theda Skocpol explains social revolutions as the product not of individual actions butted in of structural and situational conditions. "Social revolutions are rapid, basic transformations of a society's state and class structure... accompanied and in part carried through by class based revolts from below."[2] As Bachelor defines revolution as "a protest movement that manages to seize power."[3] Those who seize power are not necessarily men from below. Some are attracted to revolution from below and others from the above. However, Meusal suggests that a revolution occurs "when the upper class cannot and the lower will not continue the old system,"[4] or when both the classes are dissatisfied.

Neumann expands the definition of revolution to include a "sweeping, fundamental change in political organisation, social structure, economic property control and the predominant myths of social order (thereby) indicating a major break in the continuity of development."[5] Legality of the earlier rule is questioned. Trimberger calls revolution "an extra- legal takeover of the central state apparatus which destroys the economic and political power of the dominant social group of the old regime."[6]

All these definitions discussed above imply success in revolution. While analysing or discussing revolution many people accord violence a central role. Friedrich defines revolution as "the sudden and violent overthrow of an established political order."[7]

Huntington defines revolution as "a rapid fundamental and violent domestic change in the dominant values and myths of a society, in its political institutions, social structure, leadership, government activity and policies."[8] For John Dunn, revolution is "a form of massive, violent and rapid social change."[9]

A revolution is an attempt by subordinate groups through the use of violence to bring about (1) a change of government or of its policy, (2) a change of regime, or (3) a change of society. A.S. Cohan defines revolution as "a process by which a radical alteration of a particular society occurs over a given time span."[10]

However, the whole problem about defining the concept of revolution is that Liberals, Marxists and Fascists, do not agree about on what constitutes a radical alteration. Peter Calvert in his scholarly work, *Revolution and International Politics,* suggests that we can avoid the issue of 'radical change' etc., if we restrict ourselves to the ordinary, everyday use of the word 'revolution'. According to the ordinary usage of the word 'revolution', it refers to "events in which physical force (or the convincing threat of it) has actually been used successfully to overturn a government or regime."[11] However, we have no clear means of distinguishing different ways of using physical force. Chalmers Johnson, in his work *Revolutionary Change,* explains revolution from the point of view of the systems theory. He asserts, when a society loses its state of equilibrium or when its values and environment are not synchronised, revolution occurs. He talks about revolution as "the acceptance of violence in order to cause the system to change when all else has failed."[12] According to him, "The very idea of revolution is contingent upon the perception of social failure."[13] However, for Hannah Arendt, a true revolution is essentially a movement which aims at the creation of a republic. According to her interpretation, the revolutionary experience is a kind of restoration, whereby the insurgents attempt to restore liberties and privileges which were lost as a result of the government's temporary lapse into despotism. Certain aspects of the American Revolution as well as some recent anti-colonial revolutions may be amenable to Arendt's interpretation. But Arendt's definition of revolution does not take into serious consideration that a revolution aims at the creation not just of a new kind of society, but of a new kind of man.[14]

Tocqueville has employed a more empirical approach to the problem of revolution. He has defined it as "an overthrow of the legally constituted elites, which initiated a period of intense social, political and economic changes."[15] Crane Brinton, in *Anatomy of Revolution,* has continued this empirical thrust by differentiating between the coup d'etat, as a simple replacement of one elite by another and major revolutions such as the French or Russian which were accompanied by social, political and economic changes. Brinton defines revolution as a "drastic and sudden substitution of one group in charge of the running of a territorial political unity by another group."[16] Similarly, in respect to Latin America, George Bramksten suggests that we should distinguish between the coup d'etat and a revolution such as the Mexican experience, which eventually had a profound impact on the structure of the society.[17]

S.N. Eisenstadt in his book, *Revolution and the Transformation of Societies,* adopts a different approach. According to him, the chief legacy of the great modern revolutions to modern thought has been a certain image of revolution involving three principal components of violence, novelty and total change. As a result various historical situations are being analysed in terms of these categories and assumptions.[18] A Hegelian equates the revolution with movement or change, the manifestation of the world spirit in its quest for self-realisation and fulfillment whereas The

Marxists, see revolution as a product of irresistible historical forces, which culminate in the struggle between the bourgeoisie and the proletariat.

Albert Camus, states in his book, *The Rebel,* that, "Freedom...is the motivating principle of all revolutions."[19] Whatever be the actual outcome of revolution, its objective is always freedom.

The definitions of revolution mentioned so far, however, do not seriously consider the role of psychological factors in revolution. Ted Robert Gurr in his celebrated book, *Why Men Rebel,* discusses the psychological factors involved in revolution. He subsumes revolution under political violence and defines it as a "fundamental socio-political change accomplished through violence."[20] And civil violence takes many forms and psychological theories of aggression can help explain why individuals resort to violence to achieve political ends.

Krishan Kumar, an Indian scholar, writes that "Revolution is the sovereign means of re-structuring society and man. It is the act by means of which man asserts his ability to change totally the institutions that control him. It is an act of willed destruction and replacement of a whole system of society, to secure his freedom."[21] Thus, revolution means a process which is violent and is of the nature of a sudden shock and a breaking through or overturning, especially with regard to changes in the institutions of state and law. It has a social content, or ideology which sets a positive program of renovation further development or the progress of humanity.[22]

Roy Edgely, however, tries to discuss the concept of revolution in scientific terms. The relation between science and revolution has entered into philosophical debates in recent days after Kuhn's *Structure of Scientific Revolution*. By revolution Edgely means historical change of a fundamental and pervasive kind, a change of structure, a change of elements due to an overall change in the accepted system. A scientific revolution, as studied in the history of science, is a revolution within science, or at least within thought or theory and thus, being fundamental, pervasive and structural, it is specifically a conceptual change, a change in the basic categorical framework in terms of which reality is characterised or understood.[23]

Karl Marx studied 'revolution' in its historical context. In non-Marxian definitions discussed 'revolution' is reduced to transfer of power from one group to another. And, these definitions are moreover highly abstract and many of them are legalistic and constitutional. Revolution for Marx is a historical category and his theory of revolution is developed in the framework of the materialistic conception of history. Marxian theory of Society is a theory of society-in-history and his theory of revolution is a theory of transformation of society-in-history. A theory of history itself is a process of man's revolutionary evolution. Marx's historical materialism is above all a theory of revolution. Marxian idea of revolution has many dimensions. It involves social, economic, technological, political, legal and ideological factors. It is even seen as a natural phenomenon, as it involves the appropriation of the man-produced world of material objects. Therefore, revolution means transformation of man himself. In the words of Marx, "The whole of history is nothing but a continual transformation of human nature."[24]

Marx looks at the future communist revolution as a radical transformation of man.

> "Men make their own history, but they do not make it just as they please; they do not make it under circumstances chosen by them, but under circumstances directly encountered, given and transmitted from the past. The tradition of all the dead generations weighs like a nightmare on the brain of the living."[25]

According to Marx, revolutionary transition from one social epoch to the other involves a political revolution, the overthrow of the existing state and the conquest of the political pcwer by the revolutionary class. In some revolutions, there is a rise to power of a new exploiting class and 'progress' has been achieved only by the imposition of new forms of exploitation on the masses. In the socialist revolution when the working class takes power, all exploitation is finally abolished. Socialist revolution, once and for all ends all exploitation of man by man. The Marxian revolutionary project envisages a classless and stateless society. Marx sees social revolution as the fundamental fact which pervades the whole organic process by which a new society comes into being; the political revolution is merely a significant incident occurring at the climax of the process. However, the goal of all social revolutions, according to Marx, is freedom, which is the liberation of human creativity from all obstacles, the source of human bondage.

Reformism and Radicalism

In general, there are two dominant streams of thinking about Change which revolutions try to achieve. They are implied in the definitions of revolution. One stream is for the change of the present state of society which is corrupt. Thus the change means the restoration of the legacy of the past and is to be pursued in accordance with the political and social context of the country, its history, tradition and customs. Institutions must be reformed in accordance with their original principles, spirits and purposes. Human society is a mixture of good and evil; the good should be carefully conserved and the evil carefully remedied. Reformation or restoration is the character of revolution, according to this line of thinking. In other words it is a conservative model of change or revolution.

The other stream, on the contrary, challenges the established order as the problems of old order, according to this view cannot be solved, within the framework of that order. According to this, a fundamentally new order is to be established through the use of extreme political means to remedy the process the old order. Therefore, there should be a break from the old order. In general, the meaning of revolution is understood in this sense. This view is also known as radical.

Now, Krishnamurti is not for change through reformation or restoration. Reformation is continuation of past which is tradition and therefore, cannot solve the problems of the present, either of the individual or of society. The society or the individual is always in a state of change. Reform can never keep the world in order.

But the revolutions which claim to be radical are not really radical, according to Krishnamurti. He points out that these revolutions are based on an idea or an ideology. Revolution based on an idea is only a modified form of what was. There is nothing new in it. It cannot bring about the change in the total situation of society and the individual. The change it affects is only limited, being grounded on old patterns with slight modification. It may be the change of power from one group to another and the new group with its power becomes a new class which tries to strengthen itself by privileges and so on. Thus revolution is merely a re-structuring of the same old material within the same pattern of thought.

The Marxist principle is that in the course of development there is a conflict between thesis and anti-thesis which leads to a qualitative change. Krishnamurti questions the Marxist principle that a new society arises out of the conflict between opposite classes, namely the oppressor and the oppressed. According to Krishnamurti the opposites are not really distinct; as the anti-thesis contains within itself the element of its own thesis. Therefore, the synthesis is only a modified thesis. While the present society is based on individual acquisitiveness, in the new society, in the Marxian sense, individual acquisitiveness is opposed and replaced by state acquisitiveness. Krishnamurti thinks that in Communism the state dictates terms to the individual thus negating individual freedom.

Krishnamurti is of the view that it is unwise to sacrifice the present society—for the ideal of the future society. The present society has to be changed, but not according to speculative and intellectual ideas. It has to be changed by changing the individual psychologically. Krishnamurti questions the ends or goals to be achieved by means of revolutions. Krishnamurti says, "How can you be sure of the future? What makes you so certain of it? A religious people promise heaven and you promise a better world in the future, you have your book and your priests, as they have theirs, so there is really not much difference between you. But what makes you so sure, that you are clear sighted about future?"[26]

Krishnamurti is critical of the activities of the revolutionaries, which according to him are like religious activities, mechanical and imitative. Real change is not possible simply by applying the principles or ideas of someone. For bringing about real change, it is necessary to understand the structure of the present society and the mind which is its source or basis. He points out that the so called revolutions have used man as a means to achieve their hypothetical ends. For them ideals are more important than man. They have sacrificed man for their imaginary ends. According to Krishnamurti, the means and ends are not separate. They constitute a single and inseparable process. The means are the end: so there can be no classless society by means of class conflict. The opposites are self projected and the ideal is a reaction to '*what is*'. Conflict breeds conflict.

Krishnamurti holds that the change brought about by the so called revolution is only a reform. He reduces all of them to reform. They may bring about certain structural changes in society, but the change is not radical, total and 'final'. It needs further change. Krishanmurti therefore maintains that real change should not only be outward but also inward. The real change in society can be brought about by change within the individuals who constitute it. The outward change is brought about by the inward attitudes, thoughts and feelings.

Krishnamurti's Radical Revolution

Revolution is central to the thought of Krishnamurti. He does not use the word 'revolution' in the sense of communist or socialist. According to him, revolution involves a complete and radical transformation of the human psyche or the total structure of mind. The so called reforms and revolutions do not have total impact on the human being. The revolutions on the social, economic and political levels are limited. They do not affect the total human existence. They do not change the total structure and nature of society. Therefore, total revolution is not economic, social or political; it is not according to any pattern or idea. It presupposes a deep and fundamental revolution in the mind itself. Krishnamurti thinks that: social or economic, revolution can only change outer states and things, or in increasing or narrowing circles, but it will always be within a limited field of thought. For total revolution the brain must forsake all its inward, secret mechanism of authority, envy, fear and so on.[27]

Krishnamurti maintains that economic, political and social devolutions are a modification in the existing pattern. They are motivated and mechanical and based on the desire for comfort, adjustment, security and so on. And the change that comes through desire or motive is no real change. Fundamental revolution is quite a different process. There is fundamental revolution only in understanding the total process of action, but not at any particular level, whether economical or ideological. It is action as an integrated whole. Such action is not a reaction. Integration is not an intellectual synthesis, a verbal conclusion.

Radical revolution is not the communists' revolt against the capitalists, the son against the father, the refusal to accept the social norm to breakthrough economic and class bondage. Perhaps, these revolts are necessary but they are not very deep; they replace the old pattern by the new one which conditions and destroys the mind.[28]

There is ever increasing misery in the world; ceaseless conflict between classes and nations, between individuals and society. The world is ridden with frightful social and economic inequalities, suffering, strife and hatred, poverty, corruption, violence and war. The predicament demands an urgent need for revolution. The world crises and disintegration of humanity necessitates integral and fundamental revolution. No formula or system or ideology can bring about a fundamental revolution. A real revolution should be present at every movement of life. It will not sacrifice the present for the future. A fundamental revolution is primarily a revolution in the inner world of thoughts and feelings and radically affects the man's psychological relations with the world. Neither a system nor an institution, political or religious, however profound it may be, can bring about a real change in the world.

Krishnamurti writes:

> "In order to transform the world about us, with its misery, unemployment, starvation, class divisions and utter confusion, there must be a transformation in ourselves. The revolution must begin with oneself—but not according to any belief or ideology, because revolution based on idea or in conformity to a particular pattern, is obviously no revolution at all. To bring about fundamental revolution in oneself, one must understand the whole process of one's thought and feeling in relationship".[29]

The real change implies a radical transformation in the very nature of society. It is possible only when there is a deep and radical change in the inward being of the individual. Trying to change the outer structure of society without taking into consideration the inward conflict is meaningless. Krishnamurti explains rationally and objectively how other systems and ideologies have failed to bring about a revolution, as the real change should be at the 'centre' and not at the periphery. Change at the periphery is an inadequate and incomplete response to the challenge of real change. Real change is possible only when there is total resolution of the conflict within the individual. The integration of the human consciousness is the only revolution that is worthwhile and lasting. So the individual has to integrate himself without any choice. It needs a complete rejection of thought imposed on the mind. It means freedom from the known, from the past and the psychological time. This revolution is possible only through an understanding of the entire content of consciousness. Understanding is ending this content by having an insight into it. The content is traditional; it is built in time through thought, knowledge and memory. It is responsible for the misery, suffering, confusion, chaos and conflict in the world. The traditional mind rooted in the past can never solve any problem. Instead it makes them more complex. Real transformation implies an end to the continuity of the traditional mind and ending the continuity means the ending of tradition. Revolution, thus, according to Krishnamurti, is the ending of tradition.

Ending of Tradition

Tradition is the continuity of the past through the present towards the future. It prevents adequate response to the present, *what is*. It hinders discovery or the looking at the life anew. Tradition is a hindrance to understanding life in its totality, the perception of truth and the freedom to understand things for oneself. And the 'I' which is the product of tradition does not help and favour revolution to take place.

> "... Anything truly revolutionary is created by a few who see what is true and are willing to live according to that truth; but to discover *what is* true demands freedom from tradition, which means freedom from all fears."[30]

Ending of Knowledge

The traditional mind and its activities are always in the field of the known. They operate in the realm of knowledge. According to Krishnamurti, knowledge is of the past and it prevents understanding, because of its incompleteness. Only the mind which is free of knowledge can have insight into the tradition. Knowledge is ignorance in the psychological realm. It conditions the mind to the past; therefore the mind occupied with knowledge cannot understand and appreciate wisdom. Krishnamurti writes:

> "Wisdom is when knowledge ends. Knowledge has continuity. Without continuity there is no knowledge. That which has continuity can never be free; there is freedom only to that which has an ending. Knowledge can never be new, it is

always becoming the old.... the old must cease for the new to be".[31]

Knowledge is continuous, which involves time. The traditional mind is therefore of time and time has to end for the revolution to take place.

Ending of Thought

Thought is responsible for the continuity of division, conflict, violence and war. Thought as the product of mind or in its psychological sense is responsible for tradition which causes buffering. Thought constitutes the content of our consciousness. It is anchored to memory and is dependent on the past. There is no independent thought. On the other hand, to feel the wholeness of life, the mind should be free from thought which is limited and cannot therefore know or understand truth. Krishnamurti says, "Freedom from the known is the ending of thought; to die to thought, from moment to moment, is to be free from the known. It is this death that puts an end to decay."[32]

Insight or understanding is possible only when thought is suspended and the mind is stilled. In other words, complete suspension of thought may lead to an insight into the nature of Truth. Such ending of thought through insight is psychological revolution.

Ending of Time

The traditional mind has evolved through time. The movement is from the past to the future through the present. Time gives continuity to the content of thought. The movement of thought as memory, experience and knowledge is the movement of time, therefore; psychological transformation needs the ending of time. Sliding of time is the ending of thought as memory, experience etc. Insight can take place only when one transcends time. The realisation of the totality of time brings about an immediate radical change and that makes one transcend time and gradualness. Insight is free from thought. When there is no movement of time, there is tremendous focusing of energy. And revolution is the understanding of the movement of time in its psychological sense. Krishnamurti says:

> "Insight has no time. Insight is not the product of time, time being memory etc., that insight which is free of time acts upon memory, acts upon thought. That is, insight makes thought rational, but not thought which is based on memory."[33]

Ending of Self

Self is the result of the past and continuation of the past in the present through thought. In fact self has no substantiality; it is nothing but a bundle of memories and the projection of the psychological inheritance. Self is the consciousness of 'I' or 'Me' and comes with desire. The activity of self leads to sorrow when its desires are not fulfilled. And self always desires to be something. Human problems can be resolved by realising the non-substantiality of self.

> "If in each of us, the centre of the 'Me' is nonexistent, with its desires for power, position, authority, continuance, self-preservation, surely our problem will come to an end."[34]

It is only when one overcomes completely the sense of self that the timeless, immeasurable and the new come into being. Self can be dissolved only through self-kno

wledge. Self-knowledge helps one in understanding the instability of the self. It is the realisation of the fact that the self is the root cause of sorrow. Self-knowledge is not the knowledge of the self but seeing how the self has come into existence and how it fragments life. Self-knowledge is an insight which brings about a psychological transformation of the mind by putting an end to all options, ideas, opinions, beliefs and conclusions.

No Method for Realisation of Freedom

Krishnamurti is against any method or practice for the realisation of freedom. According to him, revolution is timeless; whereas methods, systems and paths involve time and with their help one can accomplish only something which is limited by time or involving time. To him analysis, either psychological or intellectual, is the product of thought. The analysis is the thinker which is thought itself. Analysis also implies a division between the analysis and the analysed. It involves the process of time. Time is thought, which is the product of the past. But all freedom takes place only when thought is totally absent. It takes place through insight which is beyond thought and time. Insight is free from the past and is uncaused.

Krishnamurti rejects all kinds of meditation which are adopted as the means of total revolution. According to him, systems of meditation regard freedom as an end. They accept time as the means of realising the end. But the freedom attained through a system is only a modification of the traditional mind which is conditioned. Therefore, freedom according to Krishnamurti is not a mere modification but a total ending of the conditioned mind. This is possible only when there is an insight into the origin and the structure of the conditioned mind. The conditioned mind has to perceive itself without any movement, or become aware of its own conditioning. The instantaneous knowledge of the mind without there being a known brings about radical change in the mind. To Krishnamurti, insight or choiceless observation alone is the direct and immediate way of awakening intelligence which is freedom. Krishnamurti therefore maintains that all the methods except insight are useless. Methods other than insight involve thought, time and continuity. They can only reform *what is*, but cannot radically transform *what is*.

According to Krishnamurti, transformation through a method produces the illusory division within the mind between that which transforms and that which is to be transformed. It also regards transformation as gradual or evolutionary. But gradual transformation can never be deep and radical. A method puts an end to enquiry and makes the mind mechanical. It conditions the mind to work by way of inventing and attaining the ends which are its self-projections. The mind which follows a method gets itself stuck in the method itself. Then the method becomes the framework within which the mind functions endlessly.

According to Krishnamurti, choiceless awareness alone can bring about freedom. Choiceless awareness is immediate understanding. It is perception without perceiver and experience without experiencer. It is devoid of motives and ends. Krishnamurti says:

> "The understanding of *what is* meets no motives; the motive and the means prevent understanding. Search which is choice-less awareness is not for something; it is to be aware of the craving for an end and the means of it. This choice-less awareness brings an understanding of *what is.*"[35]

Insight

Krishnamurti uses the word 'insight' with a profound meaning. For him it is an inward perception not only in the sense of looking into the very essence of the mind that is to be understood, but also in the sense of looking into the mind that is engaged in the act of knowing. The two must happen together. Only such perception makes possible the creation of new forms of response which are able to meet the challenges of new situations. From time to time new challenges arise; but the conditioned knowledge is unable to meet the challenge, instead it further complicates them. Therefore *what is* required is a creative and original response which goes beyond the known general framework. And that is possible through insight only; it provides an overall new approach to any sort of problem.

Insight has nothing to do with knowledge, memory, experience and thought. It does not involve time. It is holistic action and immediate perception. It is not a mechanical thought process. Insight is the total absence of the movement of thought. It is direct perception into *what is* and takes place in a flash and cannot be captured by thought. Action that follows insight is total; it is not fragmented. Insight is so full of vitality that it does not allow thought to operate.

Insight dissolves the mind's attachment to the illusions that bind or limit it. Insight and its energy are necessary for dissolving the blocks and barriers that prevent real understanding. They put an end to self-deception and open the mind to new perceptions which are relevant on each occasion. Insight with immense energy brings out genuine rationality. It dissolves all the conditioning:

Insight is an act of perception, permeated with intense energy and passion and brings about great clarity. It makes possible the dissolution of strong but subtle emotional, linguistic, intellectual, social and other pressures that tend to keep the mind in rigid grooves and fixed compartments. So that it cannot face fundamental challenges.[36]

Insight is passion. Passion is creative. When one has an insight into sorrow and remains with it completely without a single movement of thought, out of that comes the strange flame of passion. Sorrow is the result of the conditioning of mind which prevents insight whereas insight dissolves the conditioning of mind.

The insight in the field of science is limited to a particular area, rational and discovers new things which are universal and necessary. It has significance in the realm of matter whereas insight in art is imaginative. When imagination moves freely without any barriers it gives rise to insight. Krishnamurti insists that insight is not restricted to great scientific discoveries or artistic creation. Everybody has the capacity for insight, if they are not conditioned. Insight is possible in every area of human activity and it is of significance in all areas of life.

Insight is non-verbal. Thought cannot enter into the realm of insight. In fact, when insight takes place in thought, then it is not thought. But thought may communicate the insight or some of the data which lead to an insight. There would have to be insight into the nature of thought before thought could realise any thing. Insight is awareness of the observer as the observed. Insight sees no division between the observer and the observed. It has its own capacity for reason, logic and action. It brings about a change in understanding and puts an end to conflict and division. It is when one silently and choice-lessly observes oneself that awareness liberates the mind. Then the mind is radically transformed. Thus insight brings about revolution, which is both inner and outer.

Insight is attention. Attention is a quality of perception. The attentive mind is extra-ordinarily sensitive. It is only the sensitive mind that can be silent. Attention can wipe away the unconscious as well as the limited consciousness. For insight to take place, one has to be totally attentive to every movement of the mind. This is possible only when one knows *what is* without any conditioning. Attention involves total being, only in that state of attention the brain can function perfectly:

> "Attention means complete attention—of the body, of the psyche, of the cells; everything there is with life-alive. In that state, there is no centre, there is no time and there is no observer as the 'me'. There is no time in terms of the past, yet the past exists—because speak the language; I know my way to the room".[37]

Attention is a state of mind in which there is no contradiction. It is total movement and total action. In attention, the mind collects all its energy, or there is no fragmentation of energy. Attention is a state in which the mind is completely awake and in the state of complete attention the observer as thought does not exist. Therefore, in the state of attention, one is free from tradition and from habitual thinking. It means cessation of the division between the observer and observed. In attention, there is no interference of thought; as in it there is no image-building and concept-construction. It is communion, looking or listening non-verbally. It cannot, therefore, be cultivated. It is not a method. Attention is different from concentration. Concentration involves exclusion and resistance. It is a form of conformity. It is an act of narrowing down of thought to a particular point which makes the mind rigid and insensitive. It is incapable of grasping the whole field of life.

Perception

Insight is also called perception. The perceptive mind is the insightful mind. Perception is seeing the fact with the whole of one's being—physical, emotional, intellectual. According to Krishnamurti, perception takes place when there is no image, no symbol, no idea, no word and no form. Such perception is action itself. It is not action in terms of the actor acting in accordance with his knowledge. It is immediate and instantaneous. To the perceiving mind the very seeing is doing. It has no direction and time. It is completely free from the past. It is non-verbal and has the quality of renewing itself at every moment. It dies every moment and renews itself. Thus, in perception the ending is beginning. There is no action of the observer or perceiver in the perception, as it dies to whatever it sees and never carries it forward. So perception is ever new. It is only seeing, observing or listening without any image, conclusion, prejudice or accumulation. It perceives things clearly and totally:

> "The first perception is the last perception and the ending of the first perception is the new perception. Therefore, there is a total gap between the first perception and the second perception. In that interval, there is no movement of thought. There would be the movement of thought when the memory of the first perception remains, not when it is over. Can the mind not empty itself of every perception? Can it not die to every expression?"[38]

Perception is total and takes place when the mind is aware of its conditioning without condemning and judging it, but by merely watching it. To perceive the truth of anything, there must be a total freedom from social conditioning and influence. It must be free from acquisitiveness, of ambition, of envy and of the whole process of becoming. Perception is possible only when thought disappears and when the mind is still. In perception, there is no ego and clarity of perception means freedom from self. Krishnamurti says, "Perception can take place only in the very act of exploring. To explore implies that there is no division between the observer and observed. Therefore, watching the movement of fear and in the very watching of it there is an insight."[39]

The perceptive mind is intensely passionate. It is a state of absolute nothingness. Nothingness is not a thing put together by thought. It is the state of creative void. Perception is a flame. It is intense and a full awareness of the totality of *what is*. In words of Krishnamurti, "Perception without any qualification is a flame. It distills whatever it perceives; because it is the flame. There is that perception which distills at every minute..."[40]

Choiceless Awareness

Choiceless awareness is the key concept of Krishnamurti's Philosophy of life. It is the only way to end the conditioning of the mind and meaninglessness of life. Choiceless awareness is an observation of *what is;* the fact or actuality without any movement of thought which is knowledge of the past. It is insight into what is; or the comprehension of truth. It is a direct, pure and silent observation of the whole of *what is* without distorting it. It is an experimental approach of allowing *what is* to reveal itself as it essentially is. It is non-verbal and non-conceptual understanding. It is seeing or to be aware of *what is* without any choice. It frees the mind from contradictions. To choose is to emphasise or commit oneself to one alternative against the other. Choice may mean either indifference to, or interference with what is. Choosing is always in accordance with one's past. And where there is choice, there is no scope for complete awareness, as the mind will then be unable to think clearly, directly and objectively.

In choiceless awareness, there is direct and immediate contact with reality as it is. In such awareness, the mind is free from all symbols, images and remembrances. It comes with the understanding of the whole process of conscious and unconscious desires. Awareness is the unhindered movement of the mind that is not conditioned by identification with any idea. To be aware is to 'see' without evaluation, judgment, conformity, acceptance and denial. In such awareness, there is neither rejection, nor avoidance, nor predetermination, nor direction. There is no motive to satisfy and no problem to solve. It is just observation devoid of observer, or a center, or 'me', the self or the thinker, which is thought. It is observation without prejudice, likes and dislikes, pleasure, fear and pain. It is observation of *what is* without a perspective or a framework. Krishnamurti says that choiceless awareness is seeing the fact without distorting and dividing it. It is remaining with *what is* without moving away from it. It is the complete attention of holding the totality of *what is*, like a vessel holding water. Total attention generates the energy that regenerates *what is*.[41]

Choiceless awareness is a negative approach to *what is*. It is negative in the sense that it denies a place to knowledge in understanding. Such awareness is real revolution which radically affects our existence, our daily life and our relationships. Truth can be discovered only in the state of choiceless awareness as it leads to the discovery of the psychological structures of self and the limitations of the conditioned existence. It is true understanding in which the previous experience is totally absent. Choiceless awareness is not a result. It is not a gradual or a progressive understanding of *what is*. It does not involve intellectualisation, interpretation, explanation, theorisation or verbalisation. It is totally effortless and spontaneous. When the mind is completely aware, it becomes extraordinarily silent. In the very awareness of its own activities, the mind becomes astonishingly quiet, still and creative. It is experiencing the truth from moment to moment.

Observer is Observed

Choiceless awareness is that in which the observer is the observed. Krishnamurti maintains that there is in reality no such duality as the observer and the observed. The observer is the result of thought in which it separates itself for the sake of security. Thought is a unitary process. Thought can be ended when there is the awareness that thinker and thought are one. The observer is nothing but the movement of thought and its continuity. The observer is essentially a product of tradition, or past and therefore the observer is the movement away from that is. The observer is the result of the activity of the traditional mind. And the dualism of observer and observed leads to conflict, struggle or escape. In actuality, there is no such division. It exists only in thought. Awareness means transcending the division of the observer and the observed:

There will always be death for those who do not see that the observer is observed, the experience is experienced. It is like a vast river in which man is caught, with all his worldly goods, his vanities, pains and knowledge. Unless he leaves all the things he has accumulated (in river) and swims ashore, death will be always at his doors, waiting and watching.[42]

When there is no division of observer and observed and when one remains entirely with *what is*, there comes clarity, intensity of the mind that sees instantly the truth of *what is*.

Beauty lies in the total abandonment of observer and observed. It is a state of mind, which is wholly alone, but not in isolation. Seeing without observer is love. Krishnamurti says that observation without observer happens, quite normally and easily. In seeing, like in great danger, there is no observer separated from the observed. Psychologically also there is an immediate change when one sees inwardly, the falsity of the division between the observer and the observed.

Freedom

Choiceless awareness is not a means to an end. It is an end in itself or is itself freedom. For Krishnamurti, freedom is not freedom from something since such freedom is no freedom at all, since it is a reaction, a resistance, which only breeds further opposition. Freedom is action devoid of conditioning and contradiction. It is the total ending of thought at the psychological level. Freedom is actual, passionate and a sensitive state of an individual. It is not conforming to any beliefs, ideas or patterns. It is a state of mind which is of not-knowing. It doubts and questions everything; it is so intense, active and vigorous that it throws away every form of dependence, slavery, conformity and acceptance. It is a revolt against all inward dependence. There is no movement of desire in freedom.

Krishnamurti holds that in the state of freedom, the mind is without fear of punishment or the pleasure of reward. It is without motive. Freedom is not of choice. It is not obtaining what one chooses. Choice implies confusion and contradiction, since choice is the product of thought. Freedom is a state of clarity of immediate perception. Krishnamurti says, "Choice is the very denial of freedom. You choose when you are not clear, when there is no direct perception and so you choose out of confusion and so there is no freedom in choice psychologically, that is."[43]

Freedom is the mind which is 'unknown'. It is infinite, eternal and holistic. It is absolutely stable and orderly. Freedom is the 'emptiness' or the 'nothingness' of mind. Nothingness implies the absence of thought which is a 'thing'. Thought is confined to the realm of the known—knowledge, past or memory. The known is a material process. And total freedom is outside the realm of the known. Krishnamurti calls freedom truth; truth is that which is not thought. It is the mind which is unconditioned. Truth is not abstraction. It is living intelligently which is supremely rational. The true mind is sane in the sense that it is free from fear, irrationality and illusion. Truth is self-knowledge in action.

Self-knowledge is not in the withdrawal from life but in living in emptiness. The free mind is religious'. It is religious not in the sense of conforming to beliefs, ideals and organised religions. It is religious in the sense that it is full of energy sans self-contradiction. It is 'alone'. To be alone is to be one with all. The religious mind is full of love. Love is not sentimental; it is without attachment and detachment. Love is total; it is passion for everything, nature, birds, animals and other human beings.

For Krishnamurti freedom is absolute. Freedom is not relative since it is not freedom from some particular factors like division, fear, conflict, etc. It is absolute in the sense that it is totally free from the cause of all factors, namely thought. Freedom is the ending of thought, the very source of all problems.

Intelligence

The free mind is intelligent. The intelligent mind is integrated and perceives *what is* as a whole. To it, perceiving is doing. It is aware of the truth of everything, within and without. It is free from illusions. The intelligent mind is constantly learning without concluding and is not satisfied with explanations and arguments. It does not believe because belief is a form of conclusion. An intelligent mind is an inquiring mind. It is watchful from moment to moment. It faces life afresh. It sees *what is* as it actually is. Krishnamurti says, "Understanding the false as false, seeing the true in the false and seeing the true as the true, is the beginning of intelligence."[44]

Intelligence is not clever pursuit of argumentation. It is not the ambivalence of holding contradictory opinions. The intelligent mind is never stuck in opinions and patterns of thought. It is without fear and does not accept fully established structures but wants to discover the truth. The fulfillment of human beings can be achieved through the awakening of the intelligence.

The intelligent mind is free of tradition which has its continuity through thought. But intelligence uses thought wherever and whenever necessary. It uses physical or factual knowledge for the strictly biological well-being of humanity. It understands the limitations of thought and guides it. Intelligence alone solves the situation brought about by thought and knowledge. Intelligence is complete action as the action of intelligence is never divisive or contradictory. Intelligence, which is insight, is supremely rational. Its rationality is not that of thought as the rationality of thought is irrational and creates illusions.

Krishnamurti says, "When there is insight, there is only action, why do you want thought? Because insight is rational, Action is rational. Action becomes irrational when it is acting from thought. So insight does not use thought."[45]

Intelligence keeps the man and the world in order. It is the energy which prevents thought from making life chaotic and meaningless as intelligence alone can give meaning to life by putting thought in its right place. Human beings should develop an intelligent mind to live a peaceful and happy life in the world. Intelligent life is holistic, sane and therefore meaningful.

Right Kind of Education

Krishnamurti holds that education should help in bringing out intelligent and integrated beings. Keeping this view in mind he points out that the present education system all over the world has lost its holistic view of life. Instead of awakening the intelligence and creativity, it further cultivates the mind of the child conforming to the established social structures and traditions which are obviously responsible for the world's misery and conflict. Therefore, Krishnamurti considers that education has its importance in the development of the individual to break down all kinds of barriers-social, national, religious and so on. Its purpose should be to help the individual to understand his own psychological process and create awareness of his own mind and whole significance of life. Krishnamurti feels that any education worth its name must investigate the question of being. It should develop the spirit of critical inquiry among the young minds instead of conforming to the established structures. As Krishnamurti says, "Only by encouraging the child to question the book whatever it may be, to inquire into the validity of the social values, traditions, forms of government, religious beliefs and so on, can the educator and parents hope to awaken and sustain his critical alertness and keen insight."[46] He also says, "Education in the true sense is helping the individual to be mature and free, to flower greatly in love and goodness."[47] The right kind of education helps him in establishing harmonious relationships with others.

Silent Mind

The intelligent mind is a silent mind. The silent mind is aware of truth without the interference of thought. This silent mind is still and its stillness is not stagnation. It is not denial of action. It is the highest form of action. The silent mind looks at the vast movement of life with its full energy. It has a vast space which is immeasurable and unnamable. The silent mind is creative and is dead to the whole field of the known.

When the mind sees that silence is necessary for observation itself, then the mind becomes tranquil. Such silence is entirely different from the silence which is projected by thought. It is silence of order in which there is truth which is timeless. Krishnamurti says:

> "If you end conflict, the mind naturally becomes quiet. And when the mind is absolutely silent, without any movement of thought, then perhaps you will see something, perhaps there is something sacred beyond all words. And this man has sought everlastingly, something that is beyond measurable, beyond thought, which is incorruptible, un-nameable and eternal. That can take place when the mind is absolutely free, completely silent."[48]

Nothingness

The intelligent mind is 'nothing'. It is 'nothing' in the sense that it is not dependent on anything other than itself. It is totally empty of thought content, greed, envy, ambition, etc., all reactions and limitations of the conditioned mind.

According to Krishnamurti, "Freedom is the state of 'nothingness'. Nothing means not-a-thing, which is conditioned by thought, that is, freedom is the mind which is empty of thought-content. It is the mind in which there is no movement of thought. Thought is incomplete and therefore cannot give the mind complete security, where as "in nothingness there is complete security and stability."[49] The mind which is nothing is therefore sane. It is never irrational. It operates in the field of reality with intelligence.[50]

Meditative Mind

The intelligent mind which is revolutionary is meditative in character. For Krishnamurti, meditation is the flowering of understanding. It is actually seeing *what is*. It is emptying of the content of consciousness. Meditation is not abstraction. It is part of our daily life. It is entering into the unknown world of beauty and quietness, a world without image, symbol and without waves of memory. It is the state of freedom from the known.

For Krishnamurti meditation is the greatest art of life and one cannot learn it from anybody. It is not practice or method. Any effort to do meditation is not meditation at all. So, all the efforts to meditate are the denial of meditation. For Krishnamurti meditation is not sitting in a particular posture and repeating some phrases. It is not an isolating, self-enclosing activity but the comprehension of the world and its ways. Practice of a system makes the brain conditioned, dull and inactive. Meditation is constant learning about oneself. It is watching the way one does various things. It is a state of freedom but not from anything, since freedom from something is only the cultivation of resistance. Krishnamurti says, "Meditation is a form of self-recollected awareness, a form of discovery, a form of cutting loose from tradition, from ideas, conclusions, a sense of being completely alone which is death."[51]

To realise this state, one has to be aware of the complexities of the conditioned brain and go beyond it. The meditative mind is without friction; it is like a dynamo which is in perfect condition and operates without making any sound. There is noise only when there is friction in operation.

Meditation means the establishment of order in one's daily life, so that there is no contradiction. Thought is an impediment to meditation and only through meditation can this impediment be dissolved. Meditation is the movement of mind in stillness. In meditation, there is no attachment and it has no roots. It flowers without cause and it is a flame that burns away the boundaries or fences built around consciousness. Meditation is beauty beyond thought and feeling. It is joy and with it comes benediction.

Meditation is the capacity of the brain to operate wholly when it had freed itself from its programmed structure. It is not an intellectual coding and decoding of our perceptual capacity. It is an integration of feelings and understanding, which is devoid of self-centered activity. Meditation is going through the world of knowledge and becoming free of it to enter into the unknown. It is the mind which is light to itself. The meditative mind is a religious mind as meditation is explosive in love. Love is order and is its own virtue. Krishnamurti says:

> "The religious mind is the exposition of love. To it, Far is near. It is not the one or the many, but rather that state of love in which all divisions cease. Like beauty, it is not of the measure of words: from this silence alone the meditative mind acts."[52]

Religious Mind

The religious mind, according to Krishnamurti, does not belong to any cult, group or organised religions like Hinduism, Buddhism, Christianity, Islam etc. The religious mind does not involve itself in any kind of rituals, ceremonies and practices. It does not entertain any kind of beliefs or dogmas. To Krishnamurti, the word 'religion' means deprogramming the mind of all the systems, beliefs, dogmas, superstitions and conditionings. For Krishnamurti, the essence of religion is freedom. It is the feeling of love and compassion and the seeking of truth. The religious life is a discovery of one's own mind. To be religious is to be choicelessly aware that there is freedom from the known, while the known continues to act. So freedom from the known is the meaning of the religious life. However, it does not mean wiping out the known, but having an altogether different vision from which the known is observed. This action of seeing choicelessly is the action of love.

The religious mind is concerned with the whole and not with the particular. A religious life is possible only when one deeply understands the nature of conflict. This understanding is intelligence. It is this intelligence that acts rightly. The religious mind does not depend on anything. The religious mind is tranquil. Krishnamurti says:

> "The religious mind does not belong to any group, any sect, any belief, any church and any organised circus; therefore it is capable of looking at things directly and understanding things immediately. It is light to itself. Its light is not lit by another-the candle that is lit by another can be put out very quickly."[53]

Religious life is free from all established norms, traditions and institutional structures. It is freedom from all impressions. Therefore Krishnamurti does not consider the organised religions as religious since they are rooted in the past. Organised religions condition a person and do not allow him to think independently. And Krishnamurti holds that the religious mind only can bring about a new world-order with a new outburst of energy. To bring about a totally different culture, there must be religious revolution in each individual. There must be freedom, not only from all creeds and dogmas, but also from personal ambition and self-centered activity. Only then a new world is possible. Thus, the religious mind is whole, sane and orderly. It lives in actuality and has the awareness of *what is*. It is full of love and compassion and without the bondage of past and tradition. As Krishnamurti says:

> "A religious mind is a very factual mind; it deals with facts, with *what is* actually happening with the world outside and the world inside.....A religious life is a life of order and diligence, dealing with that which is actually within oneself, without any illusion."[54]

The religious mind is free from fear and conflict, as it does not believe in any theory, philosophy, scriptural authority or goals. It is totally attentive to every moment, both outward and inward. It is always new, innocent and without any limitations or horizons. Krishnamurti maintains that a truly religious man is not concerned with social reform since it is nothing but improving the old. Reform cannot create a new order but the truth can. So religion, according to Krishnamurti, is collecting all energy to investigate truth and to discover it out. The religious mind alone is capable of discovering something new since it is original. The religious mind is insightful. It is the realisation of one's own potentiality.

Krishnamurti holds that suffering cannot be removed by following beliefs and dogmas as beliefs and traditions enslave and prevent one from comprehending life in its momentariness.

The views of Krishnamurti with regard to religion are centred on humanism. He does not want to give a new meaning to the past/old religious traditions. He totally rejects the past as a whole in search of a fresh, new and creative life. Religious revolution does not therefore mean the revival or reformation of any particular religion but total freedom from all religions and ideologies. It is freedom from the society which has created them. That freedom is love which is free from ambition, envy, hatred and conflict. Thus Krishnamurti's approach to life is integral and not fragmentary.

Love

According to Krishnamurti, love is experiencing *what is.* When there is freedom, there is love or love comes with freedom. Love is spontaneous and is neither cultivated nor practisced. It is immeasurable and meets life anew. It is impersonal and knows no boundaries. It is free from division or conflict and in the action of love all divisions cease. Love is not different from truth. Only love has the quality of transforming the mind, life and the world. And therefore fundamental revolution is possible only through love. It is the only creative factor which can bring about real transformation in us and in society. In the words of Krishnamurti:

> "It is love, the only factor that can bring about a fundamental revolution. Love is the only true revolution. But love is not an idea; it is when thought is not. Love is not a tool of propaganda, it is not something to be cultivated and shouted about from the house tops, only when the flag, the belief, the leader, the idea as planned action, drops away, can there be love and love is the only, creative and constant revolution".[55]

Love is a state of being. Love is not pleasure. It is not desire. It is not a form of thought. Love is possible only when the sense of self is absent. Love is an end in itself and not a means to something. It is a state of living in the present. It has no yesterday and tomorrow. One can transcend all limitations, conditions, influences of tradition and the past through love. It is a state of communion with actuality. Krishnamurti says, "To be in communion is love. Without love, you cannot wipe out the past; with love, there is no past."[56]

Love is passion but not fanaticism. It is compassion for all and has no opposite. It never seeks any reward or success. It is free from imitativeness and ambition. Love comes when there is no fear. It is the absence of anxiety, loneliness, dependence and acquisition. Love is the ending of sorrow. Love is possible when one is fully aware of his hidden motives, without seeking an answer or an explanation. It is only when the mind is not caught up in words and ideas that love comes into being. Love is spontaneous action, which is not related to memory. Love is like a perfume of a flower. Krishnamurti says:

> "Love means compassion. Love, compassion means supreme intelligence, not the intelligence of books, scholars and experience. That is necessary at a certain level but there is the quintessence of all intelligence when there is love, compassion. There cannot be compassion and love without death, which is the ending of everything. Then there is creation."[57]

Love is the beginning of wisdom. Wisdom arises when knowledge comes to an end. Accoding to Krishnamurti, love and compassion only can bring about the new world order and the new culture.

We have attempted so far to formulate the problem of Tradition and Revolution according to Krishnamurti. Along with the exposition of Krishnamurti's ideas we also took note of the different formulations of 'crisis' made available by different thinkers. The problem of 'Tradition and Revolution', as Krishnamurti views it, needs a holistic approach which we find lacking in the writings of the most of the contemporary thinkers.

End Notes

1. Cited in Micheal Kimmel, *Revolution: A Sociological Interpretation* Oxford: Basil Blackwell, 1990), p. 4.
2. Theda Skocpol, *States and Social Revolutions* (Cambridge: Cambridge University Press, 1979), p. 4.
3. Cited in Micheal Kimmel, p. 4.
4. *Ibid.*, p. 5.
5. *Ibid.*, p. 4.
6. *Ibid.*, p. 4.
7. *Ibid.*, p. 5.
8. *Ibid.*, p. 5.
9. John Dunn, *Modern Revolutions* (Cambridge: Cambridge University Press, 1972), p. 12.
10. A.S. Cohan, as cited in Noel O. Sullivan "An Introductory Essay: Revolution and Modernity", In Noel O. Sullivan (ed.) *Revolutionary Theory and Political Reality* (Sussex: Wheetsheafs Books Ltd, 83), p. 8.
11. Peter Calvert, *Revolution and International Politics* (London: Francos Printer Publishers, 1984), p. 15.
12. Chalmers Johnson, *Revolutionary Change* (Bombay: Vakils Ferror and Simon Pvt. Ltd., 1966), p. 12.
13. *Ibid.*, p. 12.
14. "See Hannah Arendt, *On Revolution* (New York: Viking Press, 1965).
15. Cited in Raymand Tanter and Manus Midlarsky, "A Theory of Revolution" In Claude E. Welch Jr. and Mavis

Bunker Taintor (ed.), *Revolution And Political Change* (North Scituate: Duxbury Press, 1972), p. 155.

16. *Crane Brinton, Anatomy of Revolution,* (New York: Harper and Row, 1965), p. 34.
17. Cited in "A Theory of Revolution" in Claude E. Welch Jr. and Mavis Bunker (ed.), *Revolution And Political Change*, p. 155.
18. See S.N. Eisentadt, *Revolution And Transformation of Societies* (New York: Free Press, 1978).
19. Albert Camus, *The Rebel* (Middlessex: Penguin Books Ltd. Harmondsworth, 1973), p. 76.
20. Ted Robert Gurr, *Why Men Rebel* (Princeton: Princeton University Press, 1970). And Cited in Noel O' Sullivan (ed.) *Revolutionary Theory and Political Reality*, p. 28.
21. Krishan Kumar (ed), *Revolution: The Theory and Practice of European Idea* (London: Weidenfeld and Nicolson, 1971), p. 2.
22. Cf. Griewank Cited in E.J. Hobsbawm, "Revolution" in Roy Porter Mikulas Teich (eds.), *Revolution in History* (Cambridge: ridge University Press, 1986), p. 9.
23. See Roy Edgely, "Revolution, Reform and Dialectic", In G.H. Parkinson (ed.), *Marx and. Marxism.* (Cambridge: Cambridge University ess, 1982), p. 24.
24. Karl Marx, *Poverty of Philosophy* Cited in Robert Tucker, *Marxian Revolutionary Idea* (London: George Allen and Unwin Ltd. 1969), p. 5.
25. Karl Marx, *Eighteenth Brummaire of Louis Bonaparte, In Marx and Engels Selected Works,* Vol.1, (Moscow: Progress Publishers, 1977), p. 388.
26. J. Krishnamurti, (D. Rajagopal (ed)) *Commentaries on Living,* Second Series (Madras: KFI, 1991), p. 15.
27. J. Krishnamurti, *Krishnamurti's Note Book* (Madras: KFI, 1991), p. 11.
28. *Ibid.,* p. 186.
29. J. Krishnamurti, *First and Last Freedom.* (London: Victor Gollencz, 1987), p. 49.
30. J. Krishnamurti, This *Matter of Culture* (Madras: KFI, 1964), p. 6.

31. J. Krishnamurti, (D. Raja Gopal (ed.)), *Commentaries on Living* (New Delhi: B.I. Publications, 1972), p. 225.
32. J. Krishnamurti, *Krishnamurti's Note Book,* p. 180.
33. J. Krishnamurti and David Bohm, *The Ending of Time* (Madras: KFI, 1992), p. 73.
34. J. Krishnamurti, *First and Last Freedom,* p. 113.
35. J. Krishnamurti, [D. Raja Gopal (ed.)] *Commentaries on Living* Third series, (Madras: KFI, 1992), p. 48
36. Cf. David Bohm, "Insight, Knowledge, Science and Human Values" In Pupul Jayakar, Sunanda Patwardhan (eds.), *With in the Mind, on J. Krishnamurti* (Madras: KPI, 1988), p. 47.
37. J. Krishnamurti, (Pupul Jayakar and Sunanda Patwardhan (eds.), *Tradition and Revolution,* (Madras: KFI, 1972), p. 174.
38. *Ibid.*, p. 41.
39. J. Krishnamurti, [Mary Cadogan, Alan Kishbaugh, Mark Lee and Ray Mc Coy (eds)], *Total Freedom, The Essence of Kkrishnamurti,* (New York: Harper San Francisco, 1996), p. 243
40. J. Krishnamurti, *Tradition and Revolution,* p. 253.
41. See J. Krishnamurti, *The Way of Intelligence* (Madras: KFI, 1984), pp. 90-93.
42. J. Krishnamurti, *Krishnamurti's Journal* (Madras: KFI, 1991), p. 19.
43. J. Krishnamurti, *Truth and Actuality* (Madras: KFI, 1992), p. 149.
44. J. Krishnamurti, *Commentaries on Living,* Second Series, (Madras: IFI, 1991), p. 48.
45. J. Krishnamurti and David Bohm, *The Ending of Time,* p. 73.
46. J. Krishnamurti, *Education and Significance of Life* (Madras: KPI, 1992), pp. 41-42.
47. *Ibid.,*p. 23.
48. J. Krishnamurti, *Total Freedom,* p. 334.
49. J. Krishnamurti, *Truth and Actuality,* p. 39.

50. *Ibid.*, p. 42.
51. Krishnamurti, *Krishnamurti on Education* (Madras: KFI), p. 80.
52. Cited in, *Mary Lutyens, Krishnamurti: The Open Door* (London: John Murray, 1988), p. 103.
53. J. Krishnamurti, *Beyond Violence* (Madras: KFI, 1992), p. 125.
54. Cited in Mary Lutyens, *Krishnamurti: The Open Door,* p. 49.
55. Krishnamurti, *Commentaries on Living,* Second Series, p. 18.
56. K. Krishnamurthy (compiled), *Krishnamurti for Beginners: An Anthology* (Madras: KFI, 1995), p. 190.
57. J. Krishnamurti, Last *Talks at Saanen, 1985* (San Francisco: Harper and Row Publishers, 1986), p. 127.

6

Critical Study of J. Krishnamurti

Non-humanly religious, non-humanly moral, non-humanly intellectual and scientific, non-humanly specialised and efficient, non-humanly the business man, non-humanly the conscious individual even love. All perverts. Perverted towards goodness or badness, towards spirit or flesh but always away from central norm, always away from humanity.

— **Aldous Huxley**

In this chapter, we shall discuss Krishnamurti's views in comparison with the ideas of Plato, Marxist philosophy, the Existential philosophers like Sartre, psycho-analysis like Freud and also of the Buddhists. These thinkers represent both the East as well as the West and analyses of their writings help us to see how Krishnamurti goes beyond all of them. The attempt has also been to discuss Krishnamurti's views on cognition, relationships, mind/brain, nothingness, truth and reality and freedom. The discussion of these notions becomes important for the single reason that these concepts are closely related to the problem of 'Tradition and Revolution'.

Krishnamurti has contributed to the debate of tradition and modernity in his own way. He finds that both tradition and modernity equally problematic and they must be rejected. I discuss his views on this along with those of Gandhi and Ambedkar. This study is a serious attempt to understand a thinker and the problem of tradition and modernity which is very crucial for the healthy existence of society.

Implication of Revolution

For Krishnamurti, revolution means a total transformation of the human psyche. It is realising the unknown, through self-knowledge and understanding. The unknown is nothingness, is the real nature of the human being. It alone can bring order to the disordered and chaotic world situation. Revolution knows the truth and truth can dissolve the sorrow and misery of the world. The very nature of revolution is to have an insight into sorrowfulness of the individual which reveals the fictitious and irrational content of the mind and of the social structure.

Krishnamurti maintains that it is only through psychological revolution that global relationship can be established because the psychologically transformed mind is free from division and conflict. It is full of compassion and love. Human relationships based on love are free from any particular identification and attachment. Love will be the basis for the new world. To the transformed mind, relationship is global. It does not belong to any race, sect, nation and ideology etc. It is alone in the sense that it is all-one. The entire world is its home. Thus revolution, according to Krishnamurti, is the realisation of the essential nature of humanity which brings sanity in one's relationship to everything. Sanity is whole, healthy and holy. It is living without any image, or conclusion. It is possible only when one has self-knowledge and goes beyond verbalisation. Krishnamurti holds that, "The universal, the global feeling of all human beings and their relationship, can only comes into being when the words *nation, tribe*, *religion* have all disappeared."[1]

In freedom relationships are global. It is living without division and conflict. Freedom understands life with deep intelligence and vitality. Revolution brings about change in human consciousness, since consciousness is the consciousness of all human beings. Change in one's consciousness brings about change in the human consciousness. Krishnamurti distinguishes between two levels of consciousness. Consciousness as it appears and consciousness as it really is. Consciousness as it appears is known and consciousness as it really is unknown.[2] So the unknown is consciousness as it is which is devoid of fear, anxiety, hatred, desire, division, conflict and sorrow etc. It is of the nature of nothingness, integration, intelligence, eternity, harmony, peace and happiness. Consciousness which is nothingness is autonomous and independent. It does not depend for its existence, on something other than itself. The unknown is the timeless renewal of the nothingness which implies experiencing of wisdom.[3]

Krishnamurti maintains that the unknown is the true and real nature of consciousness. It alone can give significance to human existence. The unknown is the real and inalienable essence of consciousness. The unknown alone can render life meaningful because it is associated with goodness, love, compassion intelligence and happiness. The creative happiness of the unknown is a *sine qua non* for the peaceful co-existence of humanity. According to Krishnamurti, the individual and collective salvation or liberation is possible through the change of the structure of consciousness.

For Krishnamurti, revolution in the world can be brought about by the intelligent action of those individuals who are in the state of revolution, or who are in love with the whole. Radical change in consciousness affects a radical transformation in society. Psychological revolution should start with the individual before it manifests itself in the world since the individual is the core of the society. The deep and radical change of the individual will have its reflection on the society. Krishnamurti says, "Man is the measure of the world. You are the world not as an ideal, but factually.

As the world is yourself, in the transformation of yourself you produce a transformation of society."[4]

Krishnamurti does not give any blue print as to what happens after revolution. According to him revolution is not an idea or an ideal. It simply happens with the ending of the traditional mind. Therefore what happens after revolution cannot be put in forms of thought. However for the revolution to take place, the traditional mind which always moves in the realm of the known has to be transcended or negated. The ending of the known involves the beginning of a certainly different form of mind and society.

With revolution, there is the cessation of fear, of 'me', which is the image, the knowledge and remembrance of the past and there will be no violence and brutality. There will be love and compassion which bring clarity to one self and he/she will be free from all kinds of illusions. The action of love puts an end to every form of fear, identification and every desire for pleasure. Then man does not conform to any ideal, concept, belief or person.

The revolutionary mind meets the challenge at every moment with adequate response and intelligence. Therefore, there will be no crisis or chaos either at the individual or at the collective level. Revolution brings order in oneself and in the world. In the state of revolution, men are truly creative in living. Revolution is a total renewal, a fundamental change in the structure of consciousness which is reflected in all spheres of life.

When there is revolution, there is an end to disorder. There will be no chaos or crisis in the society or in the world since there is an ending of inner chaos. All kinds of division—political, social, religious, national, ideological, economic—cease to be when the revolution takes place. Then there will be no scope for violence and war, aggression and poverty as there will be no possessiveness and exploitation among the people. At cultural or social or political or ethnic or religious level, there will be no violent struggle and conflict since there will be only the activity of love. Love integrates both the inner and the outer world. It knows no separation and the whole humanity can survive in happiness and peace.

For Krishnamurti, revolution is total. It is not limited to any particular sphere of life, or a fragment of society. It encompasses the whole being of man and, therefore, the whole of society. A new culture is born due to revolution. Though the social institutions would exist, they would not be inhuman and violent but work for the peaceful and harmonious coexistence of people. It is the world of a new order. Krishnamurti himself has no idea of that new world. According to him the new can never be new if it is put in thought. As Krishnamurti says:

> I have no idea about the new world. The new world cannot be new if I have an idea about it. This is not just a clever argument, it is a fact. If I have an idea about it, the idea is born of my study and experience, is it not? It is born of what I have learned, of what I have read, of what other people have said the new world should be. So the new world can never be new if it is a creation of the mind, because the mind is old.[5]

Reality and Truth

Krishnamurti distinguishes between truth and reality; He calls the realm of thought as reality. Reality is that which is put together by thought. It is the knowledge of abstracted thought and includes both rational and irrational knowledge. The rational knowledge is that which is factual, logical and well-reasoned and the irrational knowledge is psychological in character. The irrational is fictitious and speculative. It is the result of invention of thought for psychological security and is responsible for division, conflict and misery in life and the world. Krishnamurti holds that the ending of reality in its psychological sense brings about a transformation in the mind. The ending of the fictitious reality is the beginning of truth. Truth is the mind which is empty of reality in its psychological sense. Truth is nothingness which gives the mind total security. The mind which is nothing acts sanely in the world of factual reality.

"There is no psychological security in reality, but only complete security in nothingness. Then if that is so, to me, my whole activity in the world of reality is entirely different".[6]

Nothingness

Krishnamurti's notion of 'nothingness' is different from the existentialist notion of nothingness in general and from Sartre's conception of nothingness in particular. Existentialists describe nothingness as a state of uncertainty, ambiguity, confusion, anxiety, dread and unhappiness. Sartre equates nothingness with consciousness which is divided, conflicting, anxious, confused and sorrowful. He says that nothingness is the cause of man's sense of emptiness or vacuity. Nothingness is like a worm in the heart of the being of man. It is the basis of man's constant struggle to become something other than him. But Krishnamurti considers nothingness in entirely different terms. To him, nothingness means a mind which is holistic and clear. It means a mind which is devoid of divisive consciousness and is totally empty of the content of thought. It is a mind which is subtle, secure and free from fear, anxiety and sorrow. Nothingness stands for freedom which transcends freedom in the Sartrean sense.

Krishnamurti concept of nothingness is very much similar to (Nagarjuna's) Madhyamika notion of nothingness (*Sunyata*). Madhyamikas like Nagarjuna, use nothingness in two senses. In one sense nothingness means the absence of any durable essence or nature in the phenomena (*Samuriti Satta*). In another sense nothingness means the transcendental truth (*Paramarta Satta*) which is beyond concepts and words. It stands for the mind which is beyond the structure of thought and its world of the phenomena. Krishnamurti's notion of nothingness also has this double sense. He says that everything is devoid of inherent nature. Like Nagarjuna, Krishnamurti shows dialectically that everything or concept is empty of inherent nature. The world of phenomena or the reality of thought is relative, limited and incomplete. That which is limited, relative and incomplete does not have an inherent being. It is nothing or empty within itself. In the world of phenomenon everything depends on every other thing, while nothingness has an independent existence. Krishnamurti's notion of 'nothingness' is also transcendental in character. It stands for truth which is absolute and ultimate. It refers to a mind which is independent and unconditional. Nothingness is timeless or eternal.

Brain and Mind Problem

Krishnamurti uses the terms 'Brain' and 'Mind' synonymously. He says that the human brain or mind is the product of evolution. Physiologically the brain has grown larger in size and psychologically the mind or brain has accumulated its content through time. In other words, the brain is conditioned not only physically but also psychologically. It is burdened not only with the factual, the rational and logical information but also with the fictitious, the irrational and the illogical knowledge. The illogical content of the mind brain includes desires, choices, anxiety, pain, loneliness, belief, fear, confusion, conflict, etc., and is due to the dominance of thought over the brain, or is due to the registration in the brain of the unnecessary part of experience. Krishnamurti calls it the old brain or mind which is traditional, imbalanced and insane. He says that "the brain or the mind with continuity of its conditioning can never find anything new. He holds that it is only when there is the ending of the old brain," that the new mind or brain comes into existence.

The new mind or brain is that which is completely changed psychologically as well as physically. Radical revolution in the brain brings about a mutation in the brain cells and such a mind or brain is free from the burden of the thought. Krishnamurti calls the free mind 'universal' and 'absolute'. It is one with the universe or the cosmos. Cosmos means perfect order and the new mind has the order of the universe. Its order is eternal and infinite. It is different from the order of thought which is actually disorder. The radically transformed brains begin contact with the universal mind and act holistically. Radical revolution awakens the brain cells which were till then inactive. The new brain is full of energy. According to Krishnamurti, the new mind is not personality; it is not yours' or mine. It is totally impersonal in the sense that it is devoid of the center called the self. It is the embodiment cf energy which is different from the energy of thought and thought itself is conflict-ridden. Therefore it is difficult to say whether Krishnamurti differentiates between the brain and the mind. He treats them as one and the same. He gives importance to holistic perspective of mind and life. We cannot say that the brain alone is sufficient to understand Krishnamurti's philosophy of life as he has not confined his analysis of life and the world to the physical brain alone. He does not like to be misunderstood as a materialistic monist. Similarly he did not choose to explain life and world in terms of the mind, because he did not want to be identified as an idealistic monist. It is possible that Krishnamurti uses the terms brain and mind synonymously in order to avoid the pitfalls of the extremes of both idealism and materialism. As Stuart Holroyd says, "Needless to say Krishnamurti himself, who regards naming and labeling as pursuits of dull mind, is indifferent as to what camp he is assigned to."

Krishnamurti on Cognition

Cognition is how we acquire and use knowledge. Cognitive process involves perception, memory, thought, knowledge and its usage. Before discussing the Cognitive theories put forwarded by psychologists, we have to understand whether the world is cognisable or not on which philosophers have different opinions. The idealists, for the most part, refuse to recognise that the world is cognisable. They argue that the reality which we fail to cognise may possibly be cognised by higher beings, namely, gods, spirits etc. Their cognition is beyond man's reach. Hence idealists come to the conclusion that the world is unknowable. Some of them, for example Berkeley, in principle admit that the world is cognisable and even work out theories of cognition. But in doing so they focus on cognising their own thoughts rather than on cognising the objective world and human society.

Agnostics doubt the possibility of cognising the world. On the other hand, materialists, particularly Marxists, hold that since the world exists objectively, it is possible to cognise it. They show that the cognitive process is carried out not by some 'pure' consciousness severed from man but by a real human being with the help of his mind; it asserts that the cognitive process is social in essence and nature. The cognitive subject is not an individual isolated from other people but a man who takes part in social life and uses forms of cognising activity developed by society.

To have a clear picture of cognition and of how Krishnamurti deals with this problem, it is useful to have a glance at general theories of cognition. Psychologists, in their effort to understand cognition, emphasise three general aspects: structure (the element and components of the intellect and their interrelationship), process (the particular activities or operations involved in taking in, interpreting, organising and retrieving knowledge or information) and function (the process or goals of a person in dealing with the available, potential knowledge). Each of these components is important for a satisfactory understanding of cognition. Broadly there are three approaches—the functional, structural and process approaches to understand cognition.

Functional theory explains human cognition in terms of functional connections between environmental conditions which stimulate the organism and the resulting behaviour. Functional analysis tends to ignore the internal structures that influence behaviour, Skinner (1957) is the representative of this approach. The objective of his approach is to predict and control behaviour. Structural approaches have generally emphasised the mental components (such as memory and emotions) and the manner in which these components are organised. Structuralists have attempted to analyse the rules of language (Chomsky, 1965) and identify the concepts that are substrata of human thought (Piaget, 1971). Piaget, the genetic epistemologist, emphasises the mental structures and knowledge of the world. He argues that an understanding of mental phenomenon can best come from looking at the development cf the mind. Chomskian theory of language ignores both functional and process components of cognition.

The psychologists who took process approach (Shiffrin and Atkinson, 1969) have been explicit about how specific activities or processes are brought to bear an input. This approach is known as information processing and views external stimuli as being altered by several kinds of process, including the recognition of a stimulus, recording into some other forms, storage of the altered stimulus, retrieval from its stored location and the like. These processes take place in different structural components. This process approach stresses on how letters and words are identified and how the combined meaning of words is calculated and how other information is retrieved and used. Its claim is that mental processes contribute to what people know and how they behave, or how knowledge is acquired and used in behaviour.

To put it more briefly, the functional explanation of Skinner regards behavioural consequences and environmental stimuli as the two factors that completely determine behaviour. For a structuralist, like Chomsky, structure takes the forms of rules for organising the input which is in this case language. According to Piaget, structure means the organisation of knowledge about experienced events and actions. All input is interpreted within the framework of such knowledge. Process accounts describe the way in which input is treated from the moment it arrives in the sensory system, enters consciousness and affects behaviour.

Krishnamurti has no specific theory about cognition, but we can form a kind of theory of cognition from his teachings. While talking about memory, knowledge, thought, perception which are included in cognition, he does not have any of the above views in his mind. He expressed his views about cognition rationally in the context of explaining how mankind and its thinking are conditioned. So there is a problem in the very nature of our understanding or in our cognitive procedure, which puts us in a chaotic situation.

Krishnamurti points out to our habitual and mechanical activity in cognition. This is the characteristic of the traditional mind; therefore humanity should become free from such a state for meaningful and intelligent way of understanding the actuality, the facts, *what is*. One should develop choiceless awareness, without having any prejudices or preconceived notions. This is possible when the mind is perceptive and attentive, as it can reveal facts or *what is*. Such a mind is always ready to meet the challenges of life as it is empty and innocent. It dies each minute and renews itself. The perceptive mind which does not have any accumulations put together by thought; is nothingness. Nothingness is the creative void. Therefore, Krishnamurti regards it as true cognition or complete comprehension of the truth. In such cognition, there is only simple experience, without image, concepts, ideas or thought or construction. It is a simple awareness of fact without any motive or desire. Therefore it is more integrated and intelligible approach to cognition than the other approaches which have their limitations. According to Krishnamurti, "To see without distortion of fact of what you are, not what you think you should be is the beginning of wisdom." And he also says, "Experience is direct; then relationship is direct and not through memory. It is this direct relationship that brings freedom from conflict and with freedom from conflict that is integration."[9] From this we can say that world is cognisable and is not something in isolation of the individual. Krishnamurti holds that "you are the world". In this sense, understanding oneself means understanding the world.

Krishnamurti and Psychoanalysis

Krishnamurti deals with the human mind and its functioning. He 'analyses' human mind, in all its dimensions but unlike the psychologists Krishnamurti does not admit the phenomena of the unconscious or sub-consciousness. Psychologists like Freud, hold that the unconscious is responsible for the abnormal functioning of the mind. Unconscious is the cause of the mental disorders like neurosis and psychosis. Freud maintains that disorders of the mind can be cured through psychoanalysis. Psychoanalysis helps to transform the unconscious into the conscious. However, Freud maintains that the unconscious mind cannot totally be transformed into the conscious mind. But Krishnamurti holds that the unconscious is not something completely different from the conscious. He says that the unconscious is the result of thought which chooses some part of the mind to be conscious. Thought has the tendency to suppress the unpleasant content of the mind. The conscious part of the mind does not want the unconscious to come into the open.

According to Krishnamurti, there is no need for psychoanalysis to bring the unconscious to the conscious level. It is enough if one realises the fact that thought is responsible for the division of the mind into conscious and unconscious. Perceiving the mind as a totality brings about freedom which is different from the freedom advocated by the psychologists. The cure of psychoanalysis is confined to making man conforming to world as it is where as Krishnamurti's notion of freedom implies that man is free from the insanity of selfishness, conflict, cowardliness, violence and war. When compared to Krishnamurti's notion of freedom, the freedom that psychologists advocate is of less significance. The aims of philosophy and psychology are not similar and Krishnamurti's task therefore has been entirely different from that of psychologists.

Krishnamurti as a Philosopher

The question, whether Krishnamurti is a philosopher or not, is debated in academic circles. However, Krishnamurti says that, "I am not concerning myself with the founding of religious or new sects, not the establishment of new theories and new philosophies."[10] There are two schools viewing the issue in two different ways. According to one school,

Krishnamurti is not a philosopher in the proper sense of the term since he does not lay claim to either system building or propounding a particular doctrine. The other school considers Krishnamurti as a philosopher as he has developed a philosophy consisting of metaphysics, epistemology, pedagogy and ethics.[11] But, we can say that the former school gives a proper estimate of Krishnamurti as a philosopher because he is against system building and propounding doctrines. He is not a philosopher of ideas, concepts and ideals and he was averse to theoretical speculation. He does not belong to a philosophical school or tradition. He does not have a philosophical predecessor. He did not identify himself with any school of thought and his teachings are not in reaction to any school of philosophy. They are also not a modified form of any theory, or an integrated view of different religious, philosophical and psychological theories. His teachings are the outcome of his direct perception of truth or an expression of the truth that he realised. To him truth is beyond speculative theories or doctrines and it cannot be comprehended through a system of concepts. Therefore, it is not correct to say that Krishnamurti developed a system of philosophy.

However, Krishnamurti talks of philosophy in its etymological sense which means love of wisdom. That is, to Krishnamurti, philosophy means, love of truth or life. Truth is the nothingness of the mind and is therefore beyond the grasp of intellect. Truth means life which is undetermined by thought. Philosophy is living life independently of systems, images, ideals and beliefs. It is living from moment to moment in the total freedom of the mind. It is the art of being nothing and living life directly, or living in the present. Krishnamurti maintains that, "This is not a philosophy, a series of theories. It is exactly what the word philosophy means the love of truth, the love of life. It is not something you go to the university to learn; we are learning the art of living in our daily life".[12]

For Krishnamurti, philosophy is an understanding of truth which is beyond thought. Philosophy is the ending of mistaking reality for truth or the end of ignorance and irrationality of approaching truth through reality. It is understood that finitude of reality and going beyond it. Krishnamurti says:

> "Philosophy means love of truth, not love of ideas, not love of speculations. And that means you have to find out for yourself where reality is and that reality cannot become the truth. You must understand the limitations of reality which is the whole process of thought."[13]

Although Krishnamurti uses the term 'Philosophy' in its epistemological sense, to him, it does not conform to the Western concept of philosophy. In Western philosophy, love is a constant quest. Wisdom is knowledge which is never final. Philosophy is a pursuit after more and more rational knowledge. It involves a series of theories about conceptual problems and stands for free intellectual life. In the West, philosophy, like science, is a quest for truth and not its conquest. It is truth-seeking and not its attainment.[14] In this sense truth is relative and in Western philosophy the answers to the seminal questions of life are not definite.

As the well known modern western philosopher Bertrand Russell puts it, "Philosophy is to be studied, not for the sake of definite answers to its questions since no definite answer can as a rule is known to be true, but rather for the sake of the questions themselves".[15]

It is clear that the western philosophy almost emphasises knowledge based on intellect. It seeks to sharpen reason or thought which is ever incomplete. The Western mind with its Greek background has not realised the importance of going beyond the intellect, by understanding its limitations, Krishnamurti holds that truth in the sense of the ending of knowledge is alien to Western philosophy.[16]

For Krishnamurti, real understanding is through ending of knowledge. Therefore for him, philosophy is not knowledge but the perception of truth in the sense of 'being' it. It is the actual realisation of truth which is beyond thought and a true philosopher is not a knower of truth, but truth itself. In the light of the above, we may say that Krishnamurti's philosophy is very much akin to the notion of Indian *darsana* which means the direct perception or seeing of the Ultimate Truth. *Darsana,* as Radhakrishnan defines it, "is the insight of the real revealed to the soul sense."[17] However, Krishnamurti's philosophy cannot be called a *darsana,* since *darsana,* also means a philosophical system. And *darsana* is also considered as an intellectual approach to life. It gives more importance to building systems of thought around truth than to its direct perception. It is concerned more with the consistency of their ideas than with the actual man and the society. Krishnamurti feels that this system of philosophy dehumanises man under the cover of theories and ideas instead of helping him live with actuality. That is why Krishnamurti has no sympathy with such systems of philosophies, Western as well as Eastern. Krishnamurti says, "These philosophies have enslaved man. They have invented what society should be and sacrificed man to their concepts; the ideals of the so-called thinker have dehumanised."[18] He wants us to perceive the truth instead of indulging in ideals, opinions and concepts. One should totally live with the actual world. So it may not be meaningful to call him an Indian or a Western philosopher. He is very much against the kinds of distinction which are verbally or psychologically constructed. Therefore, his teachings are a commentary on living. Its essence is humanism without any qualification.

Krishnamurti's philosophy is not a theory or a system about the truth. It is not a conceptual play around the concept of truth. His teachings are spontaneous and a direct commentary on life. He suggests that one should have clarity and simplicity about life and that is possible though intelligent understanding which springs from love and compassion.

Though Krishnamurti is against any act of comparison or estimation, here it may not be out of place to mention some of the parallel associations of his teachings with other well known academic/philosophical traditions. In this backdrop let us' examine what seems to be Krishnamurti's main emphasis and place it in a historical context. We want to show that his holistic approach may be connected with a long tradition.

Krishnamurti and Buddhism

Krishnamurti is often identified with the Buddha. It is held by many that Krishnamurti has taught what Buddha taught in a new idiom and a new style. His teachings are very much similar not only to Buddha's original teachings but also to the ideas of the later Buddhist philosophers. Like Buddha, Krishnamurti does not accept the notion of God as the creator, the sustainer and the destroyer of the world. Krishnamurti does not accept the Vedic idea of an eternal, everlasting and unchanging soul (*atman*). Like Buddha, Krishnamurti accepts life as a predicament of conflict and sorrow and regards the idea of self as the cause of human predicament. Like Buddha, Krishnamurti regards realisation of truth as seeing the things as they are. Seeing truth leads to freedom from conflict and the truth can be understood only by understanding the nature of thought or consciousness. The ultimate or the absolute truth cannot be perceived without perceiving the relative or conventional truth. Krishnamurti also rejects all kinds of authority and dependence.

He maintains that one must realise truth for oneself. Buddha said not accept anything just because it is said by religion or scripture or by a *guru*. One should accept anything only after seeing it for oneself. Like the Buddha, Krishnamurti also denounces the role of a *guru* in understanding the truth. Both Buddha and Krishnamurti maintain that one has to work out one's own salvation. Krishnamurti's teaching is strikingly similar in its emphasis on awareness or mindfulness. He gives importance to the concept of impermanence; both Buddha and Krishnamurti of them hold that there is nothing that permanent.

Unlike Buddha and the Buddhists, Krishnamurti never denies the reality of world. Buddha and Buddhists teach that becoming a monk and leading a life of continence is required for the realisation of nirvana whereas Krishnamurti contends that one can realise freedom by being very much in the world. Referring to Buddhism, Krishnamurti says, "They have.....denied the world. But I don't say to deny the world. On the contrary you have to live there."[19] This difference between Buddha and Krishnamurti is very significant.

Krishnamurti and Western Thought

Krishnamurti's concepts of philosophy and freedom cannot be equated with any of the Western philosophical traditions, because he contends that the Western philosophical tradition right from the Greek thought is basically intellectual. He maintains that Western thought has given importance to wisdom in the sense of knowledge and the Western philosophers have not realised the importance of wisdom in the sense of ending knowledge.

Krishnamurti's philosophy appears akin to some of the idealistic philosophers of the West like Plato, Hegel, Schopenhauer, Bradley and the evolutionists like Bergson. His notion of insight seems to be similar to the notion of intuition advocated by the Western Idealists. But upon a closer examination, it becomes evident that the intention of Western idealists is intellectual in character, whereas Krishnamurti's idea of insight transcends intellect. The implications of Krishnamurti's insights and the intention of Western idealists for human relations are entirely different. Krishnamurti's insight means a radical transformation in the structure of the mind itself. It has very profound implications for social transformation. But we cannot find such implications in the case of the western idealists.

Krishnamurti and Plato

Krishnamurti's concept of freedom is very similar to Plato's idea of Good. According to Plato, Good is a pure form which is beyond the realm of phenomena. It is eternal and timeless. To Krishnamurti, the free mind is pure consciousness, absolute and eternal. Like Plato, Krishnamurti rejects idolatry and criticises the idol worshipers. However, there is difference between Plato and Krishnamurti. Plato's pure form is intellectual, whereas Krishnamurti's pure consciousness or mind transcendent intellect. To Krishnamurti freedom is going beyond the intellect and he calls it intelligence.[20]

Krishnamurti can be compared with Plato in another aspect also. Both of them hold that free man has to necessarily work for the freedom of others. According to Plato a philosopher who has found liberation for himself must liberate everybody else. Similarly, Krishnamurti also maintains that a man who is transformed must work for the transformation of the human kind. In this respect, both Plato and Krishnamurti subscribe to the Buddhistic notion of Bodhisatva. The Bodhisatva is one who is liberated, but takes rebirth in order to liberate others from sorrow.[21]

Krishnamurti and Sartre

Krishnamurti's concept of freedom is similar to Sartre's conception of freedom to a large extent. Both of them are the champions of human freedom. Sartre says that human consciousness is ontologically free. Therefore, man is a free being. Man is the maker of himself or he is the architect of his life and the world. Krishnamurti also maintains that man is responsible for what he is. Man is the maker of his life. He is responsible for his condition and that of the world around him. Besides this similarity, there is a fundamental difference between Krishnamurti and Sartre regarding the concept of freedom. To Sartre, freedom is self-determinism. It is a voluntary choice. It is acting with a chosen motive and goal. But Krishnamurti's concept of freedom means a mind which is devoid of self-determinism, motives and ends. Freedom is a state of being in which the mind is empty of all its content. Freedom is consciousness which is without self, division, conflict and unhappiness.

Krishnamurti and Marxists

Krishnamurti's thought, is in a way close to Marxism. Krishnamurti is anti-traditional. He rejects the notions of God, heaven, hell, destiny, the scriptures, the rituals etc.

The objective of his philosophy is to liberate man from the bondage of suffering by transforming the world. He envisages a world without unnecessary differences and divisions of any kind. But Krishnamurti's concern for man and the world goes far beyond the concern of Marxism. The Marxist concept of freedom involves a civilised society which is scientifically advanced. According to Marxism, freedom is possible by bringing a change in the social structure, as it believes that man can be transformed only by transforming the environment. But according to Krishnamurti, a new world order can be brought about only by transforming or changing the individual psychologically and radically. He maintains that mind determines the environment and not vice versa. Mind has the capacity and power to overcome all the external constraints, as he says, 'inner overcomes the outer'. The outer environment or the social structure is the product of the inner man. Therefore, the world cannot be changed unless man is changed inwardly. Though Krishnamurti says that the individual is not isolated from society, yet man is the society, 'you are the world', therefore, the individual is, according to him, the collective. Transformation in the individual leads to transformation in the society. In this respect, Krishnamurti is different from Marxism. He maintains that there is no need for collective outward revolutions to achieve transformation of the world. To him, outward revolutions are not revolutions at all. They only modify the social structure and can not affect the core of social reality which is the individual or the mind. He is of firm conviction that a radical change in the individual can bring about a change in the world as change in the individual inevitably affects the world.

Unlike Marxism, Krishnamurti does not envisage class conflict and antagonism. Marxists hold that revolution is possible only by augmenting the class conflict and antagonism between the bourgeoisie and the proletariat. They treat conflict as an inevitable fact of capitalist society. They are of the view that all the problems of man are to be looked at from the economic point of view. But according to

Krishnamurti, thought is the fundamental problem of man, as it is thought which creates conflict and antagonism between bourgeoisie and the proletariat. Therefore, the change of man and society is possible by the ending of thought. It does not involve bloodshed or the vanquishing of the bourgeois by the proletariat. The revolution that Krishnamurti speaks is silent and peaceful. It does not involve any kind of violence. It is the ending of division, conflict and violence in oneself by understanding the nature and the structure of thought. Like the Marxists, Krishnamurti subscribes to the evolutionary concept of mind, man and society. He holds that man, mind and society are historical products. One should understand the evolutionary process in order to understand the present condition of the human mind and the society.

Marxism also maintains that man, mind and society are historical. The present is the product of historical development of social events. It holds that society evolves by stages—primitive communism, feudalism, capitalism, socialism and communism. An intellectual has to understand the social reality and work for its evolution towards the higher stage. But according to Krishnamurti, the radical social transformation is not evolutionary. It is not progressive and gradual, or it has no stages. It is ahistorical and timeless, the future is an illusion, it is only a product of postponement of radical revolution by thought. Future is the urge of thought to continue itself endlessly. The transformation can be brought about instantaneously, as according to him real revolution is in the 'present'. To Krishnamurti, social transformation is basically psychological in character. Individuals have to transform themselves in order to change society. If there is no change in the present, the future will be the same as the present. Therefore, he strongly opposes the social theories that advocate transformation in the future. Krishnamurti's standpoint would be very significant if we understand the results of outward or outer revolutions which ignore a radical change in the individual.

Perspectives on Freedom

The problem of freedom has been one of the fundamental questions for the philosophers. It is difficult to give a definite definition of freedom. Broadly, freedom can be distinguished as external and internal. External freedom may be equated with liberty. It stands for the civil status of an individual. It entails certain rights to have and to do certain things. It includes the civil rights like freedom to live, to property, to religion etc. Freedom in the sense of liberty means the freedom from external constraints. It signifies the absence of coercion. Liberty is not only 'freedom from', but also 'freedom to'. That is, liberty in its totality implies freedom to choose and not to choose. It is not only negative but also positive. External freedom can be assured through the establishment of the political, the economic, scientific, religious and legal institutions.

It is held that external freedom is incomplete without the internal freedom. Internal freedom is the freedom of man from 'within'. It is 'psychological' or 'spiritual' in character. It implies the freedom of mind from division, conflict and sorrow. It also means the freedom of being from the determining factors physical and psychological. The conception of inner freedom also differs from thinker to thinker. The vedantins have called it *Moksha*, which means the union of the individual self (*Jiva*) with the universal self (*Brahman*).They have identified it with pure consciousness which is truth and happiness. The Buddhists have called it Nirvana, which means the ending of desire (*Thrishna* or *Tanha*) as desire is the cause of sorrow. Inner freedom is the end of sorrow (*Dukha*).

The existentialists have equated inner freedom with the freedom of the consciousness from its essence. Freedom is the determinism of consciousness by itself. It implies the precedence of consciousness over its essence. An existentialist like Kierkegaard calls it subjectivity. He also calls it truth, which is beyond the objectivity of science. To him, freedom is a state of absolute certainty in which the individual realises his true being. An existentialist like Sartre equates freedom with consciousness itself. Consciousness is free since it is not unconscious like a thing. Freedom implies the capacity of consciousness to question and to negate its 'object' endlessly. Sartre characterises freedom with qualities like division, conflict and unhappiness and treats these characteristics as inalienable to freedom. He, therefore, says that man is condemned to be free. Man can never overcome his state of unhappy freedom.

According to Marxism, freedom is not intellectual. It is not freedom of will without freedom of action. Freedom is not the freedom of the mind alone. Freedom in its real sense is both of the will and action. It is psychological as well as social. In order to be free man has to understand not only the psychological motives of his action, but also the environmental or social factors. Freedom is the result of man's intellectual and material progress. It is not in isolation nor is it personal. It is in society and through social institutions that man attains freedom. The essential feature of society is economic production which is possible through the cooperation of fellow human beings. Man is not free alone. Economic production enables man to conform the outer reality to his inner being. It is the economic production that gives man freedom. Christopher Caudwell says, "It is because of economic production that man is free and beasts are not". This is clear from the fact that economic production is the manipulation, by means of agriculture, horse taming, road building, car construction, light, heating and other engineering, of the environment, conformably to men's will.[22]

Economic production enables man to do what he wills. Man can do what he wills, only with the help of others. Man ceases to be man without roads, food supplies, machines, houses and clothes etc. Man's free will depends on economic production because human consciousness is born of economic production which is the basis for the evolution of language, science and art. The freedom of man's acts therefore depends on his material level which is economic production. The more advanced the economic production, the more the freedom of man. This notion of freedom is based on the notion that consciousness is the result of economic production.[23]

Many people understand freedom in the sense of freedom from something or as an abstraction. In fact, freedom is the highest form of human existence. As it has been discussed in the earlier chapter, according to Krishnamurti, freedom is the total ending of thought at the psychological level since it is always in the realm of past. In other words, tradition is a hindrance to freedom. Freedom is choiceless awareness or perceiving *what is*, or 'truth'. To be free is to be clear, intelligent and rational. Freedom is an active and passionate state of mind which does not conform to or be conditioned by anything. It is self-knowledge in action. It is activity of mind which springs from 'nothingness'. And he further maintains that when man is psychologically or internally free, it finds its expression in one's own relationships with ideas, things and people. Krishnamurti calls such freedom religious. It is also called by him as revolutionary. It keeps the world in order.

Krishnamurti on Tradition, Modernity and Revolution

Modernity is opposed to the religious world view which is traditional. Tradition involves an uncritical acceptance of the past which is in the form of dogmas, beliefs and scriptural authorities. Tradition is accumulated knowledge of the past which comes to its inheritors in the form of patterned thought or formula. Basically, tradition is vested in religion and its irrational and mythical structures. Krishnamurti perceives tradition as essentially playing a negative role in man's quest for truth. Tradition is dead knowledge which ultimately manifests itself as an idol, concept or belief. Tradition as conclusion encourages dependence on it and therefore ends the spirit of challenge involved in the quest for truth. It cannot face a new situation attentively and creates attachment to the past which ultimately becomes a burden. It creates an authority to be obeyed. It results in conflict and disorder. Tradition is one of the causes of division and therefore conflict is inevitable. Krishnamurti maintains that tradition prevents free thinking, free inquiry, self-discovery and self knowing from time to time. Tradition denies freedom and prevents the mind from operating totally and attentively.

The traditional mind is a conditioned or a programmed mind which works as a hurdle to insight or intelligence. In Krishnamurti's words, "The background, the culture as the Catholic, as the Protestant, as the Communist, as the Socialist, as my family, is the centre from which one is looking. So long as one is looking at life from a particular point of view, or from a particular experience which one has cherished which is one's background, which is the 'me' one cannot see the totality."[24]

It is argued that, contrary to tradition, modernity brings change in the attitudes, values and orientation of thinking and mental makeup of the individual so as to make him/ her rational, secular, liberal, self-conscious and self-confident in a changing world. Modernity certainly involves a break with the past. Secularism, rationalism and universalism are the main characteristics of modernity. Reasoning plays a predominant role to evaluate beliefs, opinions and dogmas etc. Modernity assumes that, scientific thinking should have precedence over emotions and non-rational thought. Modernity also involves changes in the socio-economic and political structures facilitating industrialisation, urbanisation and democratisation. From the economic point of view, modernity involves reorientation of the social structure bringing about material prosperity through growing expansion of the productive forces of society and by equitable distribution of wealth. In short, the modern world view is based on empirical and scientific knowledge and is incompatible with the tradition on all important aspects of life. It can be summed up as:

Modernity embraces the idea of progress and the break from history and tradition. It subscribes to a secular meaning, the demystification and desacrilisation of knowledge and social organisation. It praises human creativity, scientific discovery and the pursuit of individual excellence. It upholds the doctrines of equality, liberty and faith in human intelligence opened up by education and universal reason.[25]

It is argued by many that scientific understanding and domination of nature would secure freedom to man from scarcity and want. Besides, transformation of the individual and control over nature, rational forms of social organisation and modes of thought would bring liberation from the irrationalities of myths, religion, superstition, arbitrary use of power and human frailties. As a result, the universal, eternal and immutable qualities of humanity will be revealed.

It is argued by some that there is a dichotomous opposition between tradition and modernity. Modernity is considered to be the anti-thesis to tradition. But many scholars for different reasons contested the view that there is any dichotomy between tradition and modernity. Also, some nationalist thinkers questioned the dichotomy between the tradition and modernity and attempted to construct the idea of modernity differently. They challenged the hitherto dominant perspectives on modernity. Nationalist thinkers argued that modernity which is equated with industrialisation, scientific and technological advancement was limited to the western countries. The so called modernity suited colonial interests at the expense of the colonised. Keeping this view in mind, the rationale of modernity, which was put forward by the Western colonial countries, was questioned. Gandhi's *Hind Swaraj*—in a fundamental sense, contested the above view. We can see in the thought of land a blend of tradition and modernity. He tried to integrate law patterns of thought and action on traditional culture. He tempted a merger of the three levels of Indian social system, viz., social stratification, culture and polity into a pattern so that the breakdown of Indian tradition could be averted. Gandhi's critique of Western civilisation "was critique of modernity and his central argument is that no enduring alternative can be pursued unless that alternative negotiated to be skills, capacities and wisdom of people."[26]

Another Indian contemporary thinker, Ambedkar has also tried to overcome the tradition-modernity dichotomy. The critique of the tradition is accompanied in Ambedkar by a refusal to accept readymade alternatives manufactured in the West. His philosophy is essentially ethical and religious and he keeps away from Western thought. At the same time, he attacked Hinduism and its claims as religion. His comment on Hinduism is illustrative of his position. "It is a misnomer to call it religion. Its philosophy is opposed to the very thing for which religion stands."[27] Hence, he considers Hinduism as anti-religious as for him, religion is love of truth. He upholds the moral basis of life while allowing critical reason to operate. He considers Buddhism as the only religion which can respond to the demands of modernity and culture. For him Buddhist teachings are infallible and they are not making a claim to supernatural origin or authority. Buddhist teachings, he believes, appeal to reason and experience. By holding on to religiousness, he goes beyond the tradition-modernity dichotomy.

"Ambedkar's conversion to Buddhism constitutes a bold attempt by a towering Indian thinker to transcend the tradition-modernity dichotomy which has a seductive grip on the colonial mind. He tried to thus create an alternative to a society which cannot be moved by the metropolis ideology of secularism and finds its traditional religion morally reprehensible."[28]

In this sense, he is critical of modernity and highlighted that the priority of social reconstruction cannot be achieved without taking into account the legacy of tradition. He further considers that legal and political institutions do not have the capacity to reconstruct social solidarity and therefore tries to provide a social basis for the liberal and political ethos which does not mean an uncritical acceptance of Western modernity or indigenous traditionalism.

Though Krishnamurti does not fit into the above framework, the discussion regarding tradition-modernity dichotomy will help us to have a better understanding and estimation of Krishnamurti. Though Krishnamurti is not a nationalist thinker, we can see the continuity between the nationalists discussed above and Krishnamurti in so far as he questions the dominant conceptions of both tradition and modernity. Though Krishnamurti is opposed to the method of comparison, it is useful to consider Krishnamurti's philosophy in the light of current debates on tradition-modernity. His major contribution has been the attempt to overcome the tradition-modernity dichotomy.

Krishnamurti totally rejects tradition and urges mankind to be free from tradition. Tradition is the product of thought and it is the continuity of the past. It cannot solve any problems since the world, society and man are changing every moment. Krishnamurti observes that from time immemorial, mankind has been living a conditioned life, which is the continuation of the traditional mind. According to him the brain is million years old. It cannot operate intelligently and totally. Krishnamurti maintains that the traditional mind or old-mind should be wiped out to make the new brain function.

In rejecting tradition, Krishnamurti does not counterpoise it to modernity, though we may see some of the modernist assumptions in his views. He maintains that there are no dualities and opposites. His only concern is that man should live with the present or with, without carrying the burden of the past over to the present or without any future expectations. One should be free of motives and ideals to follow. Man should be free from psychologically becoming something and for that man must live every moment. He should experience '*what is*' from moment to moment without having any continuity. The human brain should be totally attentive and operate intelligently. In short, the mind should be empty, should be freed from prejudice, preconceived notions and traditions so that creativity can take place.

Krishnamurti not only rejected tradition, which is built upon irrational structures, myths, dogmas, beliefs and their authority but also the reasoning or rationality which is the product of thought and psychological time. Therefore, the question does not arise of seeing rationality or reasoning or partial insights in tradition. Krishnamurti makes a differentiation between the intellect and intelligence. Intellect operates on the basis of reasoning or logic and is the result of conditioning or programming of the mind. It is also limited and partial in terms of understanding. But intelligence is not a product of thought and time. The activity of intelligence is out of love and compassion. Intelligence operates when the mind is empty or in a state of nothingness. The intelligent mind is totally attentive and works with full energy. Intelligence is freedom; it is freedom from the known, the past and the limitations of thought. An intelligent act is a creative act.

Krishnamurti observes that so far mankind lived in conflict, violence and suffering which is the nature of the traditional mind. The conditioned, programmed brain of man has created a society which is aggressive, violent, greedy, competitive, ego-centric and ambitious. So, he urges us to see the necessity of a radical and a complete change which can be called a fundamental, real and total revolution. There should be change in the brain cells or in the psyche so that the mind can operate holistically and intelligently and that is what he calls revolution. For Krishnamurti, revolution is a state of being and it is a constant transformation of the psyche. It is revolution in consciousness. Therefore, his main concern is with the change in human psyche, or its total transformation. While rejecting tradition, Krishnamurti is not in favour of creating an alternative, as for him, any alternative, ideal or ideology is an extension of the past in a different form.

As we have seen, it is generally argued by a number of scholars that change should be brought about through revolution or reform. Krishnamurti considers that reform cannot solve the problem. It is just old things put forward in a new mould, in a new pattern. He maintains that what is necessary is not a reform or revolution as we understood it, but a transformation through a total revolution, a renewal, a fundamental change in the structure of the consciousness itself. Krishnamurti's revolution is change in the inner psyche. In the words of Krishnamurti, "We are saying that human beings are now confronted with extraordinarily complex problems and to meet them adequately there must be a total revolution in the very field of consciousness itself, in very structure and the cells of brain themselves."[29]

Krishnamurti's revolution is not limited to any particular sphere of life. It encompasses the whole life and society. Therefore his revolution is not limited to legal, social, or merely economic spheres or outward revolution. To Krishnamurti, revolution is individualistic but not of the masses or collective. For him, the individual is the world and the transformation of the individual consciousness is all that is needed for a total revolution to take place. He maintains that the responsibility for bringing a radical change in human condition lies on the individual himself and not on the collective society or government or any other organisation. Only insight can cause a mutation in brain cells. The change in inward psyche automatically manifests itself in the outward world and only that brings new order. As Krishnamurti says:

> "Bloody revolution can never solve our problems. Only a profound inward revolution which alters all our values can create a different environment, an intelligent social structure and such a revolution can be brought about only by you and me. No new order will arise until we individually breakdown our own psychological barriers and are free".[30]

Krishnamurti's philosophy cannot be understood as mere individualism, it is reflexive individualism. He maintains that the individual only exists in relation to things, ideas and people. So the change in individual relationships is automatically reflected in the outer world and society.

We have seen that like Gandhi, Krishnamurti does not reconstruct tradition from a new prospective. There seems to be similarity between Ambedkar and Krishnamurti on certain issues. This similarity perhaps may be due to that both relate closely to Buddhist philosophy. At the same time, there is lot of difference between Krishnamurti and

Ambedkar. Ambedkar is critical about tradition; he has felt that Hinduism does not stand for reasoning; so he feels Hinduism is not religion. After attacking Hinduism, he proposes Buddhism as an alternative which stands for religion. He maintains that religion is ethical. In a significant way, Ambedkar holds the legacy of tradition by embracing Buddhism.

Though Krishnamurti is in favour of a religious life, his sense of religion is no way traditional, or associated with any world religions. He has given a different meaning to religion. His religion is not to be understood in terms of any organised religion. Whereas Ambedkar proposes Buddhism as a true religion, Krishnamurti's religion is humanistic and contradicts traditional and authoritative religions. His conception of religion does not follow any beliefs, idols, rituals and dogmas. Religious life is dynamic and it is the only intelligent way of living. There is no dominance, hierarchy or authority to follow in his conception of religion. It is full of love and compassion.

It is quite interesting to see that Krishnamurti is not only critical about tradition but also of scientific knowledge which is considered to be the basis for modernity. Krishnamurti accepted that scientific knowledge is useful to a certain extent but maintained that it cannot solve all the human problems since it is limited. He points out the dehumanising face of science and technology. Scientific knowledge has the potential to solve certain issues, but at the same time it is used for the purpose of dominance and destruction until man changes his nature. Therefore, Krishnamurti is critical about both tradition and science. However one has to live with actuality, *what is*, from moment to moment totally?

Humanistic Religion

According to Humanism, the distinctive character of man is that he is a rational and spiritual being. He has the capacity for self-transcendence and self-awareness and an ability to project his mind into future. Humanism recognises the human self as a cognising subject who knows itself as well as the external world. For the better understanding of Krishnamurti's views on religion it is necessary to have an understanding of what religion from humanistic perspective.

Humanistic religion is centered on man and has no concern for transcendence. It insists on man achieving full knowledge about him. Humanistic religion does not advocate pessimism and ascetic renunciation. It is opposed to authoritative and traditional religions. In authoritative religion, man surrenders himself to some higher, unseen power and is totally governed by it. According to Erich Fromm:

> "Humanistic religion ....is centered on man and his strength. Man must develop his power of reason in order to understand himself, his relationship to his fellow men and his position in the universe. He must recognise truth, both with regard to his limitations and his potentialities. He must develop his power of love for other as well as for himself and experience the solidarity of all living beings".[31]

Religious experience, according to humanistic religion, is man's experience of oneness with all. It is based on one's relatedness to the world which he comes to know through his thought and love. Humanistic religion concerns itself with the human goal of life which is to achieve greatest strength but not the greatest powerlessness. According to humanism, realisation is the greatest virtue but not obedience and surrender as in authoritative religion. It is the realisation of one's own potentiality.

One of the best examples of humanistic religion is early Buddhism. Buddha, recognises the truth about human existence and does not speak in the name of any supernatural power but in the name of reason. Zen Budhism is a better expression of humanistic religion and many of the views of Krishnamurti are strikingly similar to Zen Budhism. According to Zen Budhism, knowledge is of no value unless it grows out of man's understanding of himself. No authority, no teacher can really teach us anything except to create doubts in us. Systems of thought are dangerous because they easily turn out to be authoritative. Therefore life itself must be grasped and experienced.[32]

Erich Fromm tried to trace the elements of humanistic religion in the young Marx's writing and his socialism. Marx's concept of socialism is a protest, as is all existentialist philosophy, against the alienation of man. His socialism is a protest against the lovelessness and against man's exploitation of man. As Aldous Huxley puts it, "Our present economic, social and international arrangements are based, in large measure, upon organised lovelessness." Socialism is exactly against the loveless nature of man. And an inalienated man is one who does not dominate nature, but who becomes one with it. "Does not all this mean that Marx's socialism is the realisation of the deepest religious impulses common to the great humanistic religions of past?[33] Marx fought against religion exactly because it alienates man from his own reality and does not satisfy the true needs of man. Marx's fight against God is, in reality, a fight against the idol that is called God which is created by religion. Young Marx wrote as the motto for his dissertation, "Not those are godless who have contempt for the Gods of the masses but those who attribute the opinions of the masses to the Gods." Eric Fromm considers Marx's atheism as the most advanced form of rational mysticism, close to Meister Eckhart or to Zen Budhism than most of those who fight for god and religion and accuse Marx of 'Godlessness'.

Krishnamurti's views are centred on humanism when he talks about religion. He refutes the false notions about religion and God. He questions the irrational attitudes, dogmas and beliefs of human beings and does not want to give a new meaning to the old. Since he totally rejects the tradition as a whole for fresh, creative life, his religious revolution is not revival or reformation of any particular religion. The total freedom from all religions and ideologies which he advocates means really freedom from the society as it is the society which has created them.

Is Krishnamurti a Mystic?

It is debatable whether Krishnamurti is a mystic or not. Some people consider Krishnamurti as a kind of mystic and for others he is no mystic and there is no mystical element in his teaching. Then what is mysticism? What is its significance?

Mysticism brings to man intimations of those layers of consciousness, which are still subjective to him, that is, those on which he does not normally function. In fact, the level of consciousness just above his normal consciousness is truly the realm of mysticism.[34]

It is said that when the world is in a crisis there is scope for the emergence of mystic thought, or mystical thought helps in making religion meaningful and thus saves it. With the emergence of positivism in modern time the traditional ideas and values are questioned and discarded. This is more so in the case of religion. Religious beliefs and values are criticised in the wake of advancement of science and philosophy. Modern attitude towards religion is one of skepticism whereas mysticism is seen to be meaningful in meeting the challenge to religion as mysticism is basically experiential. So, many people look to mysticism for help and Enlightenment as mysticism provides a renewed religious life. The favourable inclination of modern man towards mystics and their teaching is to help him overcome the stress of modern life and civilisation. It appears that a new spiritual impulse comes into the life of humanity through new forms of mysticism. Mysticism reveals a higher level of consciousness which is above the normal consciousness of man.

According to Rohit Mehta, "He (Krishnamurti) is, thus a mystic of an extra ordinary type, for he cannot be fitted into any class of known mystic of the past or the present and yet his approach to life is intensely mystical. He is a person who shows paradoxical tendencies in his life and action." He also writes further that, "His (Krishnamurti) mysticism may be termed intellectual Mysticism or the mysticism of the mind. His is an intuitive approach and deals with the intuition of the mind—a state in which the beyond the mind." [35]

However, Rohit Mehta considers that in one respect it is not right to call Krishnamurti's approach intuitive, for we know nothing about intuition, which is beyond mind. But there is no better word which can mean that faculty which is beyond mind and at the same time cannot be conceptualised. But Krishnamurti is not happy with the word 'intuition' to describe his approach. Though he uses the term intuition, occasionally, for him, there is nothing mystical about the state of intuition. It is the state in which total perception takes place and the observer is observed. It is the realisation of non-duality and the act of intelligence. In one of his conversations, Krishnamurti says:

> "Intuition is the highest point of intelligence and to me keeping alive that intelligence is inspiration. Now, you can only keep alive that intelligence, of which intuition is the highest expression, by experience, by being all the time like a questioning child. Intuition, the apotheosis, the accumulation, the accumulation of intelligence."[36]

Thus according to Krishnamurti, intuition is the state of intelligence and is beyond intellect. It is the contact of actuality in a direct manner without the interpreting medium of the mind. Henri Bergson also talks about intuition which is a faculty of consciousness and is capable of knowing the reality as a whole. Zen Budhism also insists on knowing the reality from a point which is beyond intellect. Such knowing or *satori* is an unimpeded flow and means understanding the totality of things or knowing reality as a whole or in its completeness. It is the experience of reality itself without an interpretation. We will be able to perceive life from a new standpoint when the process of the mind is completely eliminated. It is an intuitive understanding of life. Krishnamurti's position is similar to the above, as according to him life manifests and fulfils itself in action every moment. He maintains that to know the truth as a whole or to have complete experience, one should go beyond all the ideas, dogmas that is imposed upon truth by the mind.

In the words of Krishnamurti, "My teaching is neither mystic nor occult" and he further affirms that, "for I hold that both mysticism and occultism are man's limitation upon truth.[38] Life is more important than any belief or dogmas and in order to allow life fruition you must liberate it from beliefs, authority and tradition. But those who are bound by these things will have a difficulty in understanding truth."[37]

It was also pointed out that, Krishnamurti's views on truth are like the mysticism of the Upanishads and Buddhism.[38] But Krishnamurti refuses to call his teaching mystical. Truth, according to him, is not other worldly. It is neither mysterious nor complex. He further says that its knowledge is not the privilege of a few but accessible to all. It does not mean accumulation of knowledge and is related to daily life. Truth is life itself. It is in the immediate present and can be known instantaneously. Truth may, however, appear to be mysterious to the mind which is burdened with past knowledge. But it ceases to be so the moment the mind becomes free from such knowledge and perceives truth directly. Krishnamurti contends that truth would be insignificant if it were to be mystical and accessible only to a few. Therefore, reducing Krishnamurti's philosophy to mysticism is to ignore its simplicity, directness universality and its relevance to the daily life of man.

Krishnamurti and His Teachings

The core of Krishnamurti's philosophy is the direct realisation of truth which is possible by ending thought. According to him, a different kind of mind and life are possible only when thought with its traditional content is completely put to an end and his entire teaching is directed towards the sole task of ending thought. Time and again he emphasises the possibility of the end of thought. The biologists and psychologists maintain that thought is the essential characteristic of the mind or the brain. Man is biologically constrained to think as long as he is alive. But Krishnamurti strongly rejects this idea. He holds that thought is not an inherent and inalienable feature of the brain or mind. It is only tradition and the habit that have made thought essential to brain. But Krishnamurti maintains that it is possible to stop thought by understanding its genesis. Krishnamurti is of the view that it is only the conditioned mind which thinks that it is impossible to end thought. It is only the sluggish, the dull and the lazy mind that accepts thought as its inseparable characteristic. But the mind which can observe itself choicelessly can discover that it is possible to end thought. Krishnamurti, therefore, says that the very assertion that it is impossible to end thought strengthens thought and such thinking is a barrier to an inquiry into the nature of thought.

The question is often asked whether Krishnamurti lived up to his teachings or not. Many people admit that Krishnamurti's teachings can be understood better by observing Krishnamurti and his life. As one who understood truth, Krishnamurti lived truth in his daily life. He was a man who conquered division, conflict, attachment and sorrow. He was also known as man or lord of love and compassion. He lived the inexpressible truth better than he expressed it in his teachings. Krishnamurti himself says that it is difficult to express the inexpressible truth in words. Truth is beyond verbalisation. On the contrary, some believe that there was a gap between the life of Krishnamurti and his teaching, or that Krishnamurti failed to live his teachings perfectly. To this criticism, Krishnamurti answered that he was only a medium through which the truth expressed itself. As a man Krishnamurti is unimportant but his life is revealing as a medium of truth. His life is like a mirror in which everyone can see themselves as they are. The mirror is not so important. As Krishnamurti says, his teaching is more important than himself. Therefore, one has to take his teaching more seriously than his life.

End Notes

1. Krishnamurti, [Mary Cadogan, Alan Kishbaugh, Mark Lee and Ray Mc Coy (eds.)] *Total Freedom—The Essential Krishnamurti* (New York: Harper San Francisco, 1996), p. 145. (and also in *Krishnamurti to Himself*).

2. The known consciousness is manifested with the burden of the past, which includes time, choice, desire, division, contradiction and sorrow. It has all the qualities of the traditional mind, where as the unknown is devoid of all these. Its nature is 'nothingness'. See G. Vedaparayana, "The Known and the Unknown: Jiddu Krishnamurti's Conception of Consciousness", *Darsana International,* Vol. XXVI No: 4, October, 1986.
3. J. Krishnamurti, [D. Raja Gopal (ed.)] *Commentaries on Living* (Hew Delhi: B.I. Publication, 1972), p. 209.
4. Cited in Mary Lutynes, *Years of Fulfilment* (New York: Avon Books, 1983), p. 74.
5. J. Krishnamurti, "Talks at Adayar: 1933-34", p. 28. as Cited in R.K. Sringy *Philosophy of J. Krishnamurti: A Systematic Study* (New Delhi: Munshiram Manoharlal, 1977), p. 326.
6. J. Krishnamurti, *Truth and Actuality* (Madras: KFI, 1992), p. 40.
7. Stuart Holroyd, *The Quest of Mind, The Philosophy of J. Krishnamurti* (Wellingborough: Aquarian Press, 1983), p. 58.
8. Luis S.R. Vas (ed.), *Mind of J. Krishnamurti* (Bombay: Jaico Publishing House, 1989), p. 30.
9. J. Krishnamurti, *Commentaries on Living,* p. 64.
10. Cited in Arundati Sardesai "Epistemology of J. Krishnamurti" *Indian Philosophical Quarterly,* Vol. XXIII, Nos. 3 and 4, July-October, 1996, p. 455.
11. *Ibid.*, p. 455.
12. J. Krishnamurti, *Letters to the Schools* (Madras: KFI, 1981), p. 72.
13. J. Krishnamurti, *Truth and Actuality*, p. 60.
14. See G. Vedaparayana, "Philosophy as the Perception of Truth—A Comment on "Epistemology of J. Krishnamurti.", *Indian Philosophical Quarterly*, Vol. XXIV, No 3, July, 1997.
15. Bertrand Russell, "The Problems of Philosophy", p. 93, Cited in Vedaparayana, (1997).

16. Cf. J. Krishnamurti and David Bohm, *The Ending of Time* (Madras: KFI, 1992), p. 98.
17. S. Radhakrishnan, *History of Indian Philosophy* Vol. I. (London: Blackie Sons, 1985), p. 43.
18. J. Krishnamurti, *Letters to the Schools*, p. 53.
19. J. Krishnamurti, *Questioning Krishnamurti, J. Krishnamurti in Dialogue* (San Francisco: Harper Collins, 1996), p. 123.
20. Cf. *Ibid.*, pp. 127-28.
21. *Ibid.*, p. 123.
22. Cf. Christopher Caudwell, *Concept of Freedom* (London: Lawrence Wishart, 1977), pp. 63-64.
23. *Ibid.*, p. 65.
24. J. Krishnamurti, *Talks in India, 1967* (California: Krishnamurti Writings Inc., 1968), p. 8.
25. Valerian Rodriegues, "Facing Post-Modernism", *Indian Journal of American Studies*, Vol. 23, No. 1, Winter 1993, p. 9.
26. Valerian Rodriuges, "Making a Tradition Critical: Ambedkar's Reading of Buddhism", In Peter Robb, *Dalit Movements and Meaning of Labour in India* (Delhi: Oxford University Press, 1993), p. 305.
27. Vasanta Moon (Comp.) Dr. *Babasaheb Ambedkar's Writings and Speeches,* Vol. 3, (Bombay: Education Department, Government of Maharastra, 1987), pp. 82-83.
28. S.G. Kulakarni, "Philosophy of Dr Ambedkar: Some Observations", (paper presented in a national seminar on *"The Relevence of Ambedkarism in India Today' September* 26, 27, 1992 at Visakhapatnam), p. 9.
29. J. Krishnamurti, *Talks in India. 1967*, p. 11.
30. J. Krishnamurti, *Education and Significance of Life* (Madras: KFI, 1992), p. 82.
31. Erich Fromm, "What is Humanistic Religion?", In George L. Abernethy and Thomas A. Langford (eds.), *Philosophy of Religion: A Book of Readings* (New York: The Mac Millan Company, 1968), p, 83.

32. Cf. *Ibid.*, p. 83.
33. Aldous Huxely, "The Perennial Philosophy", Cited in Erich Fromm, *Marx's Conception of Man* (New York: Frederick Ungar, 1961), p. 63.
34. Rohit Mehta, *The Intuitive Philosophy J. Krishnamurti Approach to Life* (Bombay: Chetana, 1988), p. 279.
35. *Ibid.*, p. 286.
36. Luis S.R. Vas (ed.), *The Mind of J. Krishnamurti* (Bombay: Jaico Publishing House, 1989), p. 82.
37. *Ibid.*, p. 21.
38. See Arundati Desai, p. 462.

7

Post Script

J. Krishnamurti: Religious or Revolutionary?

J. Krishnamurti (1895-1986) is a phenomenal figure for many people from different walks of life all over the world. From humble beginnings in a small town in India, Krishnamurti emerged as an uncompromising and unclassified teacher whose talks and writings were not linked to any specific religion—neither in the east nor in the west but for the whole world.[1] He had frequent discussions with distinguished writers, philosophers, scientists, educators and national leaders. Every word he spoke has been recorded. He is the most privileged world teacher/philosopher/psychologist/scholar/social engineer/spiritual guru/religious guru/free thinker/modern man having audience all over the world. He has constantly maintained the network with the world, from his journey from theosophical society to Krishnamurti foundations. He has never faced the problems of any common man. He has got trained to speak. He has been well versed in English, French and some world languages; of course he lost touch with his native language Telugu over the period of time. His personality has been systematically groomed. He has dramatically transformed from being a Brahmin boy of Madanapalle to become Universal teacher without belonging to any religion, nation, or political group on a mission to unifying the fragmented and conflict ridden humanity. His books have been published all over the world and translated into more than twenty languages. His works are also available on audio and video recordings and electronic disks. He is the meeting point to the diverse people such as theosophists, liberal Brahmins, socialists, environmentalists, liberal Christians, Buddhist monks, aristocrats, businessmen, women, political leaders like Nehru, Indira Gandhi, writers like George Bernard Shaw, Aldous Huxely, scientists like David Bohm etc. The phenomenon of Krishnamurti may be understood by asking simple questions such as, what is the essence of Krishnamurti's teachings? What meanings are derived by his audience from his talks? What kind of impact has it made on the social transformation?

Krishnamurti himself does not want to be classified in terms of any traditional categories as he thinks such classification of himself and his thought would be rigid and reductionist. It is really problematic to characterise Krishnamurti's thought either as philosophical, or religious or psychological. This is an attempt towards a critical assessment of Krishnamurti, though he resists this kind of exercise. His lectures are very well structured and based on certain assumptions. The method in understanding the problems of humanity and the language which he used may help us to assess him. Here I'm responding to Krishnamurti from the context of identity struggles such as gender, caste, region, religion and their limitations. In other words, these struggles came with alternative philosophical frameworks against the dominant liberal position. He exposes the limitations of liberal ideas aimed to transform the world on the path of progress and the limits of identity struggles. Liberal thought aims to eliminate the traces of the past totally from human memory and identity. Simultaneously, it formulates new bondages of mind in the form of rationality yielding freedom. This freedom is a new kind of bondage tying mind to cravings of the world. On the other hand, identity struggles invent new pasts for one self supposedly ensuring a sense of belonging in the times of swift changes in the world. Liberalism invents new desires and identity struggles offer securities in times of radical erasures of the past and construction of delusive ambitions.

Krishnamurthi's ideas can be interpreted to show that it exposes the limits of progress/predatory capitalism and other sleves inventing new pasts in the form of identity struggles. Krishnamurthi would look at both the streams as offering new forms of bondage. Freedom from bondage does not come from nervously possessing objects in the world. It comes from total end of attachments not just to things but to ideas as well. His idea of total freedom from the known is this in nutshell. It comes close to existentialism of Sartre. Both the philosophers point to intense self examination of self to see clearly fragmentations constituting core of it. By looking at divisions within the self, one could go beyond them. Both the streams assume radical individual responsibility for the kind of self one is. Their axis of thinking is an internal freedom of the mind. It emphasises the internalisation of responses to the external world. Both call attention to be critically aware of thought constructions in shaping a response to world. But, there are differences as well. Sartre focuses on the worldly affairs in achieving such freedom while Krishnamurthi totally focuses on the processes of mind for bondage as well as freedom. The individual is central to his philosophy. For him human identity devoid of any markers such as caste, class, nation, gender, etc., is ultimate. Other than the universal human identity, he considers other identities as fragmentary and misleading. He is in favour of liberation of humanity from the burden of tradition/religion/belief/knowledge of the past/thought/memory. The way he explores the logical relation between individual and world is interesting. He asserts that 'you are the world'. He believes that the change in individual automatically brings the change in the world.

Marking Krishnamurti

There are many attempts to understand Krishnamurti

through known categories by different scholars belonging to the West as well as the East. Krishnamurti's teachings are evaluated from the perspectives of Buddha and Advaita Vedanta of Indian philosophical tradition. Some scholars tried to understand him through the existentialist thinker such as Sartre. But all of them agree that Krishnamurti is something more than this.

A.P. Sharma, in *Krishnamurti, His Concept of Freedom,* tries to bring some parallels between Krishnamurti and Sankara, Budha and Sartre on certain points.[2] The state of non-awareness of duality of the self which Sankara refers to, is almost the same as is pointed out by Krishnamurti. Krishnamurti says that the consciousness in the realm of the known is always self-centered. It cannot exist without the "I" or the 'me' as its center. All its actions emanate from the center called the 'self'. Hence they are separating, self inclusive, incomplete and inadequate..... The echo of Sankara's definition of self-realisation is very often heard in Krishnamurti's definition of the term 'awareness'. He reckons that 'awareness' is a kind of process through which the self is to understand its own activities, the 'I', in relationship with people, with ideas and with things.... Unlike Sankara who is traditional in his outlook and seeks divine shelter to redeem man from ignorance, Krishnamurti is anti-traditional and does not prescribe any course for man's redemption. He seeks freedom through 'intelligent chioceless awareness', which is not a postulate of any religious dogma.[3]

Rohit Mehta, in *The Intuitive Philosophy, Krishnamurti's Aproach to Life*, considers J. Krishnamurti as a mystic—a mystic of great stature who radiates both love and power from his being. He is thus a mystic of an extra-ordinary type, for he cannot be fitted into any class of known mystics of the past or the present and yet his approach to life is intensely mystical. He is a person who shows paradoxical tendencies in his life and action for he is stern in discussions but most gentle in his behaviour with people; he is most polished and charming in his manners, but yet at the same time unconcerned with the public opinion. Are not the lives of the truly great always full of paradoxes? ....His mysticism may be termed Intellectual mysticism or the Mysticism of the Mind. His is intuitive approach and deals with the intuition of the mind—a state in which the human mind is illuminated by that which is beyond the mind. (Thinking) Krishnamurti is giving out the same old *Vedanta* is to miss the beauty of what he says today. Those who love *Vedanta* should be happy that Krishnamurti is giving out another aspect of *Vedanta*; those who do not know what *Vedanta* is, should also be happy, for a new revelation of truth that has been placed before them. K's approach to life is so fresh that one must feel it for oneself before forming judgment about it.[4]

Christine Williams in his thesis on biography of Krishnamurti has made an attempt to read Krishnamurti in the context of a stream of philosophy, *Advaita Vedanta*, based on the ancient sacred texts, the *Vedas*. And *Vedanta* was a product of Krishnamurti's home culture. He argues that Krishnamurti resonated with *Advaita Vedanta* teaching: 'The world is us and we are the world, they are not two separate states.' 'How is it possible to have no contradiction between the 'observer' and the 'observed', between the 'experiencer' and the 'experience', between love and hate?—these dualities, how is it possible to live without them? When Krishnamurti spoke, many Westerners heard a modernist language espousing individualism and revolution, yet many Indians heard the unity of classic *Advaitism*, spoken from the mouth of a radical non-traditionalist who rejected the concept of a *guru* outside of oneself, a *guru* in materialised human form.[5]

As Staurt Holroyd, in *The Quest of Quiet Mind, The philosophy of Krishamurti,* emphasises the 'wholistic' perception of Krishnamurti. Krishnamurti considers dualistic thinking as a block to the perception of truth and the concepts of 'wholeness' is central in his thinking and indeed he does sometimes seems to be speaking from *what is* known as 'a materialist monist' position, particularly in regarding thought and consciousness in terms of brain cell activity, but on the other he speaks of the silent mind generating no brain activity although it is intensely aware and in touch with reality. So, to assign him to the materialist camp, as some critics have done, is to act on a partial and superficial understanding of his thought.[6] He is not a Christian, a Hindu, or a Buddhist, although there is much in Buddhist philosophy that accords with his teaching and Aldous Huxley even compared his talks and dialogues with the discourses of Gautama.[7] Carlo Suares, the French scholar states that while Krishnamurti's message in the beginning was a simple and direct appeal to participate in a 'liberated life', Krishnamurti today is concentrating on psychological problems. At the present moment, his message is mainly concerned with the function of human consciousness. Its function, he says, is to destroy the illusion of the 'I', to liberate the individual from all self-consciousness.[8] Further, he contextualised Krishnamurti by differentiating him from Gandhi and Marxists. Krishnamurti teaches a total non-cooperation with all the values of all civilisations based on 'I' and all its desires. It is clearly realised, Saures shows, how widely different this non-co-operation is from that of Gandhi, who 'uses economic non-cooperation as a political tool and would like to have a whole people co-operating within frames established on feudal exploitation..... you are, for instance, Marxists, but your 'I's' are making compensations in other ways, you are, after all, exploiters like all the rest. But what use is it, then, to call oneself a revolutionist?'. [9]

Ada Schmidt Beil, in modern *Philosophy of Values* the German scholar argues that modern scientific research along various paths is already fumbling its way towards facts and conclusions of essential significance for a really comprehensive evaluation of Krishnamurti's world of ideas by his contemporaries. Above all, Krishnamurti elucidates these states of consciousness of the present humanity, rooted in the 'I,' the ego and he does it with wonderful accuracy and in full agreement with modern scientific knowledge. Krishnamurti has expanded modern thought on essential points, that he has gone to the root of things, he 'knows from his own experience that 'life is stronger than form'—form up till now and even during these days, being the main object of scientific research...'[10] He further explains that the philosophical feat of Krishnamurti consists primarily in the fact that he has abolished dualism, merged it into the conception of 'Reality' (life to him is a harmony in action between intellect and love) and that he has bestowed on the conception of commonly used word 'reality' a new and very distinct meaning...'[11]

The well known Buddhist scholar Walpola Rahula in dialogue with Krishnamurti argues that, what Buddha taught 2,500 years ago you teach today in a new idiom, a new style, a new garb.[12] He argues that Krishnamurti shares with Buddha on non acceptance of creator god, old Vedic, Brahminic idea an eternal soul or atman. As Buddha begins his teaching from the premise that human life is a predicament, suffering, conflict, sorrow and cause of this is the selfishness created by the wrong idea of myself, my *atman*. Buddha says that when one is free from desire, attachment, from the self, one is free from suffering and conflict. Krishnamurti, too, represents the position that freedom means freedom from all attachment. According to Buddha, realisation of truth is to see things as they are; when you do that, you see reality, you see truth and are free from conflict. This position reflects in Krishnamurti's *Truth and Actuality*. Budha said don't accept anything just because it is said by religion or scripture, or by a teacher or *guru*, only accept it if you see for yourself that it is right. Krishnamurti, too, maintains this line by saying you must not depend on authority and you must realise it yourself. Buddha's idea of impermanence is often emphasised by Krishnamurti who says that everything is impermanent, there is nothing permanent. Krishnamurti in *Freedom from the Known* says that to discern nothing is permanent is of tremendous importance—for only then is the mind free. This is in complete accordance with four noble truths of Buddha. Walpola Rahula argues with Krishnamurti that "There is no conflict between you and Buddha on these points. Of course, you are not a Buddhist, as you say".[13] Krishnamurti replies to this, "Why do you compare?"

M.M. Agrawal in *Consciousness and the Integrated Being, Sartre and Krishnamurti*, brings the parallel between western existentialist Sartre with eastern thinker J. Krishnamurti. He argues that the primary source of fragmentation in the self as a psychological construct. Following Krishnamurti, he looks upon spiritual freedom in terms of 'integration' within the fragmented being so that 'freedom' does not remain freedom *for* the self but *from* the self. The ideas of Sartre and Krishnamurti are compared in the construction of 'the integrated being.'[14] Krishnamurti's concept of freedom is similar to Sartre's conception of freedom. Sartre says that human consciousness is ontologically free. Therefore, man is a free being. Man is the maker of himself or he is the architect of his life and world. Krishnamurti also maintains that man is responsible for what he is. Man is the maker of his life. He is responsible for his condition and that the world around him. Besides this similarity, there is a fundamental difference between Krishnamurti and Sartre on the conception of freedom. To Sartre freedom is self-determininism. It is a voluntary choice. It is acting with chosen motive and end. But Krishnamurti's concept of freedom means mind which is devoid of self determinism, motives and ends. Freedom is a state of being in which the mind is empty of all its content. Freedom is consciousness which is without self, division, conflict and unhappiness.[15]

However, Krishnamurti's position is very clear by consciously keeping away from any identification except with humanity in general. 'First of all, I am nobody. That's all, it is as simple as that-I am nobody. You are the story of mankind. You are part of this whole humanity. That has a tremendous responsibility, vitality, beauty, love. And to have a mind which is totally free from comparison is to observe the whole history of humanity that is embedded in you.[16] I question that very much-whether thought is ever East or West. There is only thought, it is not Eastern thought or Western thought. The expression of thought may be different in India and the West, but it is still the process of thought. Humanity that is not Western or Eastern.[17] He considers 'Suffering is common to all humanity'. Thought is responsible for conditioning of mind and creates divisions and hatred among the humanity. 'Thought cannot solve anything psychologically'. And freedom is the negation of conditioning by any culture, by any religious division or political division.... I feel it is religious mind that can bring real unity to human beings. The religious mind is quiet, detached, non-seeking, non-believing, highly sensitive and creative.

Krishnamurti: A New Language

As Rohit Mehta noted that, there are many who find it difficult to understand Krishnamurti because of his language. No doubt, he uses the English language, but he has put a new content into the words of this language. Those who do not understand this content many a time feel utterly shocked at the language he uses. Being a mystic of very high order, he has evolved his own language and one must understand the special content of his language before accepting or rejecting his approach to life and its problems.[18]

Carlo Saures very interestingly shows how Krishnamurti gives a new significance to words, invests them with fresh nuances, how their meaning is constantly changing; in fact, how words to him no more static, but dynamic, he is all the time trying to give to the words the full meaning of his own. As Radhika Herzeberger rightly observed, Krishnamurti perceived the problems of the world as emerging from human consciousness and sought to liberate that consciousness. Even though he shared with traditional Indian thought the concept of liberation as the primary goal of human life, Krishnamurti borrowed neither his vocabulary nor his exposition from India's rich treasure house of sacred literature but, embracing modernity's iconoclastic spirit, worked out his own powerful discourse.[19]

Krishnamurti: Traditionalist or Revolutionary?

We have observed different characterisations of Krishnamurti by different thinkers, sometimes even contradictory to the other. Is he a Bhuddhist or Advaitin? Does his approach is Mystic or scientific? Is Krishnamurti idealist or materialist, atheist or theist? Does his philosophy is essentially India or western? Or a meeting point of the East and the West. Is he a typical modernist or traditionalist of different kind? Does Krishnamurti represent the Orientalist thinking? Does he cross the cultural boundaries or ignore their existence? Krishnamurti may dismiss all these questions so easily for innocently using the traditional categories or partial viewpoints to comprehend the reality. In the light of his holistic approach to *what is*, any of these approaches may look dim. His emphasis is only on universal human consciousness. One may question this very assumption of Krishnamurti regarding the sharing of this common consciousness. This may be a philosophical/theoretical ideal to follow but the concrete practical questions require different software. Existentialism of Sartre comes close to addressing this, it gives more significance to spiritual questions in the context of modern world.

It seems difficult to locate Krishnamurti and his thought in historical context since he opposes any historical constructions. He considers that history, culture and social process are responsible for conditioning the human mind. But one should not forget that he takes his audiences from the *known historical categories* to the unknown zones, i.e., freedom from the known. It is apt to bring here the dominant brahminical constructions of Indian philosophy, which is essentially idealistic. They are more concerned with abstraction or principles and totally ignore the concrete social and cultural reality. Their philosophies have often surrendered to logic. Krishnamurti is too concerned about this logical analysis. Unlike these Brahminical idealists, he is concerned about the social and political issues in order to dismiss or to show the limitations of these. Here Krishnamurti has succeeded in appealing to the larger audiences than the traditionalists through the effective use of modernist language. For instance, he gives the new meaning to the words like 'tradition', 'revolution', 'religious mind', 'awareness', 'meditation', 'thought' and 'knowledge'. The word 'religious' is identified historically with organised religions with beliefs and dogmas. He proposes this word against this kind of characterisation and identifies this with love, compassion and insight. As everybody knows the word 'revolution' identified with radical change has been propagated by the Marxists. Krishnamurti uses this word for total change in consciousness through psychological transformation. He points out the limitations of Marxian revolution. By doing this way, Krishnamurti at first reaches his audiences immediately and later takes them to his position. For better understanding of Krishnamurti, one has to understand the politics behind this.

Moreover, Krishnamurti's philosophy consciously conceals the differences, contradictions and conflicts of human society. Krishnamurti opposes any collective struggle. He treats the capitalist, communist, Indian, western, the rich and the poor in a similar fashion. He argues that they are divisive, 'I'-centred and limited. Without seeing the moral worthiness or merit of the struggle, he dismisses all the struggles with a single stroke. He elevates his position of the psychological revolution of individual through choiceless awareness to greater heights than these limited struggles based on identity. In fact, Krishnamurti's philosophy keeps the people politically neutral by not involving in any ongoing struggles. How far Krishnamurti has succeeded in his mission of setting humanity absolutely and unconditionally free is questionable. He himself answered to the questions such as, what effect had his teaching on people? Has any one been radically transformed? In eighties in New York his answer to the first question was: 'very little'. And the second one, he said, shortly before his death, that nobody had got in touch with that consciousness of which he had spoken. He added, 'perhaps they will somewhat if they live the teaching.'[20]

End Notes

1. Mary Cadogan, Alan Kishbaugh, Mark Lee, Ray McCoy, Preface, In '*Krishnamurti, J. Total Freedom, The Essential J. Krishnamurti*', Harper Sanfrancisco, 1996.
2. Sharma, A.P. *Krishnamurti, His Concept of Freedom*, New Delhi: Ajanta Publications,1993.
3. *Ibid.* pp. 73,75.
4. Rohit Mehta in *The Intuitive Philosophy, Krishnamurti's Aproach to Life*, Chetana: Bombay,1988 (First Published in 1950).
5. Williams, Christine. *J. Krishnamurti: Crossing Cultural Boarders or Ignoring their Existence?* (This paper was presented to the 15th Biennial Conference of the Asian Studies Association of Australia in Canberra 29 June 2—July 2004).
6. Holroyd, Staurt. The Quest of Quiet Mind, *The Philosophy of Krishamurti Wellingborough*: The Aquarian Press, p. 58.
7. *Ibid.*, p. 67.
8. Krishnamurti, *Contemporary Appreciations*, p. 194.
9. *Ibid.*, pp. 195, 239.
10. *Ibid.* quoted in *Krishnamurti, Contemporary Appreciations*, pp. 203, 205.
11. *Ibid.*, p. 204.
12. Rahula, Walpola. et al. 'Are You Not saying What the Budha Said?', In *Questioning Krishnamurti, J. Krishnamurti in Dialogue*, San Francisco: Thorsons,1996, p. 18.
13. *Ibid.*, pp. 19-20.
14. Agrawal, M.M. *Consciousness and the Integrated Being, Sartre and Krishnamurti*, Shimla: IIAS,1991.
15. Kesava Kumar, P. Jiddu Krishnamurti's conception of Tradition and Revolution : A Critical Study, Ph.D Thesis Submitted to University of Hyderabad, 1997. (Unpublished).
16. Anonymous. Who are you, *Questining Krishnamurti, J. Krishnamurti in Dialougue*, San Francisco: Thorsons,

1996, p. 253.

17. Pupul Jayakar, Is there an Eastern mind and a western mind? *Questioning Krishnamurti, J. Krishnamurti in Dialougue*, San Francisco: Thorsons, 1996 p. 154.
18. Mehta. Rohit *The Intuitive Philosophy, Krishnamurti's Aproach to Life*, Chetana : Bombay,1988 (First Published in 1950) p. 293.
19. Herzbeerger, Radhika. *An Overview of J. Krishnamurti's Views on Education.*
20. Skitt, David. Foreword. *Questioning Krishnamurti.* p. xii.

Reading J. Krishnamurti in the Time of War

Krishnamurti's philosophy is in simple and powerful language that offers a sort of relief and celebration of spontaneity in the world racked by divisions based on class, caste, religion or ideology. He writes, "War is the spectacular and bloody projection of our everyday life. War is merely an outward expression of our inward state, an enlargement of our daily action. It is more spectacular, more bloody, more destructive, but it is the collective result of our individual activities." *(On Conflict, 2011: 11).* His conclusion is simple, "To put an end to outward war, you must begin to put an end to war in yourself". *(On Conflict, 13*).

No room for knowledge, thought, time, history or ideology. You gain an insight into the dangers of the conditioning. At present we are suffering from fragmentation of thought which tries to act and react on the basis of past thought or knowledge or history. The ancient wisdom and scriptures have acted as fetters on human imagination and led to the dark ages in the world when religious crusades claimed the lives of millions of humans. The authority of the scriptures which have been kept beyond the reach of the common people through lack of education, the printing press, punishments to those who dared read scriptures and do *tapas* like *Sambuka* enslaved the people. History seen as the journey of human will or ridden with class conflict has led to the wars and mass killings. Modern science which has promised freedom from scarcity and endless progress has led to the dropping of atom bomb, chemical weapons, subjugation of small states and the feverish attempts to migration to the planet Mars. Krishnamurti has identified the crisis and states in the following words, "Technologically we have progressed, advanced so rapidly and psychologically our behaviour, our attitudes and actions, are more or less unevolved. We are still aggressive, brutal, cruel, thoughtless, for thousands and thousands of years. Apparently man is still behaving more or less as he behaves, 40,000 years ago". (*Mind without Measure, 34-36).*

Krishnamurti writes, "Life is meant to be lived and in that very living one begins to discover the reality, the truth, the beauty of life. To discover truth, the beauty of life, you must understand the total movement of it and to do that you have to end all this fragmentary thinking way of life." (*On Conflict, 93*). He also writes, "Only when there are no nationalities, no divisions such as Christians, Buddhists, Hindus, communists, or capitalists there will be no war. Only when man gives up his petty beliefs and prejudices, his worship of his own particular family and all the rest of it is there a possibility of peace in the world." (*On Conflict*, 57).

Many prophets, theories, isms have come and gone but the systems of oppression and the lack of awareness of the majority of the people remain intact. The psychological chains remain and here the positive effect of JK's thought needs to be appreciated. He advocates the total response to usher in an inward revolution which is absolutely necessary.

We need philosophers who are neither mechanical materialists nor idealists who throw the javelins at the windmills of ideas and neglect conditions which produce them. Idealistic philosophy has harped more on change of ideas or heart in changing the world. Though dialectical materialism has recognised the need for change in infrastructure and culture, the eventual degeneration of communism in Soviet Union, China and many east European countries turned tide in favour of idealistic philosophy. The inherent distortion of those systems and the relentless assaults directly and indirectly by the imperialist camp on all revolutionary regimes including Cuba, Chile, Nicaragua have created an ambience where idealism has gained fertile ground. In this kind of world characterised by cold war and real wars in the post-cold war, Jiddu Krishnamurti's philosophy has gained a lot of popularity.

The defeated warriors, the fatigued intellectuals and explorers of the new way have felt a need for safe haven which appeared in Krishanmurti's philosophy. He spoke the new idiom and asserted the condition beyond conflicts and schism of thought. He rejected to sit on the pedestal and be called a guru but he is seen as teacher of teachers by many including his disciples. Krihnamurti sees and criticises violence inherent in institutions such as family, religion, tradition, nationalism and State. He sees faith and truth as different. He appears like an anarchist in the best sense who refuses the reverence to authority that kills truth. Although this assertion is truthful, it also raises some questions worth considering.

He exposes the hollowness of the modern education, the meaning of real freedom, the way out of suffering. He shows the idleness in ideals and desire for power in altruism or even social revolutions. He gives no quarter for conservatives as well as revolutionaries from escaping their prejudices. He argues for infusing humanism into the system of mechanical and mercenary education that turns out skilled robots sans human heart. He also feels that "any education worth its name must investigate the question of being. It should develop the spirit of critical inquiry among the young minds instead of conforming to the established structures." (*Education and Significance of Life*). To him, "There must be freedom, not only from all creeds and dogmas, but also from personal ambition and self-centered activity. Only then a new world is possible." (*Education and Significance of Life*).

Krishnamurti also thinks that man has been violent since time immemorial and human nature has not changed. This is so not because of any immutability but due to the continuation of oppressive structures in one form or another. We cannot end this at one stroke and if we forget the valiant attempts for freedom and equality in the past and cynically claim that nothing changes, that may be acquiescing with the oppressive tradition. Krishnamurti sees tradition as the haven for the seekers of comfort and any kind of knowledge scientific or not cannot be non-tradition. If we reject future, where will we end? Witchcraft to market wizardry may not be what human wants and cynicism stems from failing to understand that every generation has to fight its battles afresh and pay the price of liberty. Continuous awareness and action are needed to preserve ideals such as freedom, equality, justice and if you reject ideals, you are also saying that the present, however, unpalatable or painful is real which is rational.

Krishnamurti's espousal of universal man and criticism of smaller identities seems right to mainly pacifists or gradualists or liberals. The working class internationalism has disappeared due to the big brotherly attitude of Soviet Union or China towards their neighbours. The grand narrative of Marxism has come under scanner or even rejected by some people. Global capitalism has emphasised national peculiarities but later on attacked third world nationalism which threatened its hegemony and now even eulogises small identities as per its convenience. The grand chariot of the market fundamentalism has been going ahead at the cost of the working classes all over the world. Some deny their very existence and others deny their ideology of emancipation and proclaim the eternal reign of Capital. Socialism has been discredited thoroughly despite the valiant efforts by Castro and Chavez. Nationalism, or even Marxism can't discount smaller identities and the struggles based on them completely. The problem is how to rejuvenate the burning hope for equality and justice from Ambedkarian, or Marxist point of view.

Krishnamurti opposes ideologies as divisive and stupid and which sacrifice humans due to conditioned response. He is not untrue. Krishnamurthy is against petrified identity politics and its resultant violence. He is a free thinker and universalist. He writes, "To be respectable, men identify themselves in terms of nationalism, religion, class, ethnicity etc." He sees the division of mind due to organised entities such as religion, nation, class or ethnic groups. He finds the conditioned response as the root cause of conflict. He advocates the total response since all are human and the earth belongs to all. His ideas are novel and exciting but can we teach the same to the predatory powers which are hell bent on creating and sustaining the world order in favour of the privileged only?

How can Krishnamaurti's ideas work in the face of the destruction of Iraq, Afghanistan, Palestinian cause, terrorism, Guantanamo bay, the harassment of Indian tribals by the State, Pogromme of the religious and national minorities in India and the rest of the world in recent times? Does he preach quietism or passive submission to the evil? Or an escape from a distorted ideology leading to gulag archipelago?

Identitarian politicians find it difficult to agree with him but even they have to accept that there is a grain of truth in his words since he preaches continuous revolution. Like Camus he advocates endless revolution and it is anathema to the narrow-minded revolutionaries who see no change after their generation. He wants change in the present and now and not in the far future. He gives the antidote to the petrifaction and self-righteousness of Revolution. He writes, "For a man to save himself from the experience, there must be a real revolution—not a bloody revolution but a revolution of inward regeneration' (*On Conflict, 23*).

Perhaps our fault lies in hoping for permanent change or heaven on the earth. Perfection is the end of life and every generation has to fight afresh to gain or sustain or expand the spheres of freedom, equality, fraternity, justice. *'The need of the hour is the rejuvenation of hope of real democracy/socialism that is not subservient to the greed private or bureaucracy'* in the present world where injustice is projected as natural and inevitable order.

Exploitation is universal or global hence the case for worldwide liberation of the working classes in the spheres of political power and culture from the grip of the global capital and theory of universalism. Exploitation takes place in specific forms and locations, hence the need for identarian politics. The issue has become complex since the concepts of internationalism or globalisation have been used by the dominant powers of the world to deny concrete truths and justice to the victims of exploitation.

Can we build a new civilisation based on political, economic, social and gender equality? Or Should we withdraw ourselves from this unjust order as the philosopher wants us to do? Can Krishnamurti's ideas help us in building better world now and here or do they merely remain ruminations of a philosopher? Can we see a free individual not in a vacuum or in his mental universe but in the real world where concrete contexts demand concrete answers?

Krishnamurti's language is new, simple, deep and also stimulating. He says that philosophies have enslaved man and sacrificed him for the sake of ideal society. His teachings are a commentary on living and their essence is humanism. Love and compassion is the means of freedom and the present is all. He talks of the annihilation of the ego and human consciousness which is indivisible. Krishnamurti's insight calls for a radical transformation in the structure of the mind itself, goes beyond intellect and has a deep implication for social change. He wants an inward revolution, a complete revolution in an individual, human consciousness and in the very structure of brain. We have to still see the transformation of world through change in human consciousness alone without any recourse to changing of oppressive structures of the world. What does the present say in this regard?

Krishnamurti's rejection of tradition including revolutionary may also lead to historical confusion since people have nothing to fall back on. It may be like a discovery of fire anew every day or the stealing of fire by Prometheus from heaven every day. Being an eternal child has its innocence and also its own share of helplessness.

Kesava Kumar has taken pains to put Krishnamurti's teachings in a historical context and in comparison to other philosophers and thinkers such as Sartre, Gandhi and Ambedkar to make sense of his teachings from his vantage point. Krishnamurti's ideas can't be dismissed off-handedly or accepted uncritically. They have to be understood in their specific context and need to be assessed on the anvil of the present. This is precisely what Kesava Kumar has done for his doctorate thesis after a careful scrutiny of Krishnamurti's ideas. Now the book is in the hands of the discerning reader for his enlightenment as well as assessment.

J. Ravindranath

Associate Professor and Head of the Department
Department of English
Gayatri Vidya Parishad College of Engineering
(Autonomous)
JNTU-Kakinada
Visakhapatnam-48.

Bibliography

Abernethy, George L. and Thomas A. Langford (eds.), (1968), *Philosophy of Religion: A Book of Readings,* New York: The Mac Millan Company.

Arendt, Hannah. (1965), *On Revolution,* New York: Viking Press.

Aggrawal, M.M. (1991), *Consciousness and the Integrated Being, Sartre and Krishnamurti,* New Delhi: National Publishing House and Shimla: IIAS.

Alcyone, (1987), (J. Krishnamurti) *At the Feet of the Master, Madras*: Theosophical Publishing House.

Allen, Douglas (1993), *Religion and Political Conflict in South Asia: India, Pakistan and Srilanka,* Delhi: Oxford University Press.

Anderson, John (1994), *Religion State and Politics in Soviet Union and Successor States,* Cambridge: Cambridge University Press.

Anderson, Mary. "Krishnamurti and Commonsense", *The Theosophist,* Vol. 116, No. 8, May 1995, pp. 316-321.

Antarkar, S.S. (1997), *An Academic Look at J. Krishnamurt (Thought, Perception and Action.),* (Unpublished Article).

Arbib, Micheal. A. and Mary B. Hesse (1987), *The Construction of Reality,* Cambridge: Cambridge University Press.

Basu, Tapan, Pradip Datta, Sumit Sarkar, Tanika Sarkar, Sam budda Sen (1993), *Khaki Shorts arid Saffron Flags, A Critique of the Hindu Right,* New Delhi: Orient Longmann.

Baranabas, Manorama, S.K. Hulbe and P.S. Jacob (eds.) (1978), *Challenges of Societies in Transition,* New Delhi: Macmillan Co. of India, Ltd.

Benzeev, Aaron (1989), "Explaining the Subject-Object Relation in Perception", *Social Research,* Vol. 56, No. 2, pp. 511-542.

Blau, Evelyne (1995), *Krishnamurti: 100 Years,* New York: A Joost Elffers Book Stenkrt, Tabori and Chang.

Brinton, Crane (1995), *Anatomy of' Revolution*, New York: Harper and Row.

Brugger, Bill and Kate Hannan (1983), *Modernisation and Revolution,* London: Croom Helm.

Burnier Radha, "Theosophy and Krishnaji", *The Theosophist,* 116, No. 8, May 1995, pp. 283-285.

Buultjens, Ralph (1974), *Rebuilding the Temple, Traditions and Change in Modern Asia,* New York: Orbis Books.

Camus, Albert (1973), *The Rebel*, Middlesex: Penguin Books Ltd. and Harmondsworth.

Canudo, Jeanne "The World Teacher is Here—(An Interview with Annie Besant, January 1928)", *The Theosophist,* Vol. 116, No. 8, May 1995, pp. 300-304.

Caudwell, Christopher (1977), *Concept of Freedom, London:* Lawrence Wishart.

——(1986), *Illusion and Reality, A Study of the Source of Poetry,* New Delhi: Peoples Publishing House.

Chinnaiah (1992), *Jiddu Krishnamurti on Human Predicament and the Way out—A Critical Study,* Ph.D. Dissertation, Sri Venkateswara University, Tirupati.

Clarke, R. Balfour (1977), *The Boyhood of J. Krishnamurti*, Bombay; Chetana.

Cornforth, Maurice (1979), *Dialectical Materialism*, Calcutta: National Book Agency.

Cynthia, Keepley Mahmood, "Rethinking Indian Communalism, Culture and Counter-Culture", *Asian Survey* No. 7, July 1993, pp. 722-737.

Dallmamyr, Fred, "Modernisation and Postmodernisation: Whither India?", *Alternatives*, No. 7, 1992, pp. 421-452.

Daniel, E. Valentine, "Three Dispositions towards the Past: One Simhala Two Tamil", *Social Analysis*, No. 25, 1989, pp. 22-41.

Das, Arvind N. (1992), *India Invented A Nation in-the-Making*, New Delhi: Manohar.

Dhopeswarkar, A.D. (1956), *Krishnamurti and the Experience of the Silent Mind*, Bombay: Chetana.

——(1976), *J. Krishnamurti and Mind in Revolt*, Bombay: Chetana.

——(1982), *Krishnamurti and the Texture of Reality*, Bombay: Chetana.

Dodd, David H. and Raymond M. White Jr. (1980), *Cognition*, Boston: Allyn and Bacon Inc.

Draper, Hal (1978), *Karl Marx's Theory of Revolution*, New York and London: Monthly Review Press.

Dube, S.C. (1988), *Modernesation and Development*, New Delhi: Vistar Publications.

Dunn, John (1972), *Modern Revolution*, Cambridge: Cambridge University Press.

Eisensteadt, S.N. (1973), "*The Influence of Traditional and Colonial Political Systems on the Development of Post-traditional Social and Political Orders*", In Hans-

Dieter Evers (ed.), *Modernisation in Southeast Asia,* London: Oxford University Press.

——(1978), *Revolutions and the Transformation of Society,* London: Free Press.

Field, Sidney (Hay, Peter [ed.]) (1989), *Krishnamurti, the Reluctant Messiah,* New York: Paragan House.

Forbes, Scott, "*Education as a Religious Activity—Krishnamurti's Insights into Education*", *The Theosophist,* Vol. 116, No. 8, May 1995, pp. 338-347.

Fouere, Rene (1973), *Krishnamurti, the Man and His Teachings,* Bombay: Chetana.

Freeman, Micheal (1980), *Edmund Burke and the Critique of Political Radicalism,* Chicago: University of Chicago Press.

Frolov, Ivan (1986), *Man—Science—Humanism a New Synthesis,* Moscow: Progress Publishers, 1986.

Fromn, Erich (1961), *Marx's Conception of Man,* New York: Frederick Ungar.

Gurr, Ted Robert (1970), *Why Men Rebel*, Princeton: Princeton University Press.

Haragopal, G. (1997), *Political Economy of Human Rights:* Emerging Dimension, New Delhi: Himalaya Publishing House.

Haynes, Jeff (1993), *Religion in Third World Polltics,* Philedelphia: Open University Press.

Heber, Lilly (1935), *Krishnamurti and the World Crisis,* London: George Allen and Unwin Ltd.

Hick, John and Lamont C. Hempel (eds.) (1989), *Gandhi's Significance for Today,* London: Macmillan Press Ltd.

Hobsbawm, Eric (1995), *Age of Extremes,* Delhi: Viking Publishers.

Hobsbawm, Eric and Terence Ranger (eds.) (1984), *Invention of Tradition*, Cambridge: Cambridge University Press.

Holroyd, Stuart (1983), *The Quest of the Quiet Mind, the Philosophy of J. Krishnamurti,* Wellingborough and Northamptenshire: Aquarian Press.

Homans, Peter (1979), *Jung in Context; Modernity and the Making of Psychology,* Chicago: Chicago University Press.

Hook, Sidney (1976), *Revolution, Reform and Social Justice,* Oxford: Basil Blackwell.

Huxley, Aldous (1937), *Ends and Means,* London: Chatto and Windus.

Jayakar, Papul (1986), *Krishnamurti: A Biography,* New Delhi: Penguin Books.

Jayakar, Papul and Sunanda Patwardhan (eds.) (1982), *Within the Mind,* On J. Krishnamurti, Madras: Krishnamurti Foundation of India.

Johnson, Chalmers (1966), *Revolutionary Change,* Bombay: Vakils, Ferrer and Simon Pvt. Ltd.

Juergensmeyer, Mark (1994), *Religious Nationalism Confronts the Secular State,* Delhi: Oxford University Press.

Kelkar, Meena. A. (1997), *The Concept of Man, the Background of Krishnamurti"s Philosophy of Education,* (Unpub Artic1e).

Kertzer, David I. (1988), *Ritual, Politics and Power* London: Yalc University Press.

Khare, Brij B (ed.) (1988), *J. Krishnamurti: Things of the Mind,* New Delhi, Motilal Banarasidas.

Kimmel, Micheal (1990), *Revolution: A Sociological Interpretation*, Oxford: Basil Blackwell.

Korner, Stephen (1979), *Fundamental Questions of Philosophy, One Philosopher's Answers,* Sussex: Harvester Press.

Krishna Kumari, M. (1992), *The Humanistic Religion with Reference to Jiddu Krishnamurti,* an UGC Project, University of Hyderabad.

Krishna, P., "Was Krishnamurti A Theosophist?" *The Theosophist,* Vol. 116, No. 8, May 1995, pp. 305-307.

Krishnamurti, J. (1968), *Talks in India, 1967,* California: Krishnamurti Writings Inc.

——(1976), *The Awakening of Intelligence,* Delhi: Motilal Banarsidass, 1973 and New York: Avon Books.

——(1977), *Life Ahead,* London: Victor Gollencz Ltd.

——(1978), *Beginnings of Learning*, Harmondsworth: Penguin Books.

——(1978), *The Impossible Question*, Harmondsworth: Penguin Books.

——(1981), *Letters to the Schools,* Madras: Krishnamurti Foundation of India.

——(1983), *Talks and Dialogue*s, New York: Avon Books.

——(1984), *The Way of Intelligence,* Madras: Krishnamurti Foundation of India.

——(1986), *Explorations into Insight,* Madras: Krishnamurti Foundation of India.

——(1985), *Last Talks At Saanen,* San Francisco: Harper and Row Publishers.

——(1986), *You are the World*, Madras: Krishnamurti Foundation of India.

——(1987), *First and Last Freedom*, London: Victor Gollancz.

——(1987), *The Flame of Attention,* Madras: Krishnamurti Foundation of India.

——(1988), *Talks with American Students,* Boston and Shaftesbury: Shambala.

——(1988), *The Flight of the Eagle,* Madras: Krishnamurti Foundation of India.

——(1990), *Mind Without Measure*, Madras: Krishnamurti Foundation of India.

——(1990), *The Wholeness of Life*, Madras: Krishnamurti Foundation of India.

——(1991), *Krishnamurti to Himself, His Last Journal*, Madras: Krishnamurti Foundation of India.

——(1991), *Krishnamurti's Journal,* Madras: Krishnamurti Foundation of India.

——(1991), *Krishnamurti's Note Book*, Madras: Krishnamurti Krishnamurti's Foundation of India.

——(1991), *Meeting Life*, London: Arkana.

——. "*Surely Freedom from the Self.... Is the True Function of Man*", (Excerpts from J. Krishnamurti's Talks and Writings), Krishnamurti Foundation of America, July 1991.

——(1992), *Beyond Violence*, Madras: Krishnamurti Foundation of India.

——(2011), *Conflict*, Chennai: Krishnamurti Foundation of India.

——(1992), *Education and Significance of Life*, Madras: Krishnamurti Foundation of India.

——(1992), *Network of Thought,* Madras: Krishnamurti Foundation of India.

——(1992), *The Last Talks,* Madras: Krishnamurti Foundation of India.

——(1992), *Truth and Actuality,* Madras: Krishnamurti Foundation of India.

——(1995), *The Book of Life,* Madras: Krishnamurti Foundation of India, (Booklet).

——(1996), *Questioning Krishnamurti: J. Krishnamurti in Dialogue*, San Francisco: Haper Collins.

—— *Krishnamurti on Education.* Madras: Krishnamurti Foundation of India.

——. *The Krishnamurti Text Collection* (CD-Rom), Madras: Krishnamurti Foundation of India.

——. (Cadogan, Mary, Alan Kishbaugh, Mark Lee and Ray McCoy) [eds.], *Total Freedom, The Essential Krishnamurti*, New York: Harper San Francisco, 1996.

——. (D. Raja Gopal (ed.) (1964), *This Matter of Culture,* Madras: Krishnamurti Foundation of India.

——. (D. Raja Gopal (ed.)) (1972), *Commentaries on Living,* New Delhi: B.I. Publications.

——. (D. Raja Gopal (ed.)) (1991), *Commentaries on Living* First Series, Madras: Krishnamurti Foundation of India.

——. (D. Raja Gopal (ed.)) (1991), *Commentaries on Living* Second Series, Madras: Krishnamurti Foundation of India.

——. (D. Raja Gopal, (ed.)) (1992), *Commentaries on Living* Third Series, Madras: Krishnamurti Foundation of India.

——. (Mary Lutyens (ed.)) (1970), *Only Revolution,* London.

——. (Mary Lutyens (ed.)) (1992), *Freedom from the Known,* Madras: Krishnamurti Foundation of India.

——. (Pupul Jayakar and Sunanda Patwardhan (eds.)) (1972), *Tradition and Revolution,* Madras: Krishnamurti Foundation of India.

Krishnamurti, J. and David Bohm (1987), *Future of Humanity*, Madras: Krishnamurti Foundation of India.

——(1992), *The Ending of Time,* Madras: Krishnamurti Foundation of India.

Krishnamurti, K. (compiled) (1995), *Krishnamurti for Beginners: An Anthology*, Madras: Krishnamurti Foundation of India.

Krishnamurti, V.G. (1990), *From J. Krishnamurti to Upanishads,* Calcutta: A Writers Workshop Publication.

Kumar, Krishan (ed.) (1971), *Revolution: The Theory and Practice of European Idea,* London: Weidenfeld and Nicolson.

Kulkarni, S.G., "Philosophy of Dr. Ambedkar: Some Observations", A Paper presented at a National Seminar on *The Relevance of Ambedkarism in India Today,* Visakhapatnam, 26-27 September 1992.

Laclau, Ernesto (1990), *New Reflection on the Revolution of Our Time,* New York: Verso.

Laxmi Narayana, S., *The Concept of Man in J. Krishnamurti and Jean Paul Satre, A Reflection*, Hyderabad: East West Research Centre, Osmania University.

Laxmi Prasad, N. (1990), *Conversations with J. Krishnamurti, the Man and the Message*, USA: Quest Books and Theosophical Publishing Books.

Lefebvre, Henri (1991), *Critique of Everyday Life* Vol. I, London: Verso.

Lenin, V.I. (1977), *Materialism and Empirico-Criticism,* Moscow: Progress Publishers.

Levi, Albert William (1974), *Philosophy as Social Expression,* London: The University of Chicago Press.

Lutyens, Mary. (Compiled), (1970), *Krishnamurti Reader,* London: Penguin Books.

Lutyens, Mary (1975), *The Years of Awakening,* London.

Lutyens, Mary (ed.) (1982), *Second Penguin Krishnamurti Reader,* Harmondsworth: Penguin Books.

Lutyens, Mary. (1983), *J. Krishnamurti, Years of Fulfilment*, New York: Avon Books.

——(1988), *Krishnamurti: The Open Door,* London: John Murray.

Marcuse, Herbert (1977), *Reason and Revolution,* London: Routledge and Kengan Paul.

Marx, Karl (1976), *The German Ideology,* Moscow: Progress Publishers.

Marx, Karl and Frederick Engels (1977), *Marx and Engels: Selected Writing* Vol. 1, Moscow: Progress Publishers.

McLean, George F. (1986), *Tradition and Contemporary Life; Hermanuatics of Personal Wisdom and Social Change*, Madras: University of Madras.

Mehta, Rohit (1988), *The Intuitive Philosophy, J. Krishnamurti's Approach to Life,* Bombay: Chetana.

——(1989), *J. Krishnamurti and Nameless Experience,* New Delhi: Motilal Banarasidas Publishers.

Mehta, Rohit and Sridevi Mehta (1990), *J. Krishnamurti and Sant Kabir,* New Delhi: Motilal Banarasidas Publishers.

Micheal, Peter (1996), *Krishnamurti, Love and Freedom Approaching Freedom*, New Delhi: Motilal Banarasidas Publishers.

Misra, Sadananda, "The Prison House of Tradition: An Inquiry into Krishnamurti, Perception", *Krishnamurti's Journal,* Vol. 1 No. 2 and 3, November 1987 and February 1988, pp. 46-53.

Mohanty, Manoranjan. (ed.) (1992), *Chinese Revolution: A Comparative Perspectives on Transformation of Non-Western Societies,* Delhi: Ajanta Publications.

Moon, Vasant (compiled) (1987), *Dr. Babasaheb Ambedkar Writings and Speeches* Vol. 3, Bombay: Education Department, Government of Maharastra.

Moore, R.J. (ed.) (1979), *Tradition and Politics in South Asia,* New Delhi: Vikas Publishing House Pvt. Ltd.

Nandy, Ashis (1987), *Tradition, Tyranny and Utopias*, New Delhi: Oxford University Press.

Neil Andre (1982), *Krishnamurti, The Man in Revolt,* Bombay: Chetana.

Nyiri, J.C. and Barry Smith (eds.) (1987), *Practical Knowledge: Outlines of Traditions and Skills*, London: Croom Helm.

O' Gorman, Frank (1973), *Edmamd Burke, His Political Philosophy,* London: George Allen and Unwin Ltd.

O'Sullivan, Noel (1983), *Revolutionary Theory and Political Reality*, Sussex: Wheatsheafs Books Limited.

Patwardhan, Sunanda (ed.) (1991), *Nature of Dialogue,* Madras: Centre for Continuing Dialogue, Krishnamurti Foundation of India.

——(1992), *Learning about Consciousness*, Madras: Krishnamurti Foundation of India.

Pandey, Rajendra (ed.) (1988), *Modernisation and Social Change,* New Delhi: Criterion Publications.

Peperzak, Adriaan Theodoor (1986), *System and History in Philosophy,* New ark: State University of New York Press.

Parkinson, G.H. (ed.) (1982), *Marx and Marxisms*, Royal Institute Philosophy Lectures Series: 14, Cambridge: Cambridge University Press.

Perera, Sasanka (1995), *Living with Tortutres and Other Essays of intervention: Srilankan Society, Culture and Politics in Perspective,* Colombo: International Centre for Ethnic Studies.

Piaget, Jean (1971), *Structuralism*, London: Routledge and Kegan Paul.

Ponnambalam Satchi (1983), *Srilanka: National. Conflict and the Tamil Liberation Struggle,* London: Zed Books Ltd.

Porter, Roy and Mikulas Teich (1986), *Revolution and History,* Cambridge; bridge University Press.

Pritchard, E.E. Evans (1972), *Social Anthropology,* London: Routledge and Kegan Paul.

Radhakrishnan, Sarvepalli (1985), *History of Indian Philosophy*, Vol. 1, London: Blackie Sons.

Rajanayagam, Dagmar Hellmann, "The Concept of a 'Tamil Homeland' in Sri Lanka—Its Meaning and Development", *South Asia,* Vol. XIII, No. 2, 1990, pp. 79-110.

Rao, O.R., *J. Krishnamurti, Philosopher of Insight, Clarity and Order*, Madras: Krishnamurti Foundation of India, June, 1988. (Unpublished Article).

Ravindra, Ravi, "Krishnamurti Speaking from the Heart", *The Theosophist*, Vol. 116, No. 8, May 1995, pp. 290-293.

Rodrigues, Valerian, "Facing Postmodernism", *Indian Journal of American Studies,* Vol. 23, No. 1, Winter 1993, pp. 7-21.

Roy, M.N. (1989), *Reason, Romanticism and Revolution,* New Delhi: Ajanta Publications.

Roy, Subrata, *Freedom for J. Krishnamurti*, (Unpublished Article).

Russian Academy of Sciences, (Translated By V. Yasinsky) "Russain Society in 1994", *Social Sciences, Russian Academy of Sciences*, No. 4, 1995, pp. 51-62.

Sardesai, Arundati, *"Epistemology of J. Krishnamurti", Indian. Philosophical Quarterly*, Vol. XXIII, No. 3 and 4, July and October 1996, pp. 455-466.

Sartre, Jean-Paul. (Tr. Philip Mairet) (1973), *Existentialism and Humanism,* London: Byre Methuen.

—— (Tr. Hal E. Barnes) (1976), *Being and Nothingness, an Essay on Phenomelogical Ontology,* London: Nethuen.

Saures, Carlo (1973), *Krishnamurti and the Unity of Man,* Bombay: Chetana.

Scokpol, Theda (1979), *States and Social Revolutions,* Cambridge: Cambridge University Press.

Sharma, A.P. (1993), *Krishnamurti, His Concept of Freedom,* New Delhi: Ajanta Publications.

Shils, Edward (1981), *Tradition*, London and Boston: Faber and Faber.

Simon, Roger (1982), *Gramsci's Political Thought, Introduction,* London: Lawrence and Wishart.

Singh, Bhaghavan R., "Born Free", *The Week,* March 2-8, 1986, pp. 16-19.

——. "Ho Comparisons", *The Week,* March 2-8, 1986, pp. 22-23.

Singh, Ramjee (ed.), (1983), *The Relevance of Gandhin Thought,* New Delhi: Classical Publishing Company.

Singh, Randhir (1976), *Reason, Revolution and Political Theory*, New Delhi: Peoples Publishing House.

Spencer, Jonathan. (ed.) (1990), *Srilanka: History and Roots of Conflict,* London: Routledge.

——, "Writing Within, Archaeology, Nationalism and Culture in Srilanka", *Current Anthropology,* Vol. 31, No. 3, June 1990, pp. 283-300.

Stingy, R.K. (1977), *Philosophy of J. Krishnamurti, A Systematic Study,* New Delhi: Munshiram Manoharlal.

Srivatsava, S.K. (ed.) (1976), *Tradition and Modernisation,* Allahabad: Indian International Publications.

Swami Anantha, "Tradition and Krishnaji", *Krishnamurti's Journal,* Vol. 1, No. 2 and 3, November 1987 and February 1988, Krishnamurti Society, Orissa, pp. 12-20.

Taylor, Micheal (1988), *Rationality and Revolution,* New York: Cambridge University Press.

Thakur, Ramesh, "Ayodhya and the Politics of India's Secularism", *Asian Survey,* No. 7, July 1993, pp. 645-661.

Third World Network, *Modern Science in Crisis—A Third World Response,* Malayasia: Third World Network, 1991.

Tucker, Robert C. (1969), *Marxian Revolutionary Idea,* London: George Allen and Unwin Ltd.

Vas, Luis S.R. (ed.) (1989), *The Mind of J. Krishnamurti,* Bombay: Jaico Publishing House.

Vedaparayana, G. (1983), *The Concept of Freedom: Comparative Study of Jean Paul Sartre and J. Krishnamurti,* Ph.D. Dissertation, Department of Philosophy, Sri Venkateswara University, Tirupati.

——, "The Known And the Unknown: Jiddu Krishnamurti's Conception of Consciousness", *Darsana International* An International Quarterly, Vol. XXVI, No. 4, October 1986, pp. 16-22.

——, "Philosophy as the Perception of Truth—A Comment on "Epistemology of J. Krishnamurti", *Indian Philosophical Quarterly,* Vol. XXIV, No. 3, July 1997, pp. 413-424.

——, "Jiddu Krishnamurti's Philosophy of Human Existence", *Krishnamurti's Journal,* Vol. 1, No. 2 and 3, November 1987 and February 1988, pp. 25-29.

Vollemer, Kurt-Mueller (1984), *The Hermeneutic Reader,* Oxford: Basil Blackwell.

Vyas, Savitri (1989), A Critical Study of *J. Krishnamjarti's Educational Thoughts,* Ahmedabad: Bhagawati Printing Press.

Weeraperuma, Susunaga (1983), *The Pathless Land, Essays on the Beauty and Uniqueness of J. Krishnamurti's Teachings*, Bombay: Chetana.

——(1984), *Bliss of Reality (Essays on J. Krishnamurti's Extraordinary Insights into Life)* Bombay: Chetana.

——(1987), *Living and Dying (From Moment to Moment.).* Bombay: Chetana.

Welch Jr, Claude (ed.) (1971), *Political Modernisation: A Reader in Comparative Political Change*, California: Wordsworth Publishing any Inc.

Welch Jr, Claude and Mavis Bunker Taintor (1972), *Revolution and Political Change,* California: Duxbury Press.

Index